HOW TO SURVIVE
MIDDLE SCHOOL
MATH

Visit us on the Web! rhcbooks.com

Educators and librarians, for a variety of teaching tools, visit us at RHTeachersLibrarians.com

Library of Congress Cataloging-in-Publication Data is available upon request.

ISBN 978-0-525-57141-4 (trade)

ISBN: 978-0-525-57146-9 (ebook)

Printed in the United States of America

10 9 8 7 6 5 4 3 2 1

First Edition

Writers: Concetta Ortiz, Matt Fazio, Sarah Cisneros, Ilse Ortabasi
Curriculum Consultant: Kimberly Coniglio
Sideshow Media Editorial and Production Team: Dan Tucker, Liz Dacey, Julia DeVarti
Penguin Random House Publishing Team: Tom Russell, Alison Stoltzfus, Brett Wright, Emily Harburg, Eugenia Lo,
Katy Miller

Produced by Sideshow Media LLC
Illustration and Design by Carpenter Collective

HOW TO SURVIVE MIDDLE SCHOOL

A DO-IT-YOURSELF STUDY GUIDE

MATH

CONCETTA ORTIZ, MATT FAZIO

BRIGHT MATTER BOOKS

NEW YORK

TABLE OF CONTENTS

CHAPTER 3   85

OPERATIONS AND RATIONAL NUMBERS: PART 1

CHAPTER 4   121

OPERATIONS AND RATIONAL NUMBERS: PART 2

CHAPTER 5   151

OPERATIONS AND RATIONAL NUMBERS: PART 3

CHAPTER 6   183

EXPRESSIONS AND EQUATIONS: PART 1

CHAPTER 7   207

EXPRESSIONS AND EQUATIONS: PART 2

CHAPTER 8   241

EXPRESSIONS AND EQUATIONS: PART 3

CHAPTER 9   283

AREA, VOLUME, AND SURFACE AREA

CHAPTER 10   323

CROSS SECTIONS, CIRCLES, VOLUME, AND ANGLES

CHAPTER 11   353

SIMILARITY, CONGRUENCE, AND ANGLE RELATIONSHIPS

CHAPTER 12   397

STATISTICS

CHAPTER 13   453

PROBABILITY

CHAPTER 14   491

BIVARIATE DATA

MATH AND THE REAL WORLD

As humans, we naturally want to describe the world we live in and all of the experiences we go through. Thanks to our five senses (touch, taste, smell, sight, and sound), we provide our brain with inputs. When we pause and look at those inputs, we learn things and develop new knowledge. Through this process, humanity has been able to establish the laws of math. These laws help us look at everything, from the stars in the sky to the invisible cells in our bodies.

CHAPTER CONTENTS

MATHEMATICS HELPS US MAKE SENSE OF THE WORLD

Through mathematics:

- meteorologists describe and predict weather

- chefs prepare and cook food

- scientists evaluate experiments

- architects design homes and buildings

- computers perform billions of computations per second

- astronomers make calculations that allow them to understand the dimensions of our solar system and hypothesize about the origins of the universe

We measure, organize, and communicate using number systems. In this way, all math is real. Even parts of the "real" world that don't seem related to math are better understood using this core. For example: *What are your top five favorite movies, in no particular order?*

MAKING SENSE OF THE MOVIES

Based on your movie preferences, you probably have a short list of favorites. If you want to rank the movies in order, you'll end up using principles of math.

How so? Well, let's say you use categories to help compare the movies. You decide to consider each movie's story, characters, visual design, etc. For each category, you assign a score out of 10.

MOVIE TITLE	
Story	__/10
Characters	__/10
Visual Design	__/10

The scores express, *in number form*, your feelings about each movie's category. Afterwards, you could add up each movie's scores, compare the totals, and see how they ranked. In this system, math structures help you better express your experiences with your favorite movies. So, although math can sometimes seem difficult, it's a natural and helpful part of our world. It's found in everything—including the things we love.

THE "PURITY" OF MATH

There's a purity and trust in math. It's comforting to know if you follow math's rules, you can rely on the answer. Although the answer can sometimes be "No Solution" or "False," at least you can trust the result. In this way, math inspires confidence.

The word confidence comes from the Latin *confidere*. Its prefix *con-* means "with" and suffix *-fidere* means "trust."

When we develop confidence with a subject like math, we're relating to it with trust.

For example, if you're working as a carpenter, how would you know to trust your measurements and calculations? Well, if the ramp you're building successfully reaches the front door, you're correct. If it doesn't, you're incorrect. There's no confusion or uncertainty; you can trust the results. Also, it's important to note these results will be the same for any carpenter anywhere in the world. It doesn't get any more pure and real than that!

HOW TO THINK LIKE A MATHEMATICIAN

Different people may use different symbols, but at its core, the language of math is always the same. As with any language, you must be fluent if you want to think in "math." In its own way, math has an alphabet and rules that allow you to build its own words, phrases, and sentences. So, it's important to practice reading, writing, and speaking math.

TALK IT OUT

It might sound silly, but *verbalizing* a math problem (saying it out loud) can help interpret the situation. As your brain focuses on how to say what you're seeing, it will help you focus on the details. You may have to do this internally if you're taking a quiz in class, but the effect is the same.

DRAW IT OUT

Sometimes it's helpful to draw a picture to help make sense of a problem or use colors to help organize information. This strategy can be helpful in finding patterns and connections.

LOOK IT UP

If you don't know the name of a symbol or the meaning of a word, take a moment to look it up. Often, the name of the symbol will tell you a key part of its function, so it's important to know what it's called. If you have difficulty with new vocabulary, remember *practice makes better*! Using study methods like flashcards or reviewing with a friend can help train your brain.

HAVE AN APPROACH

There may be times when you read a problem and you're not sure where to start. When approaching math situations, it helps to consider the following:

1. What am I given?

   - What key information is provided? Is there a diagram or chart? What are the important details in this situation?

2. What's missing?

   - What problem am I being asked to solve?

3. How can I connect the given with the missing?

   - Are there math skills or functions to join the key info with the end goal?

EXPERIMENT AND REVIEW

Once you understand what the situation calls for, the next steps are to experiment and review. A good mathematician will try out a solution method and then check their work. Once again, talking through the process can help. By retracing your steps, you may find a mistake or recognize a better path to your final goal.

CONSIDER MULTIPLE METHODS

Speaking of different paths, in math there are usually multiple ways to solve a problem. So, a good mathematician must keep an open mind. Your experiments are where you can try things out. If your ideas are based in proper math, there's nothing wrong with testing a different method. In fact, these alternate paths are opportunities to deepen your understanding!

A MATHEMATICIAN'S TOOLS

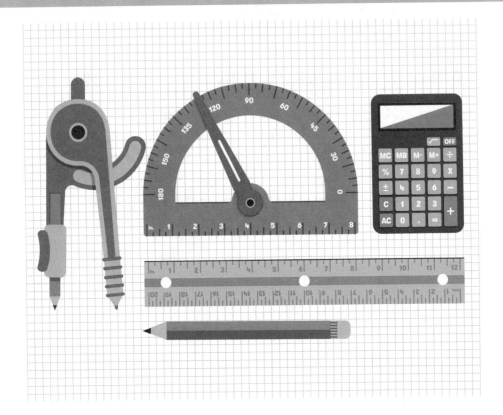

THE BASICS

In today's society, we're working more and more on digital screens. The value of a mathematician's handwritten work shouldn't be lost though. You can use paper and pencil or stylus and screen, but it's important to interact with the work. This is similar to when you read math aloud; writing math helps the brain process the situation. For example, you can get a feel for the growth and shape of a graph when you draw it. So, try using different-colored paper, colored pencils, and other supplies to aid in your process.

MEASUREMENT AND DRAWING TOOLS

- A **straight edge** is just a simple edge of book or stick that allows you to make straight lines.

- **Rulers** measure distances, usually in inches or centimeters. Since they're also **straight edges**, they can help you draw straight lines too. They're handy tools!

- **Compasses** draw circles or arcs.

- **Protractors** measure angles and, if they have a ruler on their base, distances.

- **Graph** or **grid paper** can be helpful for measuring area or distance.

CALCULATOR

No matter how great a mathematician might be, there are times when they need a calculator. If you can work without a calculator, though, you should try. It's an excellent way to build your understanding of math and logic. So when you can, keep a calculator nearby to check your work and help solve more complicated tasks.

KNOWLEDGE AND EXPERIENCE

Ultimately, your knowledge and experience are your greatest tools. Getting better at something takes time and practice, though, so be kind to yourself if you make mistakes. With more experience, you'll build ability, and this will empower your education. So, have patience and enjoy the learning process!

A THOUGHT PARTNER

While completing tough problems, it's helpful to have a thought partner—someone to discuss the problem with, such as a parent, sibling, classmate, and/or teacher. This allows you to work out **your** thinking and see if there's an idea or pathway that you may not have thought of.

EQUIPMENT FOR LEARNING

When you go on any kind of adventure, including learning about math, you need the tools that will help you survive and thrive. That's where we come in! Along with the tools we're giving you below, we'll also remind you when to use them. In the pages ahead, you'll see the tools pop up, along with some questions and ways to think about what you're reading.

SYMBOL/ TOOL	WHAT IT IS	HOW TO USE IT WHILE YOU READ
	People use a GPS so they don't get lost. It helps them figure out where they are, get directions, or explore a new area.	When you see the GPS, stop and pay attention to the big picture. You might: • Ask yourself some big picture questions before you read. • Get oriented with the basic facts. • Preview the text by skimming the headings, timelines, charts, and illustrations.
	Boots give hikers sure footing, even on rocky paths. All serious hikers pull on their boots before setting out.	Activate prior knowledge. When you see the boots, it's time to: • Think back on what you already know about the topic. • Build on what you already know with new information.
	Stop and pay attention.	• Beware of a common misconception or a common error.

	This road sign lets people know that there may be another route.	The road sign will help you find additional methods to solve the same problem. When you see the road sign: • Think about what other methods you already know that can be applied to the topic. • Use it to link new information to wider concepts.
	People use a magnifying glass to examine something up close.	The magnifying glass will remind you to stop and zoom in. Use your magnifier to: • Reflect on what you just learned. • Make conclusions based on your new information.
	A toolbox is where people store the things they always want to have on hand to solve problems, build, or fix something.	Math builds on key concepts, so when you see the toolbox, remember to: • Pay close attention to what you're learning. • Tuck it away so you can build on it later. • Think about which tool(s) might help you solve a problem.

You'll find definitions for important **vocabulary terms** in yellow boxes like this one near the first time a term is used. They're also listed for you again at the end of each chapter.

Once you've familiarized yourself with these tools, you're ready. Now, buckle your seatbelt, and off we go!

RATIO RELATIONSHIPS: PART 1

Great thinkers use comparison to better understand a subject. In mathematics, one important kind of comparison is called a ratio. You can use ratios to better understand and solve all kinds of problems, from making refreshing drinks for a bunch of people to figuring out how much time you'll need to finish an 8-mile hike!

RATIO BASICS

In mathematics, when you compare one quantity (amount) of a thing to another quantity of the same thing, it's called a **ratio**. For example, the ratio of blue stars to orange stars below is 3 to 2.

> **ratio:** the comparison between two (*or more*) groups or items with the same units (i.e., number of apples to number of oranges)

 ## TAKE A CLOSER LOOK

Did you know a spider isn't an insect?

Use the pictures on the next page and compare the spider to the humblest of all insects, the ant. Can you spot any key differences? Hint: Count the number of legs and body segments on each creature.

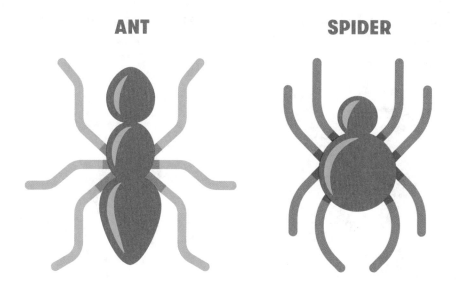

ANT

SPIDER

The ant has 6 legs and 3 body segments, while the spider has 8 legs and two body segments. One way you can compare these two creatures is to express the ratio of their legs: the ratio of **ant legs** to **spider legs** is 6 to 8.

FIRST ⟨ **ANT LEGS** 6   TO   **SPIDER LEGS** 8 ⟩ SECOND

 When you write a ratio, it's important to keep the order in the comparison. Since you started with ant legs and compared them to spider legs, the 6 goes first and the 8 goes second.

*How would you write the ratio of **spider legs** to **ant legs**?* Remember: the *order* in which they're written matters!

SPIDER LEGS   TO   **ANT LEGS**

Changing the order of the words changes the order of the ratio.

FIRST ⟨ **SPIDER LEGS** 8   TO   **ANT LEGS** 6 ⟩ SECOND

Let's take another look at the star example. Complete the second comparison.

blue stars to orange stars

3 to 2

orange stars to blue stars

_____ to _____

Because the example on the right is comparing orange stars to blue stars, the order has changed, so you write the ratio as 2 to 3.

TAKE A CLOSER LOOK

Ratios can be expressed in three different forms. The ratios in the examples above are in written form because we write the word "to" between the numbers we're comparing. Ratios can also be expressed in symbol form with a colon or as a fraction:

COMPARISON	WRITTEN	SYMBOL	FRACTION
Ant Legs *to* Spider Legs	6 to 8	6:8	$\frac{6}{8}$

TOOLS FOR SUCCESS

When working with ratios, it's important to remember:

- The order they're written in matters.
- Ratios can be expressed in written, symbol, or fractional form.

YOUR TURN!

Use your ratio knowledge to complete the following table comparing spiders and ants.

COMPARISON	WRITTEN	SYMBOL	FRACTION
Spider Legs *to* Ant Legs	8 to 6	8:6	
Spider Body Segments *to* Ant Body Segments	2 to 3		
Ant Body Segments *to* Spider Body Segments			$\frac{3}{2}$

EQUIVALENT RATIOS

Now that you know how to write ratios, let's explore equivalent ratios. That's fancy talk for two ratios that have a special relationship. Look at the two ratios below. Can you guess the relationship between them?

2:1   4:2

The first ratio has 2 blue bears and the second ratio has 4 blue bears. So, the number of blue bears doubled.

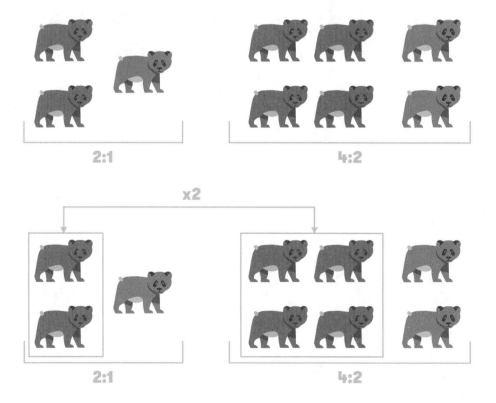

2:1   4:2

x2

2:1   4:2

Check out the orange bears. Do they also double? The first ratio has 1 orange bear and the second ratio has 2. So, yes, the number of orange bears also doubled!

When both ratios being compared are multiplied by the same number, they're called **equivalent ratios**.

> **equivalent ratios:** if one ratio can be expressed as a multiple of another, the two ratios are equal in value.

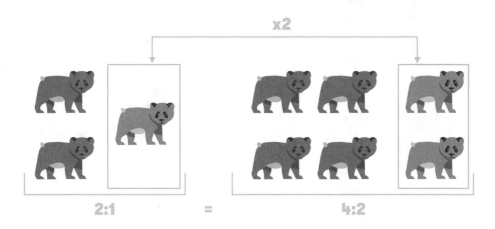

Check out the stars below—are they changing by the same amount?

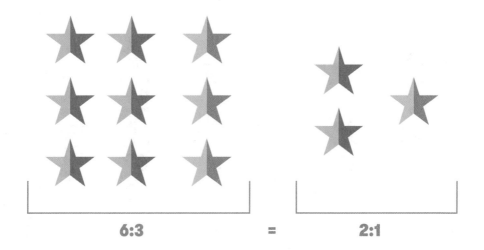

Wait a second. . . there are fewer stars this time? That's right!

Equivalent ratios can compare a larger quantity or a smaller quantity. When comparing to a larger quantity, you multiply. When comparing to a smaller quantity, you divide. In both cases, the ratios will stay equivalent.

What number can you divide the first ratio by to create the second ratio?

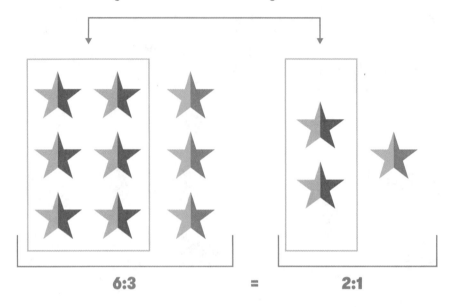

The first ratio has 6 blue stars and the second ratio has 2 blue stars. So, you could say the number of stars in the first ratio was divided by 3.

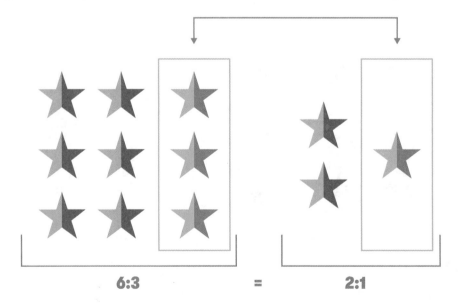

Look back at the orange stars. Do they change in the same way?
Yes, 3 ÷ 3 = 1. So, the second ratio is equivalent to the first ratio.

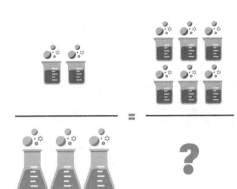

Ready for a challenge? In your science class, you notice there are 2 small beakers for every 3 large beakers. Your teacher is ordering new beakers for the next school year. If next year there are 6 small beakers, how many large beakers should there be? Find the answer with a ratio equation.

The quantity of beakers *increases*, right (6 is greater than 2)? So does that mean we multiply or divide to find the equivalent ratio? That's right! Multiply!

If 2 increased to 6, it must have been multiplied by what number? Use the answer to this question to build an equation.

$$\frac{2}{3} = \frac{6}{?}$$

As you probably know, 2 multiplied by 3 is 6. Since the two ratios must be equivalent (equals sign in-between), you also multiply the denominator by 3.

So, your teacher orders 9 large beakers.

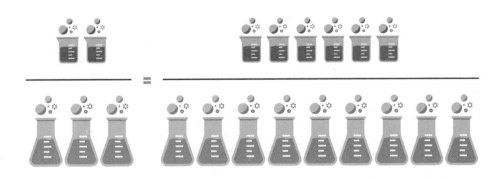

YOUR TURN!

A trail mix recipe uses two types of nuts. For every 2 almonds there are 5 peanuts. If you have 8 almonds, how many peanuts do you need to add to the trail mix?

Use these empty boxes to model (draw) the ratios in your trail mix.

BASIC RATIO		EQUIVALENT RATIO	
Almonds	Peanuts	Almonds	Peanuts

Next, write in the numbers you know to make an equation to solve for the numbers you don't know.

Almonds: _____ x _____ = _____

Peanuts: _____ x _____ = _____

So, you need to add _____ peanuts to the trail mix.

RATIOS VS. RATES

Let's look at a special type of ratio. We know that ratios compare amounts of the same type of thing, like comparing legs to legs, or body segments to body segments. But sometimes mathematicians need to compare things that are different, like pencils to markers, desks to chairs, or books to computers. This special comparison is called a **rate**.

> **rate:** the comparison between two (or more) groups or items in relation to one another with different units (i.e., 12 feet per 3 minutes)

• ratio: compares the **same** type of things

• rate: compares **different** types of things

Let's see how this looks with our ants and spiders! If you were to compare the number of an ant's legs to the number of its body segments, you would have to create a rate, being sure to label the "legs" and the "body segments" in your expression.

RATIOS	RATES
Ant Legs to Spider Legs	Ant Legs to Ant Body Segments
Cat Length (Inches) to Cat Height (Inches)	Cat Length (Inches) to Cat Weight (Pounds)
Driver Miles to Flyer Miles	Driver Miles to Driver Hours

So, looking at our ant friend below, *what would be the rate of ant legs to ant body segments?*

The rate of the number of ant legs to the number of its body segments is 6 legs for its 3 body segments. A rate is typically expressed as a fraction, so in this case it would be:

$$\frac{6 \text{ LEGS}}{3 \text{ BODY SEGMENTS}} = \frac{6}{3}$$

YOUR TURN!

Use your knowledge of ratios and rates to correctly identify a ratio versus a rate in the table below. Be sure to provide a reason for your answer.

COMPARISON	RATIO VS. RATE	REASON
A bear's weight *to* a dog's weight	Ratio	Comparing the same units (weight)
Birds *to* wings		Comparing different units
Foot length *to* foot width		
Music beats *to* minutes		

UNIT RATES

A rate that compares the number of units to *just one* of another unit is a special rate. It's called a **unit rate**. For example, our ant has 6 legs. So we could say there are 6 legs per ant. This means the unit rate of legs to ants is 6 to 1 or 6 legs for every 1 ant.

Take a look at the table to see some other examples of rates and unit rates:

RATE	UNIT RATE
120 miles for every 2 hours	60 miles per hour
$1.50 for 3 bananas	$0.50 per banana
32 legs for 4 body segments	8 legs per body segment

Can you determine which of the following are unit rates?

COMPARISON	IS IT A UNIT RATE?	REASON
$0.75 per lemon		
1,100 words read in 10 minutes		
42 pages read in 1 hour		

🔍 TAKE A CLOSER LOOK

Going back to the ant's rate of 6 legs to 3 body segments, is this a unit rate?

Nope. Since it's not comparing the legs to 1 body segment, it's not a unit rate. To find a unit rate, you can set up the rate as a fraction equal to something over 1:

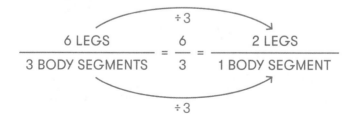

$$\frac{6 \text{ LEGS}}{3 \text{ BODY SEGMENTS}} = \frac{6}{3} = \frac{2 \text{ LEGS}}{1 \text{ BODY SEGMENT}}$$

In the equation on the previous page, dividing the denominator by 3 will get you 1, so the numerator must also be divided by 3.

This creates a unit rate of 2 legs to 1 body segment. The word *per* is another way to say you're comparing to one. So, the ant has 2 legs per body segment or 2 legs for every 1 body segment.

 ## TOOLS FOR SUCCESS

When working with unit rates, it's important to remember:

- You're comparing multiple units of something to only one unit of something else.
- The word "per" means "one."
- To find the unit rate, set up a ratio equation and solve for one unit of the item you're comparing.

Example: The rate 120 miles in 2 hours has a unit rate of 60 miles per hour.

YOUR TURN!

Find the unit rate for 1,100 words read in 10 minutes.

The unit rate is _____ per minute.

EQUIVALENT RATIOS AND RATES: FINDING THE MISSING VALUE

Here's a secret: good mathematicians like to work smart, not hard! They're always looking for the most efficient way to figure something out.

For example, you're planning to make lemonade for you and some friends. You need to juice 1 lemon for every 4 cups of water. How many lemons will you need to juice to mix with 24 cups of water?

LEMONS	WATER (CUPS)
1	4
?	24

You could keep adding the unit rate of 4 cups of water per lemon. . .

. . . but there's another way!

ACTIVATE PRIOR KNOWLEDGE

You can use your knowledge of equivalent ratios. Consider what would happen if you doubled the 1 lemon and 4 cups of water. How many lemons and cups of water would you have?

LEMONS	WATER (CUPS)
1	4
2	8

x2 (...) x2

Doubling multiplies by 2, so you would have 2 lemons and 8 cups. *If you tripled the original rate, how many lemons and cups of water would you have?*

LEMONS	WATER (CUPS)
1	4
2	8
3	12

x2 (...) x2
x3 (...) x3

Multiplying the original unit rate by 3 gives you 3 lemons and 12 cups of water. Note: each of the rates you created (2:8 and 3:12) are equivalent to the original (1:4) ratio.

$$\frac{\text{LEMONS}}{\text{WATER (CUPS)}} \quad \frac{1}{4} = \frac{2}{8} = \frac{3}{12}$$

When you create these equivalent ratios, you multiply or divide both values in the original ratio by the same number.

$$\frac{\text{LEMONS}}{\text{WATER (CUPS)}} \quad \overset{\times 2 \quad \times 3}{\underset{\times 2 \quad \times 3}{\frac{1}{4} = \frac{2}{8} = \frac{3}{12}}}$$

Using this idea, what number would you multiply 4 cups by to create the 24 cups that you need?

	LEMONS	1	2	3	?

x2 ↓ x3 ↓ x? ↓

$$\text{LEMONS} \quad \frac{1}{4} = \frac{2}{8} = \frac{3}{12} = \frac{?}{24}$$

WATER (CUPS)

x2 ↗ x3 ↗ x? ↗

	LEMONS	WATER (CUPS)	
x2	1	4	x2
	2	8	
x3	3	12	x3
x6	6	24	x6

If you multiply the 4 cups by 6, you get 24 cups of water. Don't forget: you also need to multiply the 1 lemon by 6. This creates the equivalent ratio, 6:24. This means the final mix needs 6 lemons for 24 cups of water!

⚠ ANOTHER PATH

Tables of values are super helpful, but you may not always have the time to make them. Let's set up a **ratio equation**. You can use the original lemon to cups of water ratio of 1:4 and a ratio of the unknown value compared to 24 cups.

$$\frac{1}{4} = \frac{?}{24}$$

Look familiar? That's because it's the setup for equivalent ratios! Finding the missing value requires the same multiplication (*or division*) used in the table. This will also give you the 6 lemons for the 24 cups of water.

TOOLS FOR SUCCESS

When creating equivalent ratios and rates, it's important to remember:

- All values in the original ratio will be multiplied or divided by the same value.

- You can use models, tables, or ratio equations.

RATIOS WITH THREE QUANTITIES

This time, you're going to sweeten the lemonade with sugar. You'll use
2 lemons for every 4 cups of water and 3 teaspoons of sugar. *How many
cups of water and teaspoons of sugar would you need if you have
14 lemons?*

2	4	3
14	?	?

TAKE A CLOSER LOOK

Did you notice there are three values in your lemonade recipe?
That's okay! Ratios and rates can compare more than just two things. This
time let's use a number line to find the amount of each ingredient.

LEMONS	0	2	4	6 ... 14
SUGAR (TEASPOONS)	0	4	8	12 ... ?
WATER (CUPS)	0	3	6	9 ... ?

LEMONS 0 2 4 6 ... 14

WATER (CUPS) 0 4 8 12 ... ?

SUGAR (TEASPOONS) 0 3 6 9 ... ?

Your original rate of 2 lemons to 4 cups of water to 3 teaspoons of sugar
(2:4:3) can double into 4 lemons to 8 cups of water to 6 teaspoons of
sugar (4:8:6). It can triple into 6 lemons to 12 cups of water to 9 teaspoons
of sugar (6:12:9).

How can the original 2 lemons be multiplied to become 14 lemons?

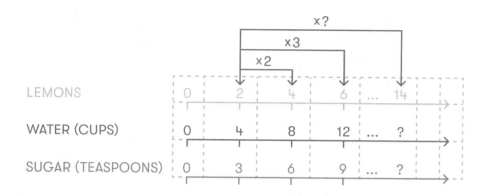

Multiplying the original 2 lemons by 7 will give you 14 lemons. To keep the ratio equivalent, you need to multiply each ingredient by 7:

Water: 4 x 7 = 28 cups

sugar: 3 x 7 = 21 teaspoons

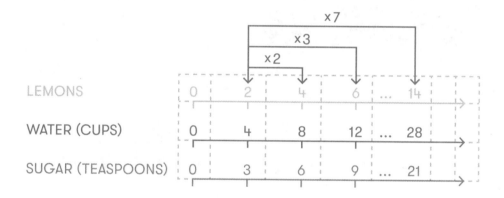

So, your final recipe will use the ratio of 14 lemons to 28 cups of water and 21 teaspoons of sugar (14:28:21).

ANOTHER PATH

You could also figure this out using an equation method. The key thing is you need to set up a ratio equation for each ingredient you're solving for. For example, using lemons and cups of water:

$$\frac{\text{LEMONS}}{\text{WATER (CUPS)}} \quad \frac{2}{4} = \frac{14}{?}$$

Since you multiplied by 7 in the numerator, you need to multiply the 4 in the denominator by 7 also. This gives you the equivalent ratio of 14:28. Or 14 lemons for 28 cups of water.

$$\frac{\text{LEMONS}}{\text{WATER (CUPS)}} \quad \frac{2}{4} = \frac{14}{28}$$

YOUR TURN!

Now your friends want to see what you can do with iced tea. You decide to use 1 tea bag for every 2.5 cups of water and 3 teaspoons of sugar. If the final recipe uses 30 cups of water, how many tea bags and teaspoons of sugar will you need?

TEA BAGS	0	1	2	3	...	?
WATER (CUPS)	0	2.5	5	7.5	...	30
SUGAR (TEASPOONS)	0	3	6	9	...	?

$$\frac{\text{TEA BAGS}}{\text{WATER (CUPS)}} \quad \frac{1}{2.5} = \frac{?}{30}$$

$$\frac{\text{WATER (CUPS)}}{\text{SUGAR (TEASPOONS)}} \quad \frac{2.5}{3} = \frac{30}{?}$$

PUTTING RATES AND RATIOS TO WORK

Late one afternoon, around 4 P.M., you decide to hike an 8-mile trail near your home. After walking for a while, you reach the 2-mile marker and look at your watch. It's 5 P.M. and you start worrying about finishing the trail by the time the sun sets at 7 P.M. You'd rather not hike after dark—plus, you don't want to be late for dinner.

ACTIVATE PRIOR KNOWLEDGE

If you know your current rate of speed, in miles per hour, you can use your knowledge of equivalent ratios to see how far along you'll be at 7 P.M. **Number lines,** like the one on the next page, help visualize your rate. You traveled two miles (blue) in the one hour (orange) from 4 to 5 P.M.

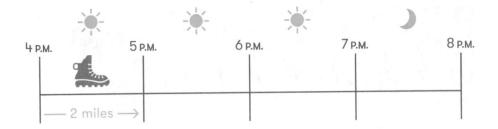

As you can see, your current speed is the unit rate of 2 miles per hour of hiking. *If you continue at a constant rate of 2 miles per hour, how many miles will you have traveled by 7 P.M.?* Will you finish the 8-mile trail by then and still make it home in time for dinner?

 ## TAKE A CLOSER LOOK

Since this is a unit rate, each additional hour you decide to hike will result in adding 2 miles to your travels.

So far, you've traveled 4 miles in the 2 hours from 4 to 6 P.M. *Will you be off the 8-mile trail by 7 P.M.?* Add one more unit rate of 2 miles for every 1 hour.

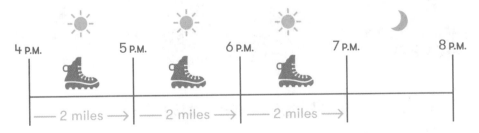

A full bite of fear sets in as you realize that in 3 hours you'll be just 6 miles along the 8-mile trail. You wisely decide to turn around and head home.

TRY A RATIO CHALLENGE

The next day you want to paint your bedroom walls. Your favorite color is purple, so you'll need a mixture of blue paint and red paint. To get the perfect shade of purple, you need a mixture of 4 parts blue paint to 3 parts red paint. In total, you need 21 pints of this mixture to paint your entire room. *How many pints of each color will you need while still keeping the 4:3 ratio?*

First, you can set up a double number line to visualize the ratio:

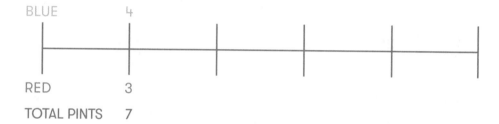

BLUE   4

RED   3
TOTAL PINTS   7

If you pour 4 pints of blue paint and 3 pints of red paint into a bucket, how many pints would you be using? This original mixture would contain 7 pints in total from the 4 blue pints plus the 3 red pints. Since you need 21 pints to paint your room, how many sets of these 7 pints would you need?

Are you thinking 3? That's correct! Three sets of 7 pints give us 21 total pints of paint.

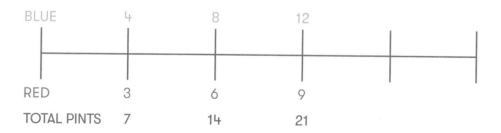

BLUE   4   8   12

RED   3   6   9
TOTAL PINTS   7   14   21

ANOTHER PATH: USING RATIO EQUATIONS

You were mixing 4 pints blue paint with 3 pints red paint in the original mixture, giving a total of 7 pints. You can also use this information to set up a ratio equation and then solve for the number of complete sets of the mixture. Since there were 7 pints here and you needed 21 pints in total, you could have set up equivalent fractions:

$$\frac{\text{TOTAL PINTS}}{\text{SETS OF THE MIXTURE}} \quad \frac{7}{1} = \frac{21}{?}$$

Using 3 sets of 7 pints will give you 21 total pints. This means you'll have 3 sets of the original mixture in total.

$$\frac{\text{TOTAL PINTS}}{\text{SETS OF THE MIXTURE}} \quad \frac{7}{1} = \frac{21}{3}$$

Since the original 4:3 mixture is being multiplied by 3, the final mixture will have 12 blue pints of paint and 9 red pints of paint.

YOUR TURN!

One day you're making a poster to hang in your room, and you decide to make a geometric design around the edge of a poster board. You create a pattern that uses 2 triangles for every 6 circles.

If you used 32 pieces total, how many of each shape did you use? Use the double number line to solve.

TRIANGLES

CIRCLES

There are _____ triangles and _____ circles in the poster board design.

TOOLS FOR SUCCESS

When using double or triple number lines to represent equivalent ratios, it's important to remember:

- Make a separate number line for each item you're comparing.

- Each number line will increase by the same value as its part of the original ratio. Each of these increases is a "hop" on the number line.

UNIT PRICING

On a hot summer day, you notice a fruit stand on the side of the road.

Next to the watermelon section, there's a sign that says "Organic Watermelon: $0.90 for 2 pounds." The good news is you have $2.00 to spend. You just need to figure out how many pounds of watermelon you can buy with your $2.00

ACTIVATE PRIOR KNOWLEDGE

If you know the cost of the watermelon per pound, you can use that information to decide how many total pounds you can purchase with $2.00.

	UNIT RATE	RATE
COST (DOLLARS)	?	0.90
POUNDS	1	2

$$\frac{COST}{POUNDS} = \frac{0.90}{2}$$

Since you're looking for cost per pound, the denominator must be 1. Dividing by 2 will give the cost of one pound.

$$\frac{COST}{POUNDS} = \frac{0.90}{2} = \frac{0.45}{1}$$

÷ 2

÷ 2

So, the unit rate of watermelon is $0.45 per pound. Using this unit rate, complete the ratio table:

	UNIT RATE	RATE			
COST (DOLLARS)	0.45	0.90	?	?	?
POUNDS	1	2	3	4	5

You can use multiplication to fill in the blanks in the table above.

$$3 \times \$0.45 = \$1.35$$
$$4 \times \$0.45 = \$1.80$$
$$5 \times \$0.45 = \$2.25$$

Let's look at this relationship when it's put into a graph. You can plot the cost per pound from the ratio table.

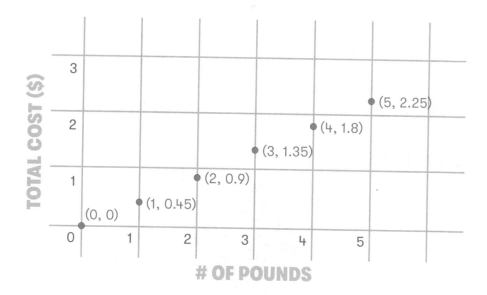

Using a graph to organize the data, you can see there's a proportional relationship to the cost and pounds. A graph uses two lines, or axes, to visually represent numbers or values. You'll learn more about graphs in Chapter 4. In this graph, the cost increases at a constant rate of $0.45.

> **graph:** a visual representation of numbers or values that is usually plotted along two lines, or axes

 ## TAKE A CLOSER LOOK

So, how does the graph help us out? Follow the "Total Cost" (the vertical, or y-axis) to the cost of $2.00. From there, move horizontally to the line of data points. $2.00 is between 4 and 5 pounds on the "# of Pounds" line (the horizontal, or x-axis). That's your answer: $2.00 will get you 4 pounds of watermelon, but it isn't enough for 5 pounds.

TOOLS FOR SUCCESS

When using graphs to represent equivalent ratios, remember:

- The constant change will form a line starting at the point 0, 0.
- Be sure to match the labels of the ratio to the labels on your graph.
- The two parts of each rate create a unique coordinate pair. The unit rate tells you how far to move horizontally and vertically.

YOUR TURN!

Ready to use your graphing skills? A new rec center has a pool, a gym, and other fun activities. The membership rate for students is $17 per month.

1. Use the table below to help find the cost for different lengths of membership.

	UNIT RATE	RATE					
COST (DOLLARS)	17						
MONTHS	1	2	3	4	5	6

2. Next, create a graph for the total cost of the membership for 1, 2, 3, 4, 5, and 6 months.

3. Based on the graph, find and label the cost of:
   a) 3 months of membership
   b) 6 months of membership

4. Bonus Question! An 8-month package costs $120. How much would you save if you purchased this package?

RATIOS AND MEASUREMENT CONVERSION

Instead of your favorite hiking trail being 8 miles, what if it was 506,880 inches long? Actually, that's not a big deal. . . because it's the same length! In math, there are different ways to represent the same measurements of length, weight, and capacity.

As you can see, it's important to know how to **convert** different forms of measurement. The good news is you already have the strategies to do this! Different forms of the same measurement are also known as equivalent ratios.

convert: change a number to a different unit of measurement

ACTIVATE PRIOR KNOWLEDGE

Let's say you end up needing 24 pints of paint to cover your room. You go to the paint store and all they have are gallons of paint. *How many gallons is 24 pints?* Luckily the paint store has a list of common measurement conversions. The key ratio to know here is there are 8 pints in 1 gallon. Now we can use any of our ratio strategies to solve for the number of gallons in 24 pints.

STRATEGY	CONVERSION
Model	8 : 1 = 24 : 3
Equation	8 × 3 = 12 3 × 1 = 3
Table	

PINTS	8	16	24
GALLONS	1	2	3

Number Line

PINTS   0   8   16   24

GALLONS   0   1   2   3

Coordinate Graph

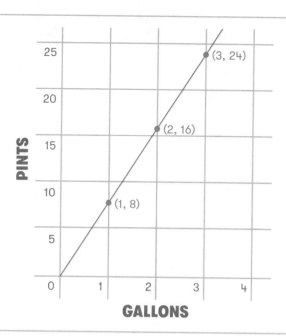

CHOOSE YOUR STRATEGY

Look closely at each strategy. Which ones do you think are the most helpful? Why?

Are you ready to give your favorite strategies a shot? Answer the following problem using two of the strategies you learned.

YOUR TURN!

You're planning to have a picnic in the park with friends, and you've volunteered to bring mini-pretzels for everyone. You have a 5-pound bag of mini-pretzels and a bunch of 6-ounce containers to separate them into. If there are 16 ounces in 1 pound, how many 6-ounce containers will you need to use for all 5 pounds of pretzels?

Use the table on the following page to do your calculations.

STRATEGY	CONVERSION
Model	
Equation	
Table	
Number Line	
Coordinate Graph	

CHAPTER SUMMARY

RATIO BASICS

When you compare one quantity (amount) of a thing to another quantity of the same thing, it's called a ratio.

- **Equivalent Ratios:** You can use equivalent (equal) ratios to make different sized groups that are equivalent in value. For example, 1:2 is equal to 2:4 and 3:6, since there is 1 item for every 2 of another item. You can achieve these equivalent ratios through multiplication or division.

RATIOS VS. RATES

Sometimes you can use these interchangeably; a rate is a specific kind of ratio. We mostly use rates to describe speed or a price.

- **Unit Rates:** This is ratio/rate for every one unit of measurement. For example, "price per 1 gallon of gas" or "5 oranges per 1 dollar." We also use unit rates to describe the "speed" of a line, or steepness.

- **Finding Missing Values:** You can use multiplication and division to complete ratio tables to find missing values. This can be done for all equivalent ratios. You can also create equivalent ratios in fraction form through a similar process.

PUTTING RATES AND RATIOS TO WORK

You can continue to use equivalent ratios to problem solve. Some models that are useful are tape diagrams, ratio tables, fraction models, and graphs.

- **Unit Pricing:** This is the same as a unit rate, but with money. You are finding the cost for 1 item (unit).

- **Ratios and Measurement Conversion:** The connection between ratios and unit/measurement conversion is very valuable. If you want to make one unit of measurement equal to another, an easy way to do that is through ratios. For example, 8 ounces equals 1 cup. Creating equivalences can be helpful in real life (for example, for baking or painting).

CHAPTER 1 VOCABULARY

convert: change a number to a different unit of measurement

equivalent ratios: if one ratio can be expressed as a multiple of another, the two ratios are equal in value

graph: a visual representation of numbers or values that is usually plotted on two lines, or axes

rate: the comparison between two (or more) groups or items in relation to one another with different units (i.e., 12 feet per 3 minutes)

ratio: the comparison between two (or more) groups or items with the same units (i.e., number of apples to number of oranges)

unit rate: the amount of one item for every one of another item (i.e., 3 lemons for $1)

CHAPTER 1 ANSWER KEY

RATIO BASICS (P. 17)

COMPARISON	WRITTEN	SYMBOL	FRACTION
Spider Legs *to* Ant Legs	8 to 6	8:6	$\frac{8}{6}$
Spider Body Segments *to* Ant Body Segments	2 to 3	2:3	$\frac{2}{3}$
Ant Body Segments *to* Spider Body Segments	3 to 2	3:2	$\frac{3}{2}$

EQUIVALENT RATIOS (P. 22)

You need to add *20* peanuts to the trail mix.

RATIOS VS. RATES (P. 24)

Birds to wings: Rate. Foot length to foot width: Ratio (same units—inches). Number of beats to number of minutes: Rate (comparing different units).

UNIT RATES (P. 25)

Since the first and last examples are rates comparing something to 1 unit, they're unit rates. The middle example isn't a unit rate because 1100 words are read in *10 minutes* (not 1 minute).

UNIT RATES (P. 26)

The unit rate is *110 words* per minute.

YOUR TURN (P. 32)

You'll need *12 tea bags* and *36 teaspoons* of sugar.

RATES AND MIXTURES (P. 36)

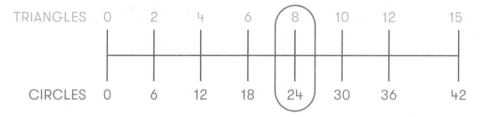

There are 8 triangles and 24 circles in the poster board design, or 32 total pieces.

UNIT PRICING (PP. 40–41)

1. The missing numbers in the table are (left to right) 34, 51, 68, and 85.

2. The line on the graph that shows monthly costs passes through these points: (0, 0); (1, 17); (2, 34); (3, 51); (4, 68); (5, 85); and (6, 102).

3. a. 3 months of membership costs $51.

   b. 6 months of membership costs $102.

4. You would save $16 if you purchased the 8-month package.

RATIOS AND MEASUREMENT CONVERSION (PP. 43–44)

There are 16 ounces in one pound, so you can multiply 5 by 16 to get 80 ounces in 5 pounds. To separate that into 6-ounce containers, you need to divide the 80 by 6. See table on following page.

STRATEGY	CONVERSION

Visual

Equation

$$\frac{80 \text{ OUNCES}}{6 \text{ OUNCES}} = 13\frac{1}{3} \text{ CONTAINERS}$$

Table of Values

CONTAINERS	1	2	3	4	10	12	13	$13\frac{1}{3}$
OUNCES	6	12	18	24	60	72	78	80

Number Line

Coordinate Graph

NOTES

2 RATIO RELATIONSHIPS: PART 2

Summertime is upon us, and the stores have so many watermelons that they decide to put them on sale. You begin to wonder—how many watermelons can you buy with the discount? Now that you understand ratios, you can build on them to use proportions and multi-step ratios— super-powerful mathematical tools— and figure out problems like this!

PROPERTIES OF PROPORTIONALITY

In Chapter 1, you used the power of equal ratios to find the cost of watermelon. These equivalent ratios are so important that they have their own name: proportions. Using proportions, you turned $0.45 for 1 pound of watermelon into $2.25 for 5 pounds of watermelon. Yes, you thought you only had $2.00 to spend, but you found an extra quarter in the pocket of your jeans!

$$\frac{\text{COST}}{\text{POUNDS}} = \frac{\$.45}{1} \overset{\times 5}{\underset{\times 5}{=}} \frac{\$2.25}{5}$$

So, when relationships increase or decrease at a constant rate, their change becomes predictable. This constant rate of change is called the constant of proportionality. That's a big title, huh? Don't worry—we'll break it down together.

proportion: two ratios that are equal to each other

constant of proportionality: the number or value, called a constant, that causes ratios to rise or fall uniformly

THE CONSTANT OF PROPORTIONALITY

Think back to the 8-mile hike from Chapter 1. The constant of proportionality in that example was 2 miles per hour. Using this rate over 4 hours became 8 miles of hiking because of this constant rate of change. It can be visualized in table or graph form:

HOURS	MILES
1	2
2	4
3	6
4	8

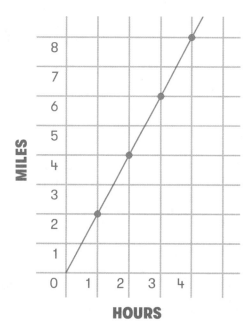

 TAKE A CLOSER LOOK

If you hiked at a constant rate of change that isn't 2 miles per hour, how would this affect your distance hiked?

For example, let's say your constant rate is 4.5 miles for every 1.5 hours.

- How can you use this information to fill in a table and graph?
- What would be the constant of proportionality?

HOURS	MILES
0	0
$1\frac{1}{2}$	$4\frac{1}{2}$
?	?

First, the new rate is for every 1.5 hours you hike 4.5 miles, so use this to start the table. Next, how could you figure out another equivalent rate?

If you hike for another 1.5 hours, how far will you have traveled?

You're doubling each value:

HOURS	MILES
$1\frac{1}{2}$	$4\frac{1}{2}$
3	9

×2 ↘   ↙ ×2

Hiking another 1.5 hours would be tripling each original value:

HOURS	MILES
$1\frac{1}{2}$	$4\frac{1}{2}$
3	9
$4\frac{1}{2}$	$13\frac{1}{2}$

×3   ×3

The information in this table is now considered constant because you're using 4.5 miles per 1.5 hours in each row.

ANOTHER PATH

Big Idea: You can use any given constant rate and multiplication to find equivalent ratios when the relationship is proportional, or crosses the y-axis at (0, 0).

$$\underset{\times 2}{\overset{\times 2}{\frac{4.5 \text{ miles}}{1.5 \text{ hours}}}} = \underset{\times 3}{\overset{\times 3}{\frac{9 \text{ miles}}{3 \text{ hours}}}} = \frac{13.5 \text{ miles}}{4.5 \text{ hours}}$$

Let's visualize this constant rate of change in graph form:

HOURS	MILES
0	0
$1\frac{1}{2}$	$4\frac{1}{2}$
3	9
$4\frac{1}{2}$	$13\frac{1}{2}$

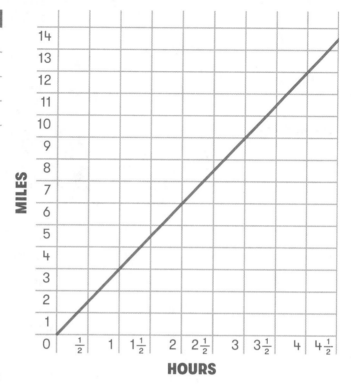

How does this graph of 4.5 miles for every 1.5 hours compare to the graph of 2 miles per hour?

- Are these relationships changing at the same rate?
- Do they represent the same constant of proportionality?
- What key features in the graphs show that the two examples have different rates of change?

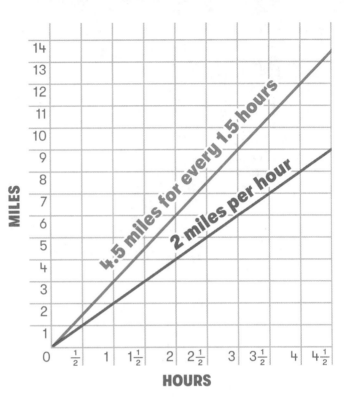

HOURS	MILES
0	0
$1\frac{1}{2}$	$4\frac{1}{2}$
3	9
$4\frac{1}{2}$	$13\frac{1}{2}$

HOURS	MILES
0	0
1	2
2	4
3	6
4	8

The straight lines graphed are not changing at the same rate. The rate of 4.5 miles for every 1.5 hours creates a steeper rise (gets taller faster) than 2 miles per hour. This shows the examples have different rates of change. The only common coordinate is (0, 0); which means they're both proportional, since directly proportional relationships always pass through (0, 0). This point is called the origin, which you'll learn about in Chapter 4.

TAKE A CLOSER LOOK

If each constant of proportionality could be expressed as a unit rate, it will be easier to compare. Consider the first example's table and graph—*what is its unit rate?*

HOURS	MILES
0	0
1	2
2	4
3	6
4	8

$$\text{UNIT RATE} = \frac{2 \text{ miles}}{1 \text{ hour}}$$

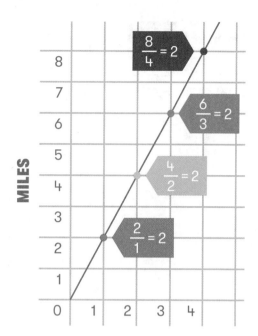

Remember, a unit rate compares an amount to 1 unit. This means the constant of proportionality, 2 miles per hour, is already in unit rate form!

Next, consider the second example's table and graph. *How can you find its unit rate?*

HOURS	MILES
0	0
$1\frac{1}{2}$	$4\frac{1}{2}$
3	9
$4\frac{1}{2}$	$13\frac{1}{2}$

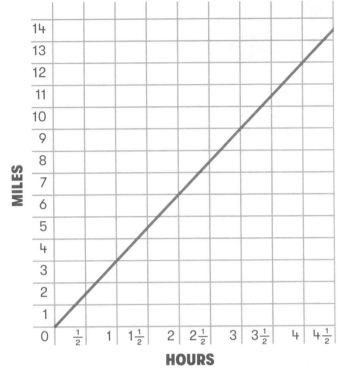

Is 4.5 miles for every 1.5 hours a unit rate? Nope. Since it's not comparing the miles to 1 hour, it's not a unit rate.

PRIOR KNOWLEDGE

To find a unit rate, use your knowledge of ratio equations. First you can set up the rate as a fraction. The denominator of a unit rate must always be one. So your equation will look like this:

$$\frac{miles}{hours} \quad \frac{4.5}{1.5} = \frac{?}{1}$$

In this example, you need to divide the denominator by 1.5 to get 1. This means the numerator must also be divided by 1.5:

$$\frac{miles}{hours} \quad \frac{4.5}{1.5} \overset{\div 1.5}{\underset{\div 1.5}{=}} \frac{3}{1}$$

This creates a unit rate of 3 miles to 1 hour, or 3 miles per hour.

Now you can easily compare the rates of change for both examples!

HIKING RATE 1	HIKING RATE 2
2 miles per hour	3 miles per hour

GRAPHING THE CONSTANT OF PROPORTIONALITY

The constant of proportionality 3 miles per hour is clearly greater than the constant of proportionality 2 miles per hour.

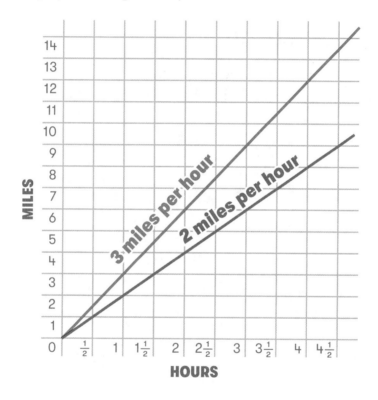

You know that 3 miles per hour is faster than 2 miles per hour when you think about it, but what does this mean for the graphs of the two lines? Revisiting the hiking comparison graph, how does a line's appearance show that one rate is faster than another?

The line for 3 miles per hour is *steeper* than the other line. Since all constant of proportionality rates share the same features, you can say the steeper the line, the greater the constant of proportionality.

TOOLS FOR SUCCESS

When you work with a constant of proportionality, it's important to remember:

1. It can be made into a unit rate.

2. As a unit rate, it's easier to compare to other constants of proportionality.

3. The constant of proportionality only exists when it's a proportional relationship. A proportional relationship always crosses the x- and y-axes at (0, 0).

ANOTHER PATH

When you need to find a unit rate, you can also use division. What happens if you divide the number of miles by the number of hours?

Divide each ratio to show the unit rate:

HOURS	MILES
0	0
$1\frac{1}{2}$	$4\frac{1}{2}$
3	9
$4\frac{1}{2}$	$13\frac{1}{2}$

$$\frac{4.5 \text{ miles}}{1.5 \text{ hours}} = 3$$

$$\frac{9}{3} = 3$$

$$\frac{13.5}{4.5} = 3$$

The results are the same and show the constant of proportionality: 3 miles per hour.

TAKE A CLOSER LOOK

Let's look at one more example with proportions in tables and graphs.

One day, you're invited to a burrito bowl feast with friends. Everyone is bringing one component for burrito bowls, and you need to make enough rice for everyone who's invited. When you make rice just for one person, you use the ratio $\frac{1}{2}$ cup of rice to $1\frac{1}{4}$ cups of water. Using your ratios skills, can you determine if the table below keeps the ratios of rice-to-water proportional?

CUPS OF RICE	CUPS OF WATER
$\frac{1}{2}$	$1\frac{1}{4}$
1	$2\frac{1}{2}$

x2 ⟲   ⟳ x2

You can start by identifying how to get from $\frac{1}{2}$ cup of rice to 1 cup of rice. This relationship is doubled (or multiplied by 2).

CUPS OF RICE	CUPS OF WATER
0	0
$\frac{1}{2}$	$1\frac{1}{4}$
1	$2\frac{1}{2}$
2	5
$2\frac{1}{2}$	$6\frac{1}{4}$

x4   x4
x5   x5

Multiplying the original ratio by 4 will result in 2:5, and multiplying it by 5 will result in $2\frac{1}{2}:6\frac{1}{4}$.

Each of the ratios are equivalent to the initial ratio. Yes, this table is showing a proportional relationship!

ANOTHER PATH

As you saw earlier, you can also determine if a relationship is proportional from its graph. Look at the rice-to-water values in graph form on page 65.

This relationship shows a constant rate of change in its graph.

PROPORTIONAL RELATIONSHIP CHECKLIST

☐ Goes through the origin (0, 0).

☐ Forms a straight line..

☐ Has a constant rate of change.

Uh-oh, it sounds like even more people are planning to attend the burrito bowl feast, and now you need to make more rice!

Look at the new row at the bottom of the table below.

CUPS OF RICE	CUPS OF WATER
0	0
$\frac{1}{2}$	$1\frac{1}{4}$
1	$2\frac{1}{2}$
2	5
$2\frac{1}{2}$	$6\frac{1}{4}$
$3\frac{1}{2}$	?

How many cups of water will you need in order to make $3\frac{1}{2}$ cups of rice?

Once again, your goal is to make a ratio that is proportional to your first ratio ($\frac{1}{2} : 1\frac{1}{4}$).

	CUPS OF RICE	CUPS OF WATER	
x?	$\frac{1}{2}$	$1\frac{1}{4}$	x?
	$3\frac{1}{2}$	?	

Focus on finding the number needed to multiply $\frac{1}{2}$ that results in $3\frac{1}{2}$. When you have that number, you can multiply it with the $1\frac{1}{4}$ cups of water and be good to go!

	CUPS OF RICE	CUPS OF WATER	
x7	$\frac{1}{2}$	$1\frac{1}{4}$	x7
	$3\frac{1}{2}$	$8\frac{3}{4}$	

You correctly determine $\frac{1}{2} \times 7 = 3\frac{1}{2}$. This means you can multiply $1\frac{1}{4}$ cups of water by 7 as well:

Good work—you're going to need $8\frac{3}{4}$ cups of water for the $3\frac{1}{2}$ cups of rice. Let the cooking for the burrito bowl feast begin!

We can also examine the graph for this relationship:

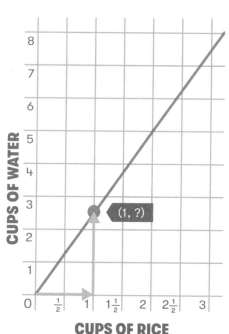

The y-value may be hard to determine if it's not a whole number. But, for this graph, if you look closely, it's easy to read as $2\frac{1}{2}$ cups of water.

Using the point $(1, 2\frac{1}{2})$, you can say the unit rate is $2\frac{1}{2}$ cups of water per cup of rice.

If you want a point that has x- and y-values that are whole numbers, you could choose (2, 5) and then write and simplify the ratio to get the unit.

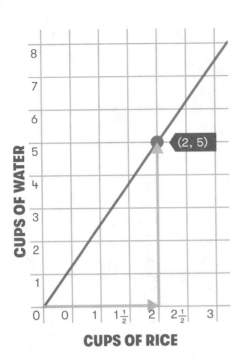

CUPS OF WATER (vertical axis)

CUPS OF RICE (horizontal axis)

Using the point (2, 5), you can find the unit rate by dividing the y-value, 5, by the x-value, 2:

$$\text{Unit Rate} = \frac{5}{2} = 2\frac{1}{2}$$

Once again, you find the constant of proportionality is the unit rate of $2\frac{1}{2}$ cups of water per cup of rice.

YOUR TURN!

Do the tables below represent proportional relationships? Explain your reasoning.

1.

NUMBER OF BEARS	POUNDS OF FOOD
1	$83\frac{1}{2}$
2	167
3	$250\frac{1}{2}$
4	334

2.

HOURS	MILES
$\frac{1}{2}$	$1\frac{3}{4}$
$1\frac{1}{2}$	$5\frac{1}{4}$
2	$6\frac{1}{2}$
$2\frac{1}{2}$	$7\frac{1}{4}$

Determine if the graphs below represent proportional relationships. Explain your reasoning.

3. **BROWNIE SALES**

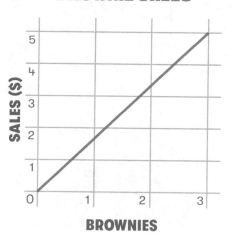

4. **STEP HEIGHT**

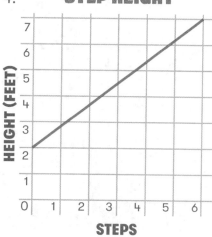

5. **DISTANCE TRAVELED**

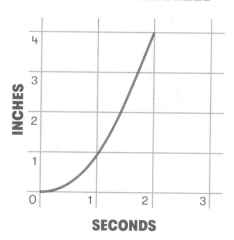

COMPARING TABLES AND GRAPHS

Now that you've reviewed how to calculate the constant of proportionality, let's compare another set of rates.

Your parents are looking to buy a used car. One of the key factors that will help them decide which car to buy is gas mileage. Since you're now great at finding the constant of proportionality, you decide to help them find the number of miles per gallon for the two cars they're considering. Using the information for the two cars in the tables below, do they have the same constant of proportionality?

CAR #1		CAR #2	
GALLONS OF GAS	MILES	GALLONS OF GAS	MILES
10.5	325.5	9.75	302.25
12.25	379.75	11.5	356.5
15	465	16	496
16.5	511.5	18.5	573.5

Set up each as a ratio equation:

CAR #1:

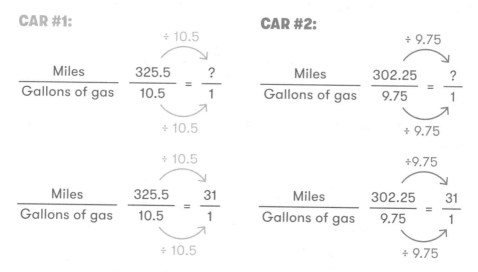

CAR #2:

$$\frac{\text{Miles}}{\text{Gallons of gas}} \quad \frac{325.5}{10.5} = \frac{?}{1}$$

$$\frac{\text{Miles}}{\text{Gallons of gas}} \quad \frac{302.25}{9.75} = \frac{?}{1}$$

$$\frac{\text{Miles}}{\text{Gallons of gas}} \quad \frac{325.5}{10.5} = \frac{31}{1}$$

$$\frac{\text{Miles}}{\text{Gallons of gas}} \quad \frac{302.25}{9.75} = \frac{31}{1}$$

Car #1 has a constant of proportionality of 31 miles per gallon and **Car #2** also has a constant of proportionality of 31 miles per gallon. Since both cars get the same gas mileage, the car being sold for less is going to be the better buy.

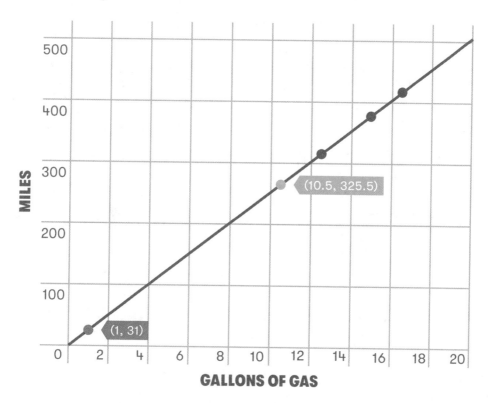

Finally, you can also determine the constant of proportionality from a graph. The graph on p. 70 uses car #1 as an example of how to do this.

You know that 10.5 gallons gives you 325.5 miles driven. So, if you divide 325.5 by 10.5, you can calculate that 1 gallon will take you 31 miles.

TOOLS FOR SUCCESS

When finding a constant of proportionality from a graph, remember:

- The graph relationship must include (0, 0).
- For each coordinate (x, y), when you divide them y ÷ x or y/x, the values must be equivalent.
- If this is true, the value that you calculated is the constant of proportionality.

YOUR TURN!

Fill in the constants of proportionality in the tables below.

1.

CUPS	FLUID OUNCES	CONSTANT OF PROPORTIONALITY
3	24	
5	40	
8	64	
9	72	

2.

GALLONS	FLUID OUNCES	CONSTANT OF PROPORTIONALITY
2	256	
3	384	
4	512	
5	640	

3. Identify the graph below that has a constant of proportionality of 1.75.

a. Cost of Lemons

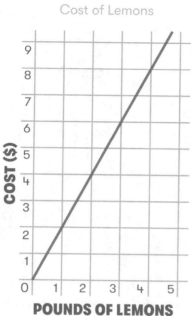

COST ($) vs POUNDS OF LEMONS

b. Rate of Travel

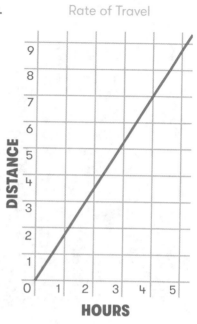

DISTANCE vs HOURS

c. Fish Caught with Worms

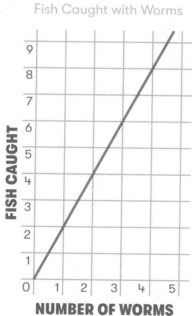

FISH CAUGHT vs NUMBER OF WORMS

d. Cookie Sales

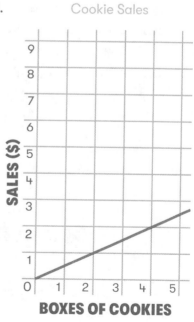

SALES ($) vs BOXES OF COOKIES

WRITING PROPORTIONAL EQUATIONS

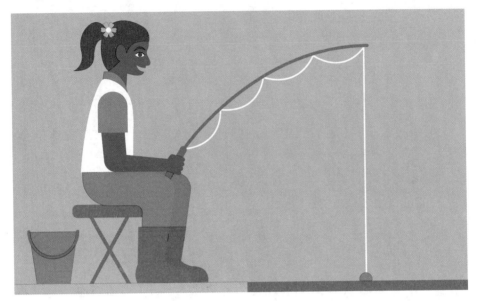

One day, you walk to a nearby lake to do some fishing. You find the perfect spot, set up your gear and fish for about 4 hours. As you walk home, you wonder how many fish you caught per hour. You remember that you caught 3 fish the first hour.

So, how does this information help you find out how many fish you caught per hour?

HOURS	FISH CAUGHT
0	0
1	3
2	?
3	?
4	12

PRIOR KNOWLEDGE

You can use any complete row of information to set up a proportion to find out how many fish you caught after 2 hours. Let's use 12 fish in 4 hours:

$$\frac{\text{fish}}{\text{hours}} \quad \frac{?}{2} = \frac{12}{4}$$

The challenge now is to figure out what number will make these fractions equivalent. Let's start with something we do know: $2 \times ? = 4$.

Since $2 \times 2 = 4$, the denominators are related by a factor of 2. So, let's use that to find the unknown denominator. What number times 2 gives you 12?

$$? \times 2 = 12$$
$$6 \times 2 = 12$$

Not too difficult, right? The missing numerator is 6. Let's put that into the proportion:

$$\frac{fish}{hours} \quad \frac{6}{2} = \frac{12}{4} = 3 \text{ fish per hour}$$

How can you verify that this belongs in the table? This is where it's good to notice that the table gives you the constant of proportionality, 3 fish per hour. If each of the ratios in the proportion simplify to the constant of proportionality, then you're on the right track.

Good work! Fill in the rest of the table now that you know the constant of proportionality:

HOURS	FISH CAUGHT
0	0
1	3
2	6
3	9
4	12

$$\frac{3}{1} = \frac{6}{2} = \frac{9}{3} = \frac{12}{4}$$

You had a great day of fishing!

YOUR TURN!

1. Use the constant of proportionality $\frac{6}{9}$ *fish caught per piece of popcorn* to find how many fish would be caught with 36 pieces of popcorn.

2. Use the constant of proportionality $\frac{7}{12}$ *chocolate candies to total candies* to calculate how many chocolate candies you would get if you got 48 total pieces of candy on Halloween.

3. Playing basketball, you make 5 baskets out of every 6. If this constant of proportionality continues, how many baskets would you make in 48 attempts?

SIMPLE INTEREST

Simple interest is a percentage of the original amount (called the **principal**) applied at the end of each time period. For example, $100 invested at 6% simple yearly interest means there will be 6% of 100 applied at the end of each year. Since 6% of 100 is $6, the first three years would look like this:

YEAR	BALANCE OR PRINCIPAL AMOUNT	SIMPLE INTEREST	NEW ACCOUNT BALANCE
1	$100	+ $6	$106
2	$106	+ $6	$112
3	$112	+ $6	$118

simple interest: the amount paid on the starting sum of money that is borrowed or loaned to someone for a specific period of time

principal: the starting amount in a bank account, investment, or loan

To find the total amount of money that the interest generated, you can add $6 repeatedly. But also...

ANOTHER PATH

Is there a faster way to add the same number repeatedly? Yes, multiplication! With that in mind, you can instead use this formula:

THE SIMPLE INTEREST FORMULA

$$I = P \times r \times t$$

I: interest total amount

P: principal (starting) amount

r: interest rate (as a decimal)

t: time

🔍 TAKE A CLOSER LOOK

Have you ever thought about how much money you want when you're older? Did you know that what you do with your money now at a young age can positively or negatively affect how much you have later in life? Here's a good piece of money-saving advice: the earlier you start saving, the more time your money will have to grow!

Let's say, at the end of the summer, you've saved $500. You shop around to see which local bank offers the best savings account. You find the following offers:

NIFTY BANK

NOW!

Offering high interest savings!

Simple interest rate of **6.5%** per year for 10 years

Call Nifty Bank today!

THRIFTY BANK

WOW! WOW! WOW!

Offering long term savings!

Simple interest rate of **5.25%** per year for 15 years

Call Thrifty Bank today!

Which bank has the better offer? There are a couple of things to consider here:

- If you deposit $500, how much will you earn every year in interest?
- How much money will you have at the end of each time period?

 ## PRIOR KNOWLEDGE

First, it's a good idea to organize the key information for the formula, $I = P \times r \times t$.

	I	P	R	T
NIFTY	?	$500	6.5%	10
THRIFTY	?	$500	5.25%	15

Use the formula to find the simple interest after 1 year for each bank:

BANK	SIMPLE INTEREST	YEARLY INTEREST
Nifty	$I = \$500 \times 0.065 \times 1$	$I = \$32.50$
Thrifty	$I = \$500 \times 0.0525 \times 1$	$I = \$26.25$

At the end of the first year, Nifty Bank will earn $32.50 in interest and Thrifty Bank will earn $26.25 in interest.

Since this is simple interest, during the second year each bank will earn the same amount as in the first year. So, multiply the yearly interest by 10 to find the total money earned at the end of a 10-year investment.

BANK	SIMPLE INTEREST	YEARLY INTEREST	INTEREST OVER 10 YEARS
Nifty	$I = \$500 \times 0.065 \times 1$	$I = \$32.50$	$\$32.50 \times 10 = \$325$
Thrifty	$I = \$500 \times 0.0525 \times 1$	$I = \$26.25$	$\$26.25 \times 10 = \$262.50$

Over 10 years, you earn more money with Nifty Bank, with an extra $62.50. But at Thrifty Bank, the money collects interest for 15 years instead of 10. If you calculate that:

Thrifty Bank: $26.25 × 15 = $393.75

So, how do you decide which bank to choose? It depends on how long you want to keep your money in the bank. If you want to take your money out after 10 years, choose Nifty Bank. If you want to leave it in for 15 years, choose Thrifty Bank.

ANOTHER PATH

You could also find the total amount of interest for all 10 years for Nifty Bank using the formula. In this method, make $t = 10$:

$$I = \$500 \times 0.065 \times 10 = \$325$$

Now, let's also use the formula for all 15 years for Thrifty Bank, making $t = 15$:

$$I = \$500 \times 0.0525 \times 15 = \$393.75$$

TOOLS FOR SUCCESS

When working with simple interest, it's important to remember:

- Interest is a percentage and should be written in decimal form in calculations.

    - Example: An interest rate of 5.25% is the decimal 0.0525.

- Simple interest is basically just repeated addition. It's a set percentage of the original amount that gets applied to the end of each week, month, year, etc.

    - Example: 10% simple yearly interest for a $2,000 investment will result in $200 (10% of $2,000) applied at the end of each year.

- There's a helpful formula for simple interest: $I = P \times r \times t$.

YOUR TURN!

Calculate the amount of interest earned each year and the total interest at the end of the full time period for each of the following:

INVESTMENT	YEARLY INTEREST	INTEREST OVER FULL TIME PERIOD
A $1,500 invested at 6.5% for 15 years		
B $1,500 invested at 8.5% for 10 years		

PROPERTIES OF PROPORTIONALITY

For a relationship to be proportional, it must include the origin (0, 0) and have a constant unit rate: for every increase of 1 for one of the variables, there will be a constant increase in the other.

THE CONSTANT OF PROPORTIONALITY

You can visualize the constant of proportionality in tables, graphs, and equations.

COMPARING TABLES AND GRAPHS

CAR #1	
GALLONS OF GAS	MILES
10.5	325.5
12.25	379.75
15	465
16.5	511.5

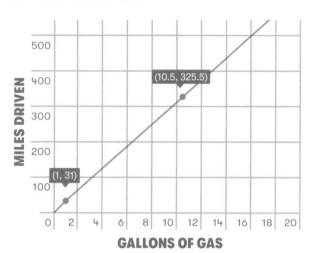

WRITING PROPORTIONAL EQUATIONS

Unit 1/unit 2 = unit 1/unit 2 as long as the left side and right side of the equation represent equal relationships. Example:

$$\frac{5 \text{ miles}}{1 \text{ gallon}} = \frac{10 \text{ miles}}{2 \text{ gallons}}$$

SIMPLE INTEREST

This is a type of interest that you can apply to a situation where you have a principal (beginning amount), a rate of interest (usually a percentage), and an amount of time that the money is earning interest.

THE SIMPLE INTEREST FORMULA

$$I = P \times r \times t$$

I: interest total amount

r: interest rate (as a decimal)

P: principal (starting) amount

t: time

CHAPTER 2 VOCABULARY

constant of proportionality: the number or value, called a constant, that causes ratios to rise or fall uniformly

principal: starting amount in an account or investment

proportion: two ratios that are equal to each other

simple interest: the amount paid on a starting amount of money ("principal") that is borrowed or loaned to someone

CHAPTER 2 ANSWER KEY

PROPORTIONAL RELATIONSHIPS (PP. 66–67)

1. Yes, this table represents a proportional relationship. There's a constant change in the pounds of food as the number of bears increases.

2. No, this table doesn't represent a proportional relationship. There's not a constant change in the miles at 2 and $2\frac{1}{2}$ hours.

3. Yes, this graph represents a proportional relationship. It starts at the origin (0, 0) and changes at a constant rate, as shown by the straight line.

4. No, this graph doesn't represent a proportional relationship. It doesn't start at the origin (0, 0).

5. No, this graph doesn't represent a proportional relationship. It starts at the origin (0, 0), but it doesn't change at a constant rate. The shape of the graph isn't a straight line.

COMPARING TABLES AND GRAPHS (PP. 70–71)

1. All have a constant of proportionality of 8.

2. All have a constant of proportionality of 128.

3. Graph *b* (Rate of Travel) has a constant of proportionality of 1.75.

WRITING PROPORTIONAL EQUATIONS (P. 73)

1. 36 pieces of popcorn would catch 24 fish at the rate $\frac{6}{9}$ fish per piece of popcorn.

2. If you got 48 total pieces of candy, 28 of them would be chocolate at the rate $\frac{7}{12}$ chocolate candies to total candies.

3. If you make 5 baskets out of every 6, 48 attempts would result in 40 baskets.

SIMPLE INTEREST (P. 78)

Investment A: $1,500 invested at 6.5% for 15 years.

     The interest each year will be $97.50.

     The total interest after 15 years will be $1,462.50.

Investment B: $1,500 invested at 8.5% for 10 years.

     The interest each year will be $127.50.

     The total interest after 10 years will be $1,275.00.

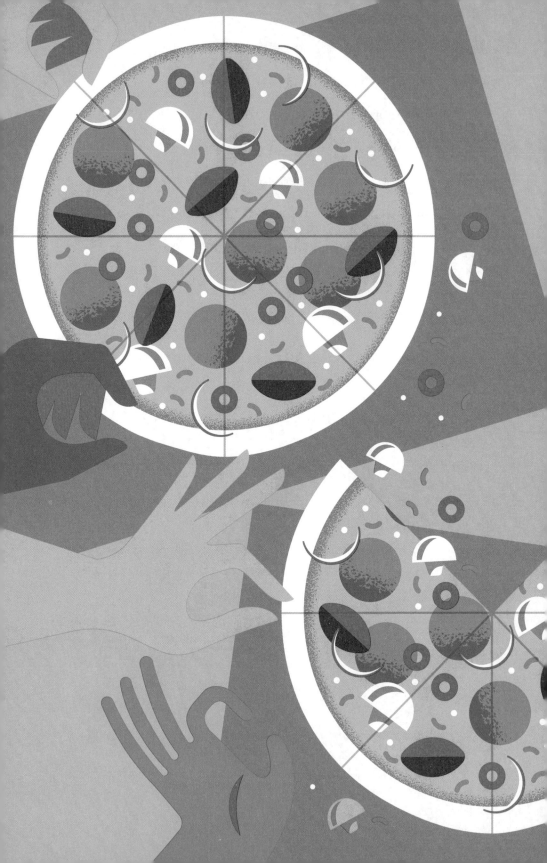

3 OPERATIONS AND RATIONAL NUMBERS: PART 1

As you've seen, numbers are a useful way to better understand the world. The more kinds of operations you're able to perform with numbers, the greater your power!

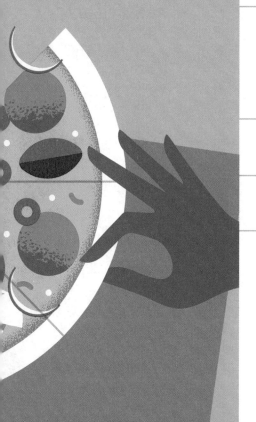

CHAPTER CONTENTS

DIVISION: GOING BEYOND WHOLE NUMBERS

You and a few friends decide to join the Environmental Club at your school. At your first meeting, the club president brings two large pizzas for the group. Each one will be divided equally into eighths. How many $\frac{1}{8}$-slices will there be in 2 large pizzas?

Use the diagrams above to find the number of slices in 2 whole pizzas. Remember, each of these slices represents $\frac{1}{8}$ of a whole pizza.

 ## TAKE A CLOSER LOOK

So, what is the result of dividing 2 by $\frac{1}{8}$? Count the slices of pizza.

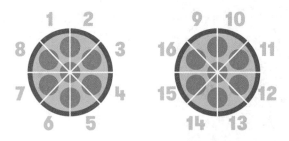

If you found that there were 16 $\frac{1}{8}$ slices in 2 whole pizzas, you're correct!

You might be thinking, "Isn't division supposed to separate a number into equal smaller pieces?" This time, when you divided 2 by the fraction $\frac{1}{8}$, the result was a number greater than 2.

By dividing the 2 pizzas into $\frac{1}{8}$ -parts, you divided the pizzas into 16 equal slices, making them easier to share.

DIVIDING A WHOLE NUMBER BY A FRACTION

You just saw a visual model showing a whole number divided by a fraction. Now, let's look at how to use numbers and operations to get the same result. This process is called the standard algorithm (see page 89).

> **operations:** ways of manipulating numbers that allow you to calculate a new value (multiplication, division, subtraction, addition, etc.)

Since you're dividing each pizza into 8 pieces, there will be 8 slices per pizza. So, change the division into multiplication.

2 pizzas divided into $\frac{1}{8}$ slices.

2 pizzas ÷ $\frac{1}{8}$ size slices = ?

When setting up the equation, the 2 will go first because it's being divided into $\frac{1}{8}$ parts.

$$2 \times \frac{8}{1} = ?$$ *Find the reciprocal of $\frac{1}{8}$.*

$$\frac{2}{1} \times \frac{8}{1} = ?$$ *Rewrite 2 as a fraction.*

$$\frac{2}{1} \times \frac{8}{1} = 16$$ *Multiply across for the answer.*

$$2 \div \frac{1}{8} = 16$$ *Division, for reference.*

Good work! As you saw in the illustration, there will be 16 slices when 2 pizzas are divided into $\frac{1}{8}$-slices. The key math property here is called multiplying by the **reciprocal**. It means the first fraction is multiplied by the flip (reciprocal) of the second fraction.

reciprocal: the number resulting from "flipping" the numerator and denominator of the target number.

$$a \div \frac{b}{c} = ? \quad \Rightarrow \quad a \times \frac{c}{b} = ?$$

Next, your friends decide to cut each pizza slice in half—so there will be more of them! Right now, one slice of pizza is $\frac{1}{8}$ of the whole pizza. What will be the size of each new slice after dividing the $\frac{1}{8}$ slice in half?

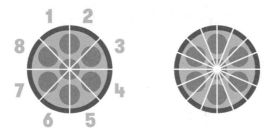

This time, the fraction, $\frac{1}{8}$, will go first because it's being divided into 2 parts (halved).

$$\frac{1}{8} \div 2 = ?$$

$$\frac{1}{8} \div \frac{2}{1} = ? \qquad \text{\textit{Rewrite 2 as a fraction.}}$$

$$\frac{1}{8} \times \frac{1}{2} = ? \qquad \text{\textit{$\frac{1}{8}$ will multiply the reciprocal of $\frac{2}{1}$.}}$$

$$\frac{1 \times 1}{8 \times 2} = \frac{1}{16} \qquad \text{\textit{Multiply across.}}$$

Nice job—each slice will be $\frac{1}{16}$ of the whole pie!

YOUR TURN!

1. The football team is planning a cookout, and you have 5 pounds of ground meat to make $\frac{1}{4}$-pound burgers. How many $\frac{1}{4}$-pound burgers can you make from 5 pounds of meat? Use the diagram provided to solve this problem.

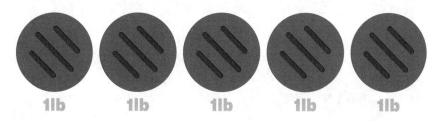

1lb   1lb   1lb   1lb   1lb

Use the standard algorithm to solve the following problems:

2. $7 \div \frac{1}{3}$

3. $\frac{3}{5} \div 4$

> **standard algorithm:** this is a general term that mathematicians use to describe the traditional way of completing a procedure

DIVIDING A FRACTION BY A FRACTION

For Earth Day, your Environmental Club has a $\frac{2}{3}$-acre plot of land to plant pine trees. You decide to split the land into sections that are each $\frac{1}{6}$ of an acre. *How many rows measuring $\frac{1}{6}$-acre will you have?*

ACTIVATE PRIOR KNOWLEDGE

This may seem a little hard to wrap your mind around. That's okay—an area model will help visualize what's going on. You know that the land measures $\frac{2}{3}$ of an acre in total and that it will be divided into $\frac{1}{6}$-acre sections.

This time let's use a rectangular-shaped model.

ONE UNIT (1 ACRE)

The club's land is $\frac{2}{3}$ of an acre, so begin by dividing the one-unit model into thirds.

Shade 2 out of 3 parts to represent $\frac{2}{3}$.

Now you're ready to divide the land into $\frac{1}{6}$-acre sections for pine trees. Remember, you'll need to divide the *entire* acre into 6 parts to make $\frac{1}{6}$-acre sections!

$$\frac{2}{3} \div \frac{1}{6} = ?$$

Each two-third block would be divided into 6 rows.

So, how many $\frac{1}{6}$-acre sections will make up the $\frac{2}{3}$ acre of land?

Two-thirds of an acre divided into $\frac{1}{6}$-acre sections shows that there will be **4 sections** on which the club can plant pine trees.

Since there are 4 groups of $\frac{1}{6}$-acre sections, $\frac{2}{3} \div \frac{1}{6} = 4.$

There you go! You successfully divided the $\frac{2}{3}$ of an acre into $\frac{1}{6}$-acre spaces and made 4 sections for pine trees.

ANOTHER PATH

You can also use a number line diagram to illustrate the division of two fractions. To divide $\frac{2}{3}$ of an acre into $\frac{1}{6}$-acre spaces:

$\frac{2}{3}$ **OF AN ACRE**

Shade 2 out of 3 parts.

Divide the one acre into 6 sections. Shade 4 out of 6 parts, which represents two-thirds.

$\frac{1}{6}$ **OF AN ACRE**

How many $\frac{1}{6}$-acre spaces fit in the $\frac{2}{3}$ of an acre?

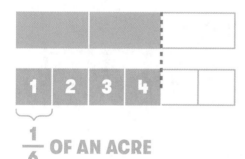

Continue to shade blocks and count.

$\frac{1}{6}$ **OF AN ACRE**

Again, you see $\dfrac{2}{3} \div \dfrac{1}{6} = 4$.

DIVIDING A FRACTION BY A FRACTION USING AN EQUATION

Let's work the pine tree problem again using an equation. The goal is to find the result of dividing $\frac{2}{3}$ of an acre of land into $\frac{1}{6}$-acre sections:

$$\frac{2}{3} \div \frac{1}{6} = ?$$
Set up the equation.

$$\frac{2}{3} \times \frac{6}{1} = ?$$
$\frac{2}{3}$ will multiply the reciprocal of $\frac{1}{6}$.

$$\frac{2 \times 6}{3 \times 1} = \frac{12}{3} = 4$$
Muliply and simplify if possible.

Done! As in the model and with the line diagram, $\frac{2}{3}$ of an acre can be divided into four $\frac{1}{6}$-acre sections.

YOUR TURN!

The Environmental Club wants to plant more trees along a trail at another park. The trail is $\frac{3}{4}$ of a mile in total.

$\frac{3}{4}$ OF A MILE

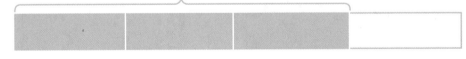

If you plant a tree every $\frac{1}{8}$ of a mile, how many trees will there be along the $\frac{3}{4}$-mile trail?

- Use the diagram above to help solve with the area model method.

- Then, check your answer using the standard algorithm.

DIVIDING A MIXED NUMBER BY A FRACTION

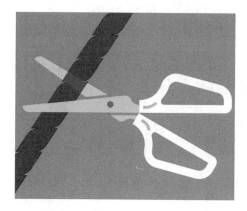

You're preparing supplies for a craft project. The project calls for pieces of rope that measure $\frac{1}{9}$ of a yard. You're given a long length of rope that measures $2\frac{2}{3}$ yards. *How many pieces of rope measuring $\frac{1}{9}$ yard can you cut?*

ACTIVATE PRIOR KNOWLEDGE

You can use your number line model skills to visualize this division of two fractions. The mixed number $2\frac{2}{3}$ will be created first to represent the rope.

$$2\frac{2}{3} \text{ yards of rope} \div \frac{1}{9} \text{ yard pieces} = ? \text{ number of pieces}$$

Create two, 1 yard spaces. Divide into ⅓ blocks. **Create $\frac{2}{3}$ yard with two $\frac{1}{3}$ blocks.**

Create $\frac{1}{9}$ yard by dividing 1 yard into 9 blocks. Shade the $\frac{1}{9}$-yard block.

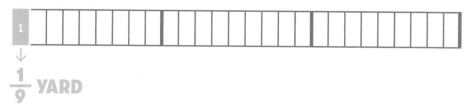

Perfect. Now you can use the pieces of $\frac{1}{9}$ yard to overlay them on top of the $2\frac{2}{3}$-yards rope and *count* the number of $\frac{1}{9}$-yard pieces that fit inside or on top of the rope.

How many ⅑-yard pieces of rope are in $2\frac{2}{3}$ yards?

Great! You have 24 pieces of $\frac{1}{9}$-yard rope for your craft project!

TAKE A CLOSER LOOK

Drawing a visual model can sometimes be difficult with mixed numbers. Dividing $2\frac{2}{3}$ by $\frac{1}{9}$ could also be solved using an equation if you use an improper fraction in place of the mixed fraction $2\frac{2}{3}$.

In an **improper fraction**, the numerator is greater than the denominator (i.e. greater than 1), so $2\frac{2}{3}$ becomes $\frac{8}{3}$. Take a look at how:

$$2\frac{2}{3} \div \frac{1}{9} = ?$$

$$2\frac{+2}{\times 3} = \frac{8}{3} \longrightarrow \frac{8}{3} \div \frac{1}{9} = ? \qquad \textit{Create an improper fraction.}$$

$$\frac{8}{3} \times \frac{9}{1} = \frac{72}{3} \qquad \textit{Multiply.}$$

$$\frac{72}{3} = 24 \qquad \textit{Simplify.}$$

Again, you find that the $2\frac{2}{3}$ yards of rope have 24 pieces measuring $\frac{1}{9}$ yard.

YOUR TURN!

When you were planting trees, you decided to hang bird feeders along the walking trail, and now it's time to refill them. There are $2\frac{5}{8}$ cups of birdseed left.

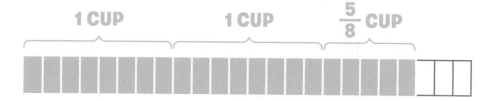

1 CUP   **1 CUP** $\frac{5}{8}$ **CUP**

If each bird feeder holds $\frac{3}{4}$ cup of birdseed, how many bird feeders can you fill using $2\frac{5}{8}$ cups of birdseed?

- Use the diagram above to help solve with the area model method.

- Then, check your answer using the standard algorithm.

OPERATIONS WITH DECIMALS

The decimal system has many uses in everyday life, whether it be with money, measurements, or time. Knowing how to add, subtract, multiply, and divide with decimals is a great skill to have!

ADDING DECIMALS

As thanks for planting the trees, the city is paying for a picnic for the Environmental Club. You're helping the club advisor organize the picnic, so you purchase a few items online. What is the total cost of your groceries?

GROCERY	PRICE
(1) Watermelon	$2.42
(1) Gallon of Water	$1.99
(1) Box of Granola Bars	$2.84
(1) Apple	$0.80
(1) Loaf of Bread	$3.75
(1) Jar of Peanut Butter	$5.44
(1) Jar of Jelly	$2.98

```
   5 3
  $2. 4 2
 +$1. 9 9
 +$2. 8 4
 +$0. 8 0
 +$3. 7 5
 +$5. 4 4
 +$2. 9 8
 ─────────
 $20. 2 2
```

The decimals are lined up for easy addition. Take a moment, using a pen or pencil, to add-up the cost of your items.

Your groceries cost $20.22.

The store charges a delivery fee of $6.50. You also give the delivery person a $4 tip. After the fee and the tip, *how much do you end of up paying?*

$20.22 + $6.50 + $4.00 = $30.72   *Write all numbers as monetary amounts.*

```
      1
  $ 2 0 . 2 2
+ $   6 . 5 0
+ $   4 . 0 0
  $ 3 0 . 7 2
```

Line up all decimals and add as usual.

The total cost of groceries including tip and delivery fee is $30.72.

SUBTRACTING DECIMALS

Your advisor says you can spend up to $40, and whatever is left can go into the club treasury.

How much money do you have left over?

$40 − $30.72 = *money left over*

First, rewrite $40 with two decimal places for cents as $40.00.

Second, line up the decimal points, just as you would for addition.

Subtract the the numbers as usual, remembering to borrow as you would in the traditional subtraction algorithm. The total amount left over is $9.28.

```
    3 9 . 9 10
  $ 4 0 . 0 0
− $ 3 0 . 7 2
  $ 0 9 . 2 8
```

MULTIPLYING DECIMALS

Now use your multiplication skills to figure out how much money you could have saved if you remembered to use a coupon with a 15% discount.

Discount only applies to the cost of the goods, not delivery fee and tip. So, what is 15% of $20.22?

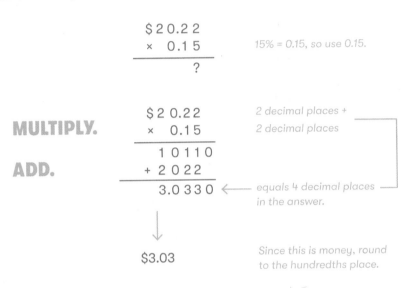

$20.22
× 0.15
——————
    ?

15% = 0.15, so use 0.15.

MULTIPLY.

ADD.

$20.22
× 0.15
——————
  10110
+ 2022
——————
 3.0330

2 decimal places +
2 decimal places

equals 4 decimal places in the answer.

$3.03

Since this is money, round to the hundredths place.

DIVIDING DECIMALS

A few days after the picnic, your neighbors organize a party at the park. They give you $20 to buy some sandwiches for the party. Today, sandwiches are on sale for $2.50 each.

How many can you buy?

Are you thinking of division? Fantastic.

You could divide the $20 by the cost of each sandwich, $2.50. It's difficult to *divide by a decimal*, but it is much easier when the divisor is a whole number. Let's see:

$$2.50 \overline{)20}$$

Move the decimal 2 places to the right in the divisor and dividend.

$$2.50, \overline{)20.0.0,}$$

Insert zeroes as placeholders.

$$\begin{array}{r} 8 \\ 250 \overline{)2000} \\ -2000 \\ \hline 0 \end{array}$$

Move the decimal up and divide.

Nice job! You can buy 8 sandwiches for your neighborhood's party in the park.

You invite some friends to the neighborhood's party to share the 8 sandwiches. There are 16 people in total. *How will you split up the sandwiches?*

8 sandwiches ÷ 16 people = amount of sandwich per person

$$8 \div 16 = ?$$

Since 16 cannot go into 8, so you must add decimal place values in the dividend until you find a number that 16 can go into.

$$\begin{array}{r} 0.5 \\ 16 \overline{)8.0} \\ -80 \\ \hline 0 \end{array}$$

Bring the original position of the decimal up to the quotient.

Divide normally.

Since your answer is 0.5, each person would get half a sandwich.

TAKE A CLOSER LOOK

For the upcoming party, you also spent $9.50 on decorations. Five of your neighbors offer to split the cost. *How much does each person need to contribute for the decorations?*

$9.50 ÷ 5 people = $ for decorations per person

```
      1.9
  5 ⌐9.50
    - 5
    ─────
      4 5 0
    - 4 5 0
    ─────
          0
```

Bring the original position of the decimal up to the quotient.

Divide normally.

Each person will need to contribute $1.90 for decorations.

YOUR TURN!

Try some practice examples with all four operations for numbers in decimal form:

1. Two pieces of yarn are in a scrap pile, one measuring 7.235 inches and the other 17.92 inches. What is the total length of yarn that can be reused for another project?

2. If 16.2 gallons of gasoline are purchased at $2.09 per gallon, how much is the total gasoline purchase?

3. There are 48.6 ft available on an ocean jetty for people to fish 8 ft apart from one another. How many people can safely fish along the jetty?

4. How many packs of gum costing $1.98 each can be purchased with $266?

TERMINATING AND REPEATING DECIMALS

The decimal system in mathematics uses the number 10 as its base and helps us understand the larger number system. One way this is true is for the remainders of division.

- Whether a number is rational or irrational, it can always be represented in **decimal form**.

- Only rational numbers can be written as fractions.

> **rational number:** a number that has a value that can be written as a fraction, repeating decimal, terminating decimal, or integer

TAKE A CLOSER LOOK

When decimals are used to express rational numbers, their remainders either *terminate* or *display a repeating pattern*.

Terminating decimal remainders are those that end or stop:

$$\longrightarrow \frac{1}{10} = 0.1 \qquad \longrightarrow 4\frac{7}{100} = 4.07$$

$$\longrightarrow \frac{1}{4} = 0.25 \qquad \longrightarrow \frac{37}{16} = 2.3125$$

$$\longrightarrow \frac{11}{8} = 1.375$$

Repeating decimal remainders display a pattern of one or more numbers. Both a bar above the numbers or an ellipsis (. . .) can show that a pattern continues.

$$\frac{1}{3} = 0.\overline{3} \longleftarrow \textbf{BAR ABOVE}$$

When a pattern has more than one number, look closely to see that the pattern is repeating:

$$\frac{7}{11} = 0.636363 = 0.\overline{63}$$

1st → (first 6) 3rd → (second 6) 2nd ↑ (3)

YOUR TURN!

Can you identify which numbers are terminating and which are repeating? Write T above the terminating numbers and R above the repeating numbers:

YOUR CHOICE:			
0.7575. . .	4.5625	5.125	$1.\overline{267}$

GREATEST COMMON FACTOR OF WHOLE NUMBERS 100 OR LESS

The Environmental Club is planning a work day to tend to some of the trees you planted, and you're in charge of making trail mix. After shopping for supplies, you have 36 ounces of granola, 72 ounces of dried cranberries, 96 ounces of almonds, and 48 ounces of chocolate chips. You want every batch to have the same proportions. *How many batches can you make?*

As you look at different sets of numbers, you should think about what they have in common. What do 36, 72, 96, and 48 all have in common? They're even numbers. Let's use 48 (chocolate chips) as an example to look at how multiplication applies.

PRODUCT $\longrightarrow$ 48 = 12 × 4 $\longleftarrow$ **FACTORS**

The numbers that are multiplied to get 48 are called *factors*. The result, or answer, is the *product*. To figure out sets of factors, you start with 1 and 2 and move on up the list to find their factor partner. *Let's look for the greatest factor.*

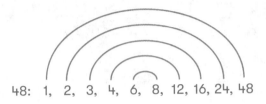

48: 1, 2, 3, 4, 6, 8, 12, 16, 24, 48

Factor Rainbow Method

The diagram above connects the factors of 48 to each other. You can use this method to find any common factors when you compare more than one number.

Let's try to find the common factors between the 36 ounces of granola and the 48 ounces of chocolate chips.

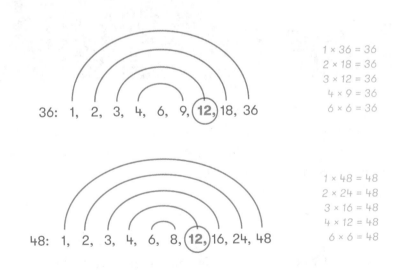

36: 1, 2, 3, 4, 6, 9, (12,)18, 36

1 × 36 = 36
2 × 18 = 36
3 × 12 = 36
4 × 9 = 36
6 × 6 = 36

48: 1, 2, 3, 4, 6, 8,(12,)16, 24, 48

1 × 48 = 48
2 × 24 = 48
3 × 16 = 48
4 × 12 = 48
6 × 6 = 48

After creating the sets of factors, you can identify their greatest common factor, 12. The **greatest common factor (GCF)** is the greatest number in the factor lists that are in common between both lists.

ANOTHER PATH

You can also use a number line diagram to illustrate the division of two fractions:

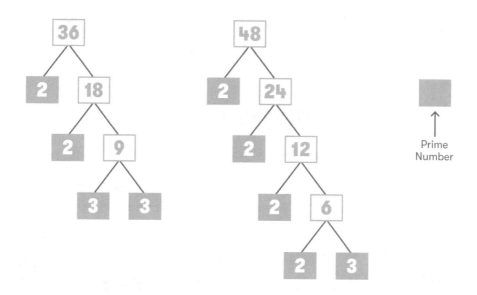

Identify sets of prime factors common to both numbers:

Prime factors of 36: 2 × 2 × 3 × 3
Prime factors of 48: 2 × 2 × 2 × 2 × 3

Multiply those common prime factors together to find your GCF:

GCF of 36 and 48: 2 × 2 × 3 = 12

Nice work! 12 is the *greatest common factor* of 36 and 48.

What is the greatest number of batches you can make using these ingredients: *72 ounces of dried cranberries, 96 ounces of almonds, and 48 ounces of chocolate chips?*

Create a list of factors for 72, 96, 48.

48: 1, 2, 3, 4, 6, 8, 12, 16, (24) 48

72: 1, 2, 3, 4, 6, 8, 9, 12, 18, (24) 36, 72

96: 1, 2, 3, 4, 6, 8, 12, 18, (24) 32, 48, 96

The greatest number that is in each set of factors is 24.

The GCF of 72, 96, and 48 is 24. This means that you can make at most 24 batches of trail mix using the ingredients you have on hand.

 ## TAKE A CLOSER LOOK

How can we use GCF to rewrite expressions?

For example, how can the expression 25 + 80 be rewritten using the **distributive property**? (You'll get more on the distributive property in Chapter 5, but it's so important we're going to define it here as well.)

> **distributive property:** holds that multiplying a number (a) by a group of numbers added together (b + c) is equivalent to multiplying that number by each number separately: a(b + c) = ab + ac. This also holds true for subtraction: a(b – c) = ab – ac

The distributive property can also be used to rewrite expressions:

$$ab + ac = a(b + c).$$

Start by finding the GCF for 25 and 80:

25: 1, 5, 25
80: 1, 2, 4, 5, 8, 10, 16, 20, 40, 80

Use a list of factor pairs to find the GCF.

Use the distributive property to show GCF(factor 1 + factor 2).

25 + 80

(5 × 5) + (5 × 16)   *Rewrite using the GCF factor pairs for each.*

5(5 + 16)   *Respective factor pairs.*

↓

25 + 80 = 5(5 + 16) = 105

expanded form = factored form = standard form

If you were to distribute the GCF(5) over the other factors (5 + 16), it would create the original expression, 25 + 80!

BATCHES: *WHAT ABOUT THE INGREDIENTS?*

Let's think about the trail mix recipe you used for the Environment Club again. *How many ounces of each ingredient will there be in each batch of the trail mix you made?*

You know that you're making 24 batches, but let's review where this number came from. Since the GCF of 72, 96, and 48 is 24, this means there must be 24 groups of each ingredient.

Note: *Each batch has the same ingredients.*

24 × (batch)

24 × (dried cranberries + almonds + chocolate chips)

24 (dried cranberry ounces) + 24 (almonds ounces) + 24 (chocolate chips ounces)

24 × ___ = 72   24 × ___ = 96   24 × ___ = 48

The factor pairs for 24 in each of the 3 ingredients are the number of ounces of each used per batch. You'll need 3 ounces of dried cranberries, 4 ounces of almonds, and 2 ounces of chocolate chips for each batch of trail mix to make 24 portions.

YOUR TURN!

1. It's a hot summer day, and the gatherings don't stop. Your mom is making fruit cups for a family reunion. You decide to help and find there are 72 whole grapes, 90 pieces of watermelon, 54 half strawberries, and 36 pieces of pineapple.

   a. How many fruit cups can you make if each cup has the same ingredients?

   b. How many pieces of each fruit will there be in a cup?

2. Use the distributive property to rewrite the expressions as the product of their GCF and the respective factors.

   a. 35 + 42

   b. 28 + 70

   c. 54 + 36 + 72

LEAST COMMON MULTIPLES OF WHOLE NUMBERS 12 OR LESS

Have you ever noticed that sometimes hot dogs come in packs of 6, but the buns are in packs of 8? What are you supposed to do with the extra buns? *How many packs of hot dogs and how many packs of buns would you need so that there's the same number of each without leftovers?* Before we can solve this, we need to understand multiples.

USING A DOUBLE NUMBER LINE

Multiples are the products of two factors.

$$\overset{+2\ \ +2\ \ +2\ \ +2\ \ +2}{\frown\frown\frown\frown\frown}$$
multiples of 2: 2, 4, **6**, 8, 10, **12**, . . .

$$\overset{+3\ \ +3\ \ +3\ \ +3}{\frown\frown\frown\frown}$$
multiples of 3: 3, **6**, 9, **12**, 15, . . .

Listing the multiples of two numbers and finding the lowest one that they have in common is called finding the **least common multiple (LCM)**.

Use the number line to find the LCM of 3 and 7. Start by listing all the multiples for each number until a common one appears.

MULTIPLES OF 3

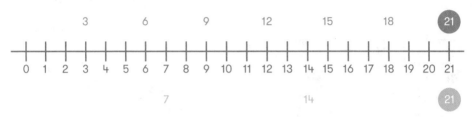

MULTIPLES OF 7

List the multiples of the first number on the top of the number line and the multiples for the second number below the number line. For the top, jump in multiples of 3. For the bottom, jump in multiples of 7. Continue jumping along the line until you hit the first number that they have in common. The least common multiple of 3 and 7 is 21.

Let's apply this method to the hot dogs and buns situation. In our example, hot dogs come in packs of 6 and buns come in packs of 8. So, you want to find the *least common multiple of 6 and 8*.

HOT DOG PACKAGES: MULTIPLES OF 6

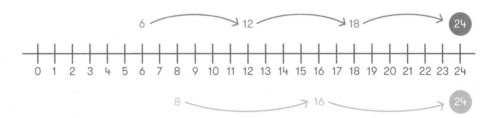

HOT DOG BUN PACKAGES: MULTIPLES OF 8

Start with 6 and make your first jump to the next multiple, 12. Go to 8 and make the first jump to 16. Do the destination numbers match? Since 12 ≠ 16, jump again one at a time. The multiples of 8 grow faster than the multiples of 6, so you need to make an extra jump for 6 to reach 24.

The least common multiple of 6 and 8 is 24. This means that you'll need to buy *4 packages of hot dogs and 3 packages of buns* to have an equal number of buns and hot dogs.

ANOTHER PATH

You can also organize multiples in list or table form to identify the least common multiple.

PACKAGES OF HOT DOGS multiples of 6	HOT DOG BUNS multiples of 8
6	8
12	16
18	24
24	

4 packages of hot dogs

3 packages of hot dog buns

This confirms your result from the previous method, 24 is the least common multiple, which translates to 24 items of each. You can use a list to determine how many packs of hot dogs and buns you need.

Packs of hot dogs   6 × 4 = 24   24 is the fourth number in the list.

Packs of buns   8 × 3 = 24   24 is the third number in the list.

So, you'll need to buy 4 packs of hot dogs and 3 packs of hot dog buns.

YOUR TURN!

1. At the local park where you planted trees, a ranger refills the bird feeders every 2 days. Every 4 days, they water the trees. Every 6 days, they perform grounds maintenance.

PARK RANGER'S TASK	FREQUENCY (DAYS)
Refill the bird feeders	2
Water trees	4
Grounds maintenance	6

If the ranger completed all 3 tasks today, how many days from now will he complete all 3 tasks again?

CHAPTER SUMMARY

FRACTIONS

- Area Models for Division

- Standard Algorithm for Division of a Fraction by a Fraction:

$$\frac{a}{b} \div \frac{c}{d} = \frac{a}{b} \times \frac{d}{c} = \frac{ad}{bc}$$

- Standard Algorithm for Division of Whole Numbers by Fractions:

$$\frac{a}{1} \div \frac{c}{d} = \frac{a}{1} \times \frac{d}{c} = \frac{ad}{c}$$

DECIMALS

- Add, Subtract, Multiply, and Divide with Decimals

  - **Add and Subtract:** Line up the decimals; subtract or add as normal.

  - **Multiply:** Multiply as normal; include the total number of decimal places in the final answer.

  - **Division:** The position of the decimal point will depend on the original position in the dividend.

- Terminating and Repeating Decimals: When decimals are used to express **rational numbers,** their remainders either *terminate* or *display a repeating pattern.*

THE DISTRIBUTIVE PROPERTY

The distributive property can be used to rewrite expressions:

$$ab + ac = a(b + c)$$

GREATEST COMMON FACTOR OF WHOLE NUMBERS 100 OR LESS

- The **greatest common factor (GCF)** is the greatest number in the factor lists that are in common between both lists.

- **GCF Methods:** Factor tree, prime factorization, and factor rainbow (connected list)

LEAST COMMON MULTIPLES OF WHOLE NUMBERS 12 OR LESS

- Multiples are the products of two factors.

- To find the least common multiple (LCM), list the multiples of two numbers and find the one with the lowest value that they have in common.

- **LCM Methods:** Double number line method, multiples list, and table/chart method

CHAPTER 3 VOCABULARY

distributive property: holds that multiplying a number (a) by a group of numbers added together (b + c) is equivalent to multiplying that number by each number separately. a(b + c) = ab + ac. This also holds true for subtraction: a(b − c) = ab − ac

greatest common factor (GCF): the number with the greatest value that is a factor of (i.e., it can be multiplied to produce) two or more target numbers

improper fraction: a fraction in which the numerator is greater than the denominator, for example $\frac{5}{4}$ is an improper fraction equivalent to $1\frac{1}{4}$

least common multiple (LCM): the number with the lowest value that is a shared multiple of two (or more) target numbers

operations: ways to manipulate numbers that allow you to calculate a new value (multiplication, division, subtraction, addition, etc.)

rational number: a number that has a value that can be written as a fraction, repeating decimal, terminating decimal, or whole number

reciprocal: the number resulting from "flipping" the numerator and denominator of the target number. Multiplying any number by its reciprocal always equals 1

standard algorithm: this is a general term that mathematicians use to describe the traditional way of completing a procedure

CHAPTER 3 ANSWER KEY

DIVISION OF WHOLE NUMBERS BY FRACTIONS (P. 89)

1. You can make 20 burgers.

2. 21

3. $\frac{3}{20}$

If you used a calculator to help you with these examples or if you're familiar with decimal representations, you might have gotten other equivalent answers for examples 2 and 3. We'll talk more about this later!

DIVIDING A FRACTION BY A FRACTION (P. 94)

You planted 6 trees along the hiking trail.

STANDARD ALGORITHM FOR DIVIDING A MIXED NUMBER BY A FRACTION (P. 97)

$3\frac{1}{2}$ bird feeders can be filled.

OPERATIONS WITH DECIMALS (P. 102)

1. 25.155 inches

2. 33.858 is rounded up to $33.86 because money follows the rounding rules of decimals when finding cost.

3. 6 people is rounded down from 6.075 because you can only have whole people.

4. 134 packs of gum is rounded down from 134.34 because you can't buy part of a pack of gum.

TERMINATING AND REPEATING DECIMALS (P. 104)

R	T	T	R
0.$\overline{7575}$...	4.5625	5.125	1.2$\overline{67}$

GREATEST COMMON FACTOR OF WHOLE NUMBERS 100 OR LESS (P. 110)

You can make 18 fruit cups. Each cup will contain: 2 pineapple pieces, 3 strawberry halves, 4 grapes, and 5 watermelon pieces.

LEAST COMMON MULTIPLES OF WHOLE NUMBERS 12 OR LESS (P. 114)

1. On the 12th day, the park ranger will perform all 3 tasks.

2a. $35 + 42 = 7(5 + 6)$

2b. $28 + 70 = 4(7 + 10)$

2c. $54 + 36 + 72 = 9(6 + 4 + 8)$

4

OPERATIONS AND RATIONAL NUMBERS: PART 2

Above ground / Below ground. Lending Money / Borrowing Money. Up to the Attic / Down to the Basement. Above Freezing / Below Freezing. There are two sides to every story. How can you best describe these phrases? Can you think of any more to add? All these phrases represent examples of things that oppose one another. Math helps you describe many opposing things using integers: positive and negative whole numbers.

POSITIVE AND NEGATIVE INTEGERS

One hot summer day you walk to a nearby lake to cool down. As you get closer to the water, you realize that it might be colder than you prefer. Your toes touch the water and—yep—it's so shockingly cold you'd think that it's wintertime!

PRIOR KNOWLEDGE

As you walk into the lake, you can practically feel the difference in temperature with every inch you move above or below water. The numbers that measure those precious inches above and below the waterline are integers.

> integers: positive and negative whole numbers

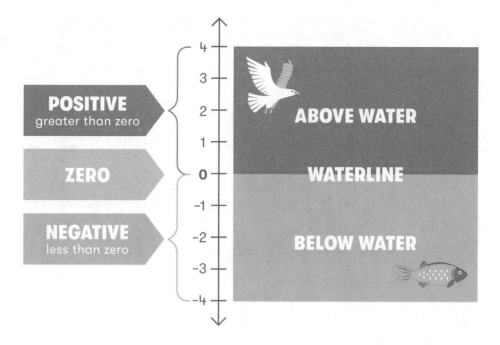

Heights above the water are positive numbers (greater than 0). Depths below the water are negative numbers (less than 0). To talk about the different parts of this diagram, you can rotate the image to be horizontal instead of vertical. That way you can take a closer look at the numbers labeled on a familiar number line. Positive whole numbers are greater than 0, and they increase in value by 1 from left to right.

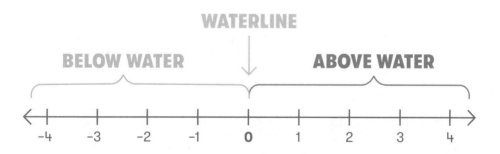

Negative numbers are less than 0, and they decrease in value by 1 on the number line from right to left. Think of the movement along the number line as being *steps* away from zero.

As you can see on the number line, numbers 1, 2, 3, and 4 each have a match that's the same distance from zero, only on the *left* side of 0. Every positive number has a negative match, or an opposite.

> **opposites:** numbers that are the same distance from 0 on the number line, but on different (opposite) sides of 0

Positive numbers have opposites on the other side of zero. Zero, whole numbers, and the opposites of whole numbers make up the category of numbers called integers.

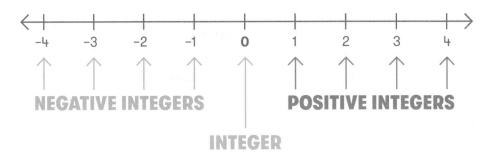

LOCATING RATIONAL NUMBERS ON A NUMBER LINE

If you want to locate a target number on the number line, start by asking yourself:

- Is this number greater than 0 or less than 0? *This will allow you to position the number on the correct side of 0.*

- What number is *greater* than the target number?

- What number is *less* than the target number?

Let's give it a try! Target Number: −2.5

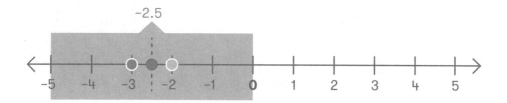

a. Is this number *greater than* 0 or *less than* 0?

- *Since the number is negative, the number is less than 0. The target number should be positioned to the left of the zero.*

b. What number is *greater than* the target number?

- *A number that is greater than −2.5 is* **−2**. *This is the closest* friendly number *that is greater than −2.5.*

c. What number is *less than* the target number?

- *A number that is less than −2.5 is* **−3**. *This is the closest friendly number that is less than −2.5.*

- With this information, you can begin to place this information on the number line to narrow down the position of the target number. Since −2.5 represents the halfway mark, position the −2.5 halfway between the −2 and −3.

friendly or benchmark number: a number that is easy to work with, often a multiple of ten or a single-digit whole number

On the number line below, how can you describe the location of the following integers?

$$-1, 6, 0, -5$$

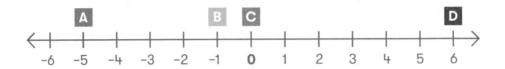

Focus on one integer at a time and remember to move to the *left* for *less* than 0 and to the *right* for *more* than 0.

- −1 is 1 space to the *left* of 0, so it's *less* than 0, at position B.

- 6 is 6 spaces to the *right* of 0, so it's *more* than 0, at position D.

- 0 is the middle of all opposites, the *start* of the positive integers and the start of all negative integers, at position C.

- −5 is 5 spaces to the *left* of 0, so it's *less* than 0, at position A.

COMPARING INTEGERS USING A NUMBER LINE

Here are some examples of how to compare integers:

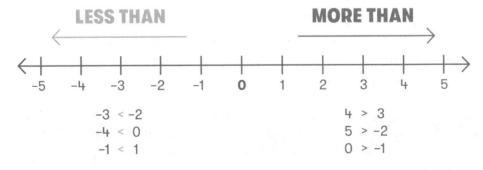

A number to the *left* of another number will always be the *lesser* value and a number to the *right* of another number will always be the *greater value*.

When you plot a negative number on the number line, remember that *left* means *less* than 0. Positive or negative signs tell you the direction to move. The number tells you the number of units to move away from 0.

TOOLS FOR SUCCESS

When working with positive and negative rational numbers, it's important to remember:

• Numbers greater than 0 are positive.

INCREASING
positive numbers to the right of 0

• Numbers less than 0 are negative and marked with a minus symbol in front of the number.

DECREASING
negative numbers to the left of 0

• The number 0 is the anchor number for determining which integers are positive or negative. The number 0 is neither positive nor negative.

• Integers are positive whole numbers, negative whole numbers, and 0.

• The same numbers with different signs are considered opposite.

    • For example, –4 and 4 are opposites.

YOUR TURN!

Try solving these problems:

1. Is this number greater than 0 or less than 0?

    a. 1

    b. –3

    c. 8

2. Plot each integer on the number line: 3, –6, 5, –5.

    a. Which number is the smallest? How do you know?

    b. Which number is the largest? How do you know?

    c. For the numbers in between the smallest and largest,
       which is the larger number? How do you know?

3. Place the following integers on the number line.

    a. –5

    b. 3.5

ABSOLUTE VALUE

Your best friend moved 50 miles east from where you live to another town, and the following weekend your favorite cousins moved 50 miles west to a different town. Are east and west opposites of each other? It's not a trick question—they are! So that makes where you live the "0" location on the number line. But then, how do you decide if east or west represents the positive/negative integers? Have you ever heard someone say they traveled "negative 50 miles?" Probably not. When it comes to distance, it's never referred to as *negative*: this is absolute value.

absolute value: the distance between a value on the number line to 0 (for example, 6 and −6 are both 6 units away from the 0 on a number line)

When you're referring to distance, you can say left/right, up/down, north/south, east/west, above/below, etc., but never negative. Whether you are traveling from the North Pole to the South Pole or vice versa, the distance between the two poles is about 8,595 miles.

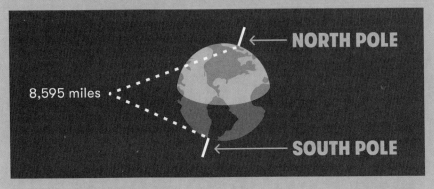

8,595 miles

NORTH POLE

SOUTH POLE

TAKE A CLOSER LOOK

When the distance from 0 is described symbolically, the | | symbol is used: for example, |10| and |−10|. These are said to be "the absolute value of 10" and the "absolute value of −10." They both represent 10 spaces from 0.

The absolute value of both 10 and −10 is 10, because both integers are 10 units away from 0. On a number line:

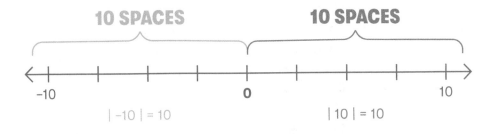

10 SPACES   **10 SPACES**

−10   0   10

| −10 | = 10 | 10 | = 10

Use the given number line to find |-4| and |5|.

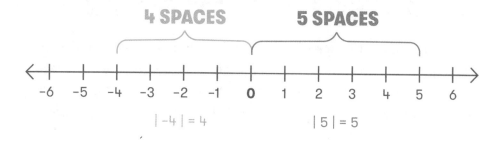

$|-4| = 4$

$|5| = 5$

-4 is 4 spaces from 0 to the *left*, and 5 is 5 spaces from 0 to the *right*.

TOOLS FOR SUCCESS

It's important to remember that absolute value:

- represents a number's distance from zero

- will always be a positive value

- uses the symbol | |, as in |50| or |-50|

YOUR TURN!

With your newfound knowledge, determine the absolute value of the numbers below.

- $|-12|$
- $|\frac{1}{5}|$
- $|-1.6|$
- $|3|$

HORIZONTAL OR VERTICAL LINE DISTANCE BETWEEN TWO POINTS

You can use absolute value to help find the distance between two points on a horizontal or vertical line. Think back to when you were in the lake. If your feet were 27 inches below the water line and the top of your head was 27 inches above the water line, *how tall are you?*

Because distance (height) is never negative, the 27 inches under water will be the absolute value of –27, which is 27 since it represents distance. Therefore, your total height (the distance from the bottom of your feet to the top of your head) is

$$|27| + |-27| = 54 \text{ inches}$$

$$27 + 27 = 54 \text{ inches}$$

TAKE A CLOSER LOOK

After your dip in a lake, you come out to the shore and set up an umbrella to give you some shade. The umbrella's instructions say, "Dig a hole at least 10 inches deep to secure the pole." You bury the bottom of the umbrella about 10 inches into the sand and stand up. The part of the umbrella remaining above ground is as tall as you are, 54 inches. Can you figure out the total length of the umbrella?

You realize that 10 inches of the umbrella are below ground and 54 inches are above ground. Using absolute value here would allow you to write a mathematical statement:

$$|-10| + |54|$$

$$= 10 + 54$$

$$= 64$$

The distance of 10 inches underground plus the distance of 54 inches above ground equals 64 inches in total. This means the total length of the umbrella is 64 inches.

YOUR TURN!

Use an absolute value statement to represent each scenario and answer each question.

1. Your friend is standing 9 feet to the left of a light pole and you're standing 5 feet to the right of the light pole. *What is the distance between you and your friend?*

2. A fishing pier on the shore is 10 feet above sea level and a fish is swimming 2 feet below the surface. *What is the distance from the pier to the fish?* You can use the number line for the problem below to help you calculate.

3. Write an absolute value statement according to the diagram below. *What distance does a cormorant flying 30 feet in the air have to travel to snag his lunch?*

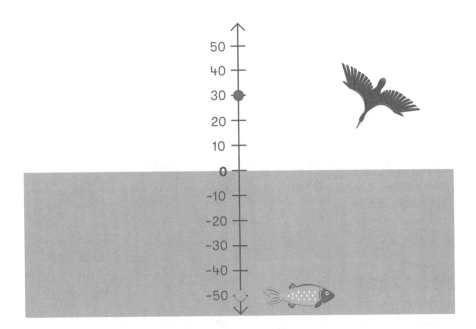

POSITIVE AND NEGATIVE NUMBERS ON THE COORDINATE PLANE

Putting together the horizontal number line (**x-axis**) and the vertical number line (**y-axis**) creates the coordinate plane. The intersection of the x- and y-axis is called the **origin**. It represents where both the x- and y-values are zero, the coordinate (0,0). Look familiar? It's a type of graph.

x-axis: the horizontal axis of integers

y-axis: the vertical axis of integers

origin: the intersection point of the x- and y-axis on the coordinate plane, (0, 0)

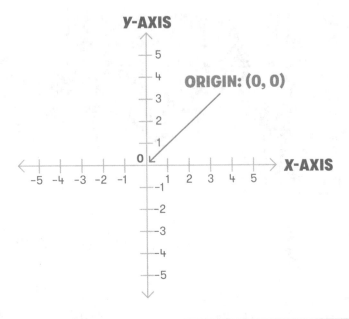

Fun fact! The coordinate plane is called the **Cartesian plane**, named by its creator, René Descartes.

PRIOR KNOWLEDGE

The coordinate plane allows you to describe a position in two dimensions. The x-value tells you the number of horizontal units (left/right). The y-value tells you the number of vertical units (up/down).

> **coordinate plane:** the two-dimensional plane formed by an x-axis and y-axis

When plotting a point, it's important to remember:

x-value comes first ⟶ (x, y) ⟵ y-value comes second

One way to remember x is first and y is second is that (x, y) are in alphabetical order.

For example, plot the point (6, 4):

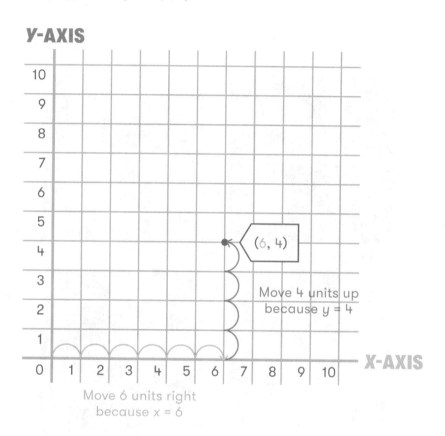

Y-AXIS

Move 4 units up because y = 4

Move 6 units right because x = 6

X-AXIS

TAKE A CLOSER LOOK

When the x- and y-values are both positive, the point exists inside of **quadrant I**. Think about the prefix *quad-*. Have you ever ridden a "quad," a sporting vehicle with four wheels? Maybe the word *quadrilateral* sounds more familiar to you, a polygon with four sides. The prefix, *quad-* means four. With that in mind, the coordinate plane has four quadrants.

> **quadrant:** sections of the coordinate plane formed by the vertical, y-axis and horizontal, x-axis; there are four in the coordinate plane

Traditionally, quadrants are written with Roman numerals: I, II, III, IV.

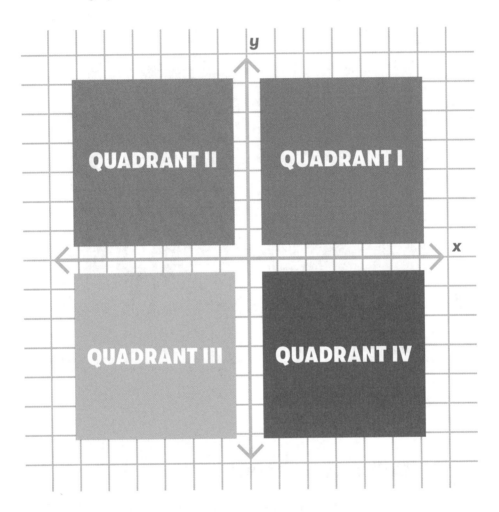

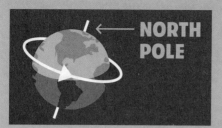

You may have noticed the quadrants are in counterclockwise order. They rotate in the opposite direction of the hands on a clock. Although nobody knows for sure why the ancient Babylonians rotated angles in this way, it may have to do with the rotation of Earth. If you were way above the North Pole viewing Earth from space, you would notice that Earth revolves counterclockwise.

It's time to update your time capsule. Using your favorite tree as (0, 0), the spot where you buried it last was 5 feet east from the tree and 2 feet underground. *(Note: Underground would be a negative direction vertically.)*

If you laid an *xy*-coordinate plane on top of your map, *what quadrant would your time capsule be in?*

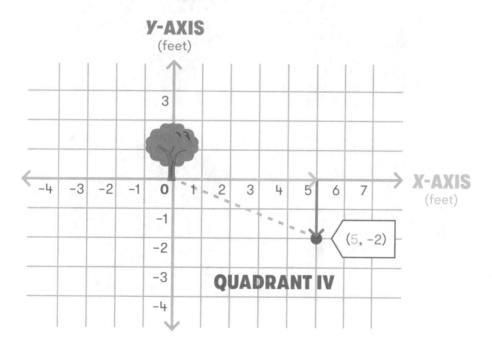

Your time capsule is located at the coordinates for the point (5, −2) in Quadrant IV.

> **coordinates:** values used to describe the location of a point on a graph and written in the form (x, y)

TAKE A CLOSER LOOK

In Quadrant IV, all coordinates have a positive x-value and a negative y-value, (+, –). What about the other quadrants? See if you can determine the signs (positive or negative) for the x- and y-values in Quadrants I, II, and III.

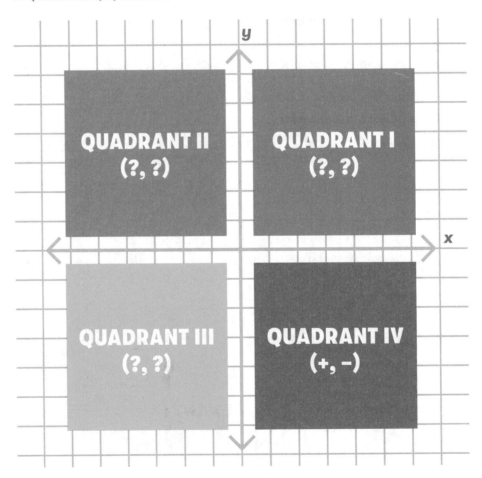

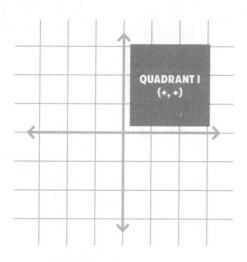

In Quadrant I, both x- and y-values are greater than zero: (*positive*, *positive*).

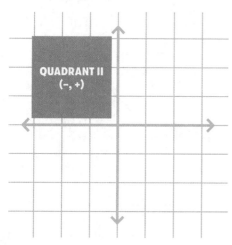

In Quadrant II, x-values are less than zero, but y-values are greater than zero: (*negative*, *positive*).

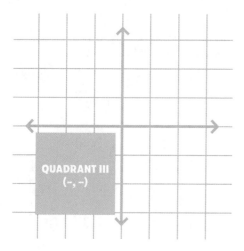

In Quadrant III, both x- and y-values are less than zero, so the coordinates are (*negative*, *negative*).

YOUR TURN!

1. Determine the quadrant of each coordinate below. Then plot the points on the coordinate graph. Each unit on the grid = 1.

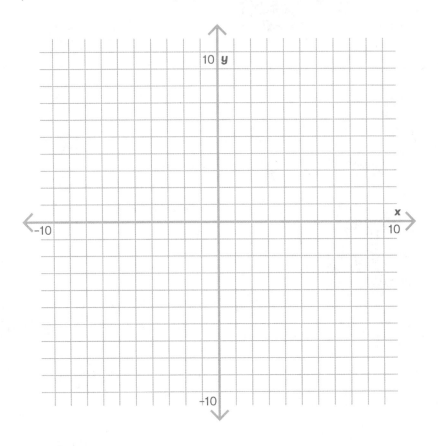

COORDINATE	QUADRANT
(5, –2)	IV
(–2, –5)	
(–10, 5)	
(4, 5)	
(0, 5)	

2. While visiting a national park, you're up in a lookout station at the origin (0, 0) on the coordinate plane. Looking through your binoculars, you spot several animals. Write the coordinates and quadrants for each of the following:

- Gray wolf

- White-tailed deer

- Brown bear

- Big horn sheep

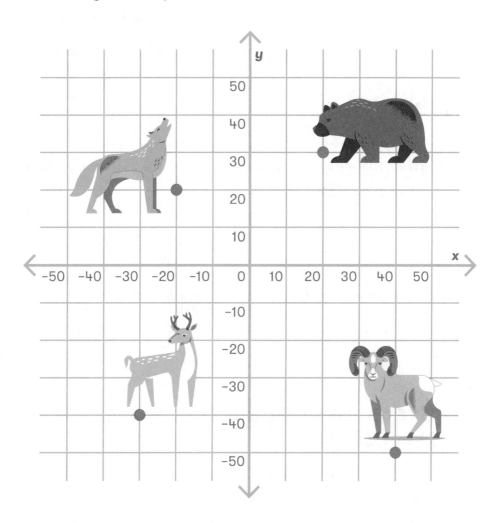

CHAPTER SUMMARY

POSITIVE AND NEGATIVE INTEGERS

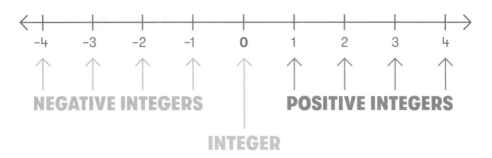

ABSOLUTE VALUE

Absolute value represents distance on a number line from zero. You can use the absolute values to find horizontal or vertical line distances between any two points or positions.

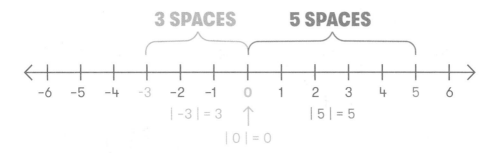

POSITIVE AND NEGATIVE NUMBERS ON THE COORDINATE PLANE

You can use the coordinate plane to describe the positions and distance between two or more points. The coordinate plane allows you to use negative values, which directionally would represent south and west. The coordinate plane has 4 quadrants.

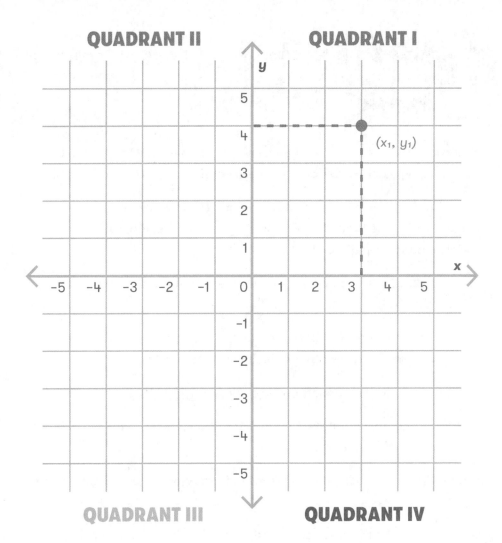

CHAPTER 4 VOCABULARY

absolute value: the distance between a value on the number line to 0 (for example, 6 and −6 are both 6 units away from the 0 on a number line)

coordinate plane: otherwise known as the "Cartesian Plane"; a two-dimensional plane formed by intersecting perpendicular axes, which intersect at the **origin** (0, 0)

coordinates: locations in the coordinate plane; they must have an x- and y-value (x, y)

friendly or benchmark number: a number that is easy to work with, often a multiple of ten or a single-digit whole number

integers: positive and negative whole numbers

opposites: numbers that are the same distance from 0 on the number line, but on different (opposite) sides of 0

origin: the intersection point of the x- and y-axis on the coordinate plane, (0, 0)

quadrant: sections of the coordinate plane formed by the vertical, y-axis and horizontal, x-axis; there are four in the coordinate plane

x-axis: the horizontal axis of integers

y-axis: the vertical axis of integers

CHAPTER 4
ANSWER KEY

POSITIVE AND NEGATIVE NUMBERS (P. 128)

1a. greater than

1b. less than

1c. greater than

2.   a. –6 is the smallest because it's farthest to the left.

   b. 5 is the largest because it's the farthest to the right.

   c. 3 is larger than –5 because 3 is to the right of –5.

3.

ABSOLUTE VALUE (P. 131)

• |–12| = 12

• |$\frac{1}{5}$| = $\frac{1}{5}$

• |–1.6| = 1.6

• |3| = 3

HORIZONTAL OR VERTICAL LINE DISTANCE BETWEEN TWO POINTS (PP. 133–134)

1. |–9| + |5| = 9 + 5 = 14. You and your friend are 14 feet apart.

2. |10| + |–2| = 10 + 2 = 12. The pier and the fish are 12 feet apart.

3. |30| + |–50| = 30 + 50 = 80. The cormorant must travel 80 feet.

POSITIVE AND NEGATIVE NUMBERS ON THE COORDINATE PLANE (P. 142–143)

1.

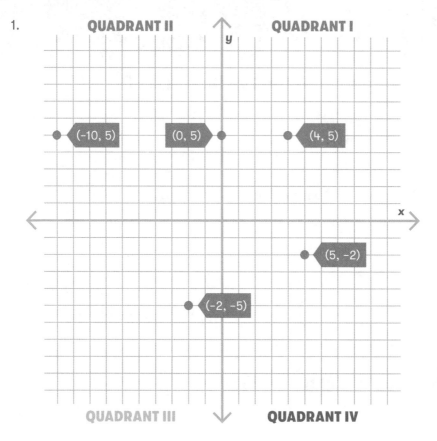

(0, 5) is on the border between Quadrant I and Quadrant II. You can see where the other coordinates fall!

2. • Gray wolf: (–20, 20); Quadrant II

   • White-tailed deer: (–30, –40); Quadrant III

   • Brown bear: (20, 30); Quadrant I

   • Big horn sheep: (40, –50); Quadrant IV

NOTES

BITE OFF S'MORE THAN YOU CAN CHEW

OOEY-GOOEY GOODS!

OPERATIONS AND RATIONAL NUMBERS: PART 3

You're finally going on an overnight camping trip with a friend. But you need a new tent, and you have no money. So, you come up with a business idea called "The Bite Off S'More Than You Can Chew" homemade DIY dessert kit—perfect for a sweet treat reminiscent of a campfire, even if you're not near one. In order to make and sell these kits, you need supplies. Luckily, your parent offers to loan you $20 to get your business started. How can you put your math skills to work to turn a profit? Read on!

CHAPTER CONTENTS

ADDING AND SUBTRACTING RATIONAL NUMBERS

STARTING BELOW ZERO

Since you'll have to repay the loan, it's like your business has "negative" 20 dollars. Borrowing money means you have less than zero dollars, and the borrowed $20 could be shown on a horizontal number line like this:

-20

-20 -18 -16 -14 -12 -10 -8 -6 -4 -2 **0** 2

DOLLARS

$20 is a good amount of money to start a business, but you decide to borrow $10 more from a friend. *What amount of money would now represent your business' balance?*

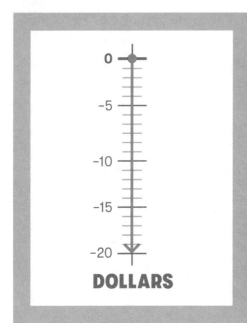

DOLLARS

This information can also be shown on a vertical number line:

When you use a vertical number line to represent money, the negative integers below 0 represent what is owed, borrowed, or the overall cost.

INTEGER CHIP MODEL

Let's look at the money borrowed using integer chips. Use blue integer chips for positive numbers and red integer chips for negative numbers.

$20 borrowed from parent (–20)

PLUS (+)

$10 borrowed from a friend (–10)

–20 + (–10)

How many integer chips are there total? Why are they all red? You started by owing your parent $20 (20 red integer chips), and then you added owing your friend $10 (10 more red integer chips). So, all of the chips are red because that represents the total that you owe people. If you count all of the integer chips, there are 30 in total:

$$-20 + (-10) = -30$$

You **owe** a total of $30. You can think of adding a negative integer to another negative integer as making the group of negatives increase, in the negative direction. *To generalize this, when you add integers that are negative, the result is still negative.*

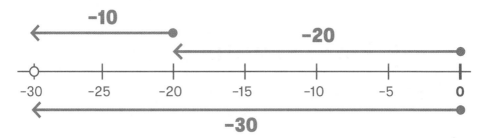

You can also use a number line to find and/or confirm your answer.

−10

−20

−30	−25	−20	−15	−10	−5	0

−30

Both representations match the equation: $(-20) + (-10) = -30$.

So, after borrowing $20 and then borrowing $10, it makes sense that you now owe $30.

Your business has a balance of −$30.

Next, using the borrowed money, you go to the local market to buy supplies. You purchase graham crackers, chocolate bars, marshmallows, clear bags, and string. After giving the cashier $30, she returns $8 back to you. With this, you can start to pay back your loans. You then wonder: *How much of the borrowed money do I still owe?*

🔍 TAKE A CLOSER LOOK

Since the $8 is used toward repaying your loan, it's positive. This means you'll *combine* −$30 with $8. You can model this by continuing to use the *integer chip model*, this time using positive and negative chips. You'll need 30 red chips and 8 blue chips. Align the chips so that 1 negative is paired with 1 positive to help you figure out how much you still owe:

ZERO PAIR

Since −1 + 1 = 0, each red integer chip cancels out each blue integer chip.

How many red integer chips remain? This will be the amount you still owe.

Looking again to the number line, confirm your answer.

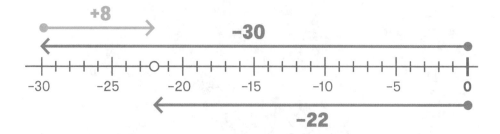

Tie both models together with the equation: (–30) + (8) = -22.

So, after borrowing $30 and then repaying $8, you now owe just $22. Your business has a balance of –$22.

YOUR TURN!

You can use either model—integer chips or the number line—to add integers.

1. Use integer chips: (–5) + (–2) = ?

2. Use integer chips: 10 + (–4) = ?

3. Use a number line: (–9) + 3 = ?

4. Solve using any method: (–12) + 15 + (–8) + 3

TOOLS FOR SUCCESS

When adding signed numbers, it's important to remember:

1. If you add 1 positive integer chip to 1 negative integer chip, they cancel out to give you 0.

2. The signs of the numbers being added show you their location on the number line or the direction of movement.

ADDING DIFFERENT-SIGNED NUMBERS

There are specific rules when the signs are different.

HOW IT ADDS UP	
+ + **−** = **+**	*A larger positive number combined with a smaller negative number is a positive.*
+ + **−** = **−**	*A smaller positive number combined with a larger negative number is a negative.*
− + **+** = **−**	*A larger negative number combined with a smaller positive number is a negative.*
− + **+** = **+**	*A smaller negative number combined with a larger positive number is a positive.*

Using your supplies, you plan to sell enough s'mores kits to pay back the $22 that you still owe. Then, after paying back the loan, you can start to earn the profit needed to buy a new tent.

FIRST WEEKEND

During the first weekend, you make sales of $9 on Friday and $17 on Saturday, but then realize you're out of clear bags. After purchasing more bags for $4, you make a profit of $21 on Sunday.

What is your balance now?

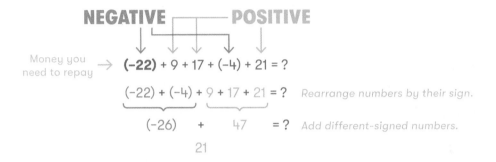

Good work—your business has made a profit of $21 in a single weekend!

After a successful weekend, you've paid back your $22 loan (or –$22) and now things are getting fun since you have $21 in profit. It's a good start, but nowhere near the cost of the tent. You'll need to sell more s'mores kits, so you decide to purchase supplies for a second weekend.

SECOND WEEKEND

The additional supplies cost you $18, (or –$18). You then make sales on the second weekend of $11 on Friday, $20 on Saturday, and $29 on Sunday.

What is your balance after your new expenses and sales?

$$21 + (-18) + 11 + 20 + 29 = ?$$

$21 + (-18) + 11 + 20 + 29 = ?$ *Add numbers of the same sign.*

$(-18) + 81 = ?$ *Add different-signed numbers.*

63

After your successful second weekend, your business now has **$63 in profit!**

YOUR TURN!

1. The last time you went camping, you dug a circular hole for a fire pit 6 inches deep. The camp counselor noticed it might not be deep enough and dug down another 4 inches. How many inches below ground was the fire pit after the counselor's work?

$$(-6) + (-4) = ?$$

2. Starting at an elevation of 50 feet, you start your hike by going down a path that drops 10 feet in elevation. The next hill rises 31.5 feet then drops 11.8 feet. What is your elevation at this part of the hike? Show how you rearranged your integers.

$$50 + (-10) + 31.5 + (-11.8) = ?$$

SUBTRACTING RATIONAL NUMBERS

Your money-making idea with the s'mores kit started with a negative amount because you borrowed money from others. What if that debt was erased? What if your parent and friend decided you didn't have to pay them back? (Now, wouldn't *that* be awesome?!) Let's pretend they *take away* your debt—*what is your new profit total?*

🔍 TAKE A CLOSER LOOK

In math, subtraction has very often been described as *take away*. If you apply this to your debt being *taken away* by your loved ones, this means –30 is being subtracted from your profit.

$$Balance = 21 - (-30)$$

Hold up! What does it mean to subtract a negative? If you don't have to pay back the borrowed money, then the $30 you used to start your business is now added to your profit.

Graphically, look at what happens if your $30 debt is taken away:

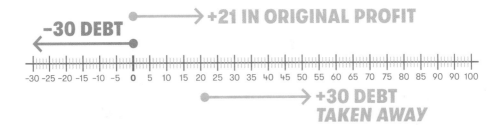

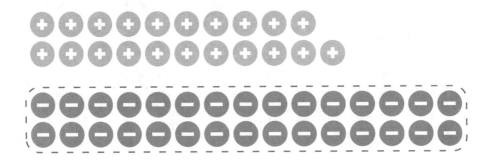

In this problem, you went from 21 + (–30) = –9 to 21 – (–30) = 51.

Since we have a double negative (*take away a negative*), it gets transformed into addition:

$$21 + (+30) = 51$$

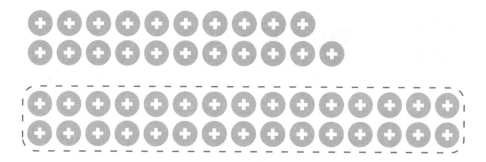

If your debt is forgiven, after the first weekend your balance is $51.

TEMPERATURE CHANGES

With a fresh wad of bills in your hand, you're eager to get to the camping store. Before you head out, you check your weather app and notice that the temperature is 85 degrees. Halfway through the trip, though, there's a rainstorm that causes the temperature to drop 15 degrees. When you get back into the car, your parent turns the heat on to match the temperature from earlier. All of a sudden the Sun comes out, and the temperature increases by 5 degrees. *What is the temperature now?*

Work through each temperature change:

$85 - 15 = 70$ *The temperature drops by 15 degrees.*

$70 - (-15) = 85$ *Turn on the heater to restore the temperature to what it was originally.*

$85 + 5 = 90$ *The sun comes out.*

The temperature at the end of the trip is 90 degrees.

TOOLS FOR SUCCESS

When subtracting negative integers, it's best to rewrite each problem as adding the opposite while thinking about it as taking away a loss, or reversing an amount owed.

SUBTRACTING NEGATIVE NUMBERS		
➕ − ➖	*becomes*	➕ + ➕
➖ − ➖	*becomes*	➖ + ➕

Notice that only the number *after* the subtraction symbol changes.

YOUR TURN!

You can use either model—integer chips or the number line—to add integers.

1. Use integer chips: (−5) − (−2) = ?

2. Use integer chips: 10 − (−4) = ?

3. Use a number line: (−9) − (−3) = ?

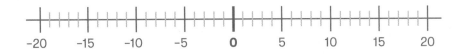

4. On a super cold night, you hear on the radio that the temperature is predicted to be 8°F by midnight. If you last checked the temperature at the beginning of the evening and it was 27°F, by what number will the temperature drop?

MULTIPLYING AND DIVIDING RATIONAL NUMBERS

For the camping trip, you and your friends want to purchase 3 packs of hot dogs. You've volunteered to buy the hot dogs:

$3 per pack of hot dogs

For the cost of the hot dogs, you could add the costs repeatedly, or you could multiply instead because multiplying is repeated addition.

For 3 packs of hot dogs at $3 per pack, you figure out

$$\$3 \times 3$$

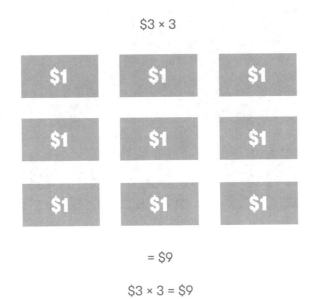

$$= \$9$$

$$\$3 \times 3 = \$9$$

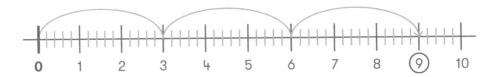

So, for the hot dogs, the cost will be $9. Note: repeatedly adding a positive gets you a positive result. You can also say multiplying a positive by a positive gives a positive result.

As you walk up to the cashier, you start thinking about how these costs will lower the amount of money you have. The dollars you had in your pocket will now be in the store's cash register—you won't be able to use them! So to you, the cost of each of the 3 packs of hot dogs is negative:

−$3 per pack of hot dogs

They will now represent repeatedly adding a negative. You could also say you're multiplying by a negative. You have 3 packs of hot dogs at −$3 each:

3 × (−$3) or add (−$3), 3 times

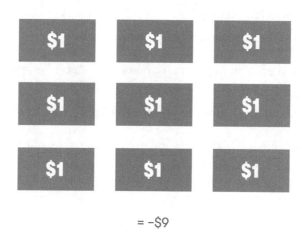

= −$9

3 × (−$3) = −$9

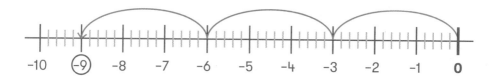

Good work! The cost of the hot dogs could be represented as –$9. So, when you walk up to the cashier, you'll have to hand over $9 of that hard-earned cash.

Repeatedly adding a negative gets you a negative result, and repeatedly subtracting a positive also gives a negative result. You can also think of it as multiplying a positive by a negative and multiplying a negative by a positive gets you a negative result.

$$(+) \times (-) = (-)$$

$$(-) \times (+) = (-)$$

TAKE A CLOSER LOOK

Surprise! At checkout, the cashier has good news: there is a "Buy 2, Get 1 Free" special on hot dogs!

So, how will your cost change? You remember from earlier, subtracting a negative is a positive thing. This means repeatedly subtracting a negative (multiplying by a negative) works the same way!

The cashier will remove (subtract) one of the –$3 packs of hot dogs:

–1 × -$3

$1 $1 $1

= +$3

–1 × (–$3) = +$3

Multiplying by Negative → Flips Over the 0

The cost of the hot dogs will be added back to your total. Note: repeatedly subtracting a negative makes a positive result. Or, multiplying a negative by a negative gets you a positive result.

$$ \ominus \times \ominus = \oplus $$

With the $3 returned, the total cost of your hot dogs will be −$9 + $3 = −$6.

After leaving the grocery store, you begin to wonder how much it would cost each person if they decided to pay an equal share for the hot dogs. Since there are 5 of you all together, you divide the $6 by 5.

$$ -\$6 \div 5 $$

$$ 5\overline{)6} $$

$$
\begin{array}{r}
1.20 \\
5\overline{)6.0} \\
-5.0 \\
\hline
1.0 \\
-1.0 \\
\hline
0
\end{array}
$$

Awesome! If each person in the camping group wanted to help pay for the hot dogs, they will owe $1.20.

$$ -\$6 \div 5 = -\$1.20 $$

Each person's portion is still $1.20, but now that's considered −$1.20. In fact, the rules for dividing by negative and positive rational numbers are the same as multiplying by them!

TOOLS FOR SUCCESS

Here is a summary of the rules for multiplying or dividing negative and positive rational numbers:

MULTIPLYING OR DIVIDING SIGNED NUMBERS				
+	× or ÷	+	=	+
+	× or ÷	−	=	−
−	× or ÷	+	=	−
−	× or ÷	−	=	+

YOUR TURN!

1. Solve the following problems:

   a. Each scoop of your shovel digs 2.5 inches down into the dirt. After 10 scoops, how deep do you expect to be?

   $$10 \times (-2.5) = ?$$

   b. Using the same shovel, you can fill in 3.1 inches of dirt per scoop. After 8 scoops, will there be enough dirt to refill the hole?

   $$-8 \times (-3.1) = ?$$

2. A local park limits the total weight of fish you can take away from the lake. After a day of fishing, you and two friends will have to remove 14.5 pounds of fish from your catch. How much weight will each person have to get rid of to meet the limit of the park?

   $$-14.5 \div 3 = ?$$

THE DISTRIBUTIVE PROPERTY

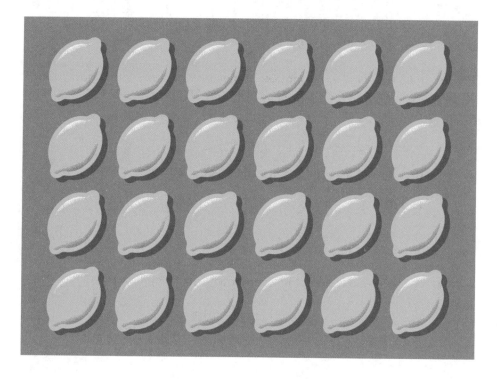

You know what every hot dog needs? A refreshing beverage to wash it down! You're about to see the power of the distributive property, using an example you might remember from when you were little: a lemonade stand! Pretend it's a sweltering summer day and you've just constructed your lemonade stand. Now, let's use the distributive property (touched on in Chapter 3) to help you *expand* the ingredients in your delicious lemonade!

distributive property: holds that multiplying a number (a) by a group of numbers added together (b + c) is equivalent to multiplying that number by each number separately. a(b + c) = ab + ac. This also holds true for subtraction: a(b – c) = ab – ac

🔍 TAKE A CLOSER LOOK

Distribution allows you to multiply a group of terms being added (or *subtracted*) together.

For example, you find that to make 5 times the amount of lemonade you need 5 times the original ingredients.

5 (**3** cups of lemon juice + **9** cups of ice + **20** cups of water)

(5 × 3) + (5 × 9) + (5 × 20)   *5 will multiply all the terms inside.*

15   +   45   +   100

After the distribution is complete, you now have 5 times as many ingredients!

15 cups of lemon juice + 45 cups of ice + 100 cups of water

How many cups of lemonade will this make?

15 **cups** of lemon juice + 45 **cups** of ice + 100 **cups** of water

(15 + 45 + 100)   *Like terms (all "cups"),*
                     so they can be added together.

160 cups of ingredients

Using the distributive property, and making certain that you are adding together like terms, you can calculate that this recipe will make 160 cups of lemonade.

like terms: variables with the same exponent or constants

ANOTHER PATH

There's a way to double-check this total. First, combine the ingredients, then multiply by 5:

5 (3 **cups** of lemon juice + 9 **cups** of ice + 20 **cups** of water)

5 (3 **cups** + 9 **cups** + 20 **cups**) = 5 (32 **cups**)

Again, like terms (all "cups"), so they can be added together.

160 cups of ingredients

ACTIVATE PRIOR KNOWLEDGE

The distributive property makes use of a concept you already know: equivalent expressions.

This was shown when you created 5 times the ingredients:

EQUIVALENT EXPRESSIONS

$$5 (3 + 9 + 2) = (5 \times 3) + (5 \times 9) + (5 \times 20)$$

EQUIVALENT EXPRESSIONS

$$5 (3 + 9 + 2) = 5 (32)$$

$$160 = 160$$

By distributing, you're just creating another version of the same expression. So, it makes sense that they're equal!

equivalent expressions: two or more expressions that are equal in value

Next, if you're using a negative number when distributing, it's important to bring that negative along for the ride. For example,

$$-2\ (9 + 5 + 4)$$

-2 multiplies each term.

$$(-2 \times 9) + (-2 \times 5) + (-2 \times 4)$$

$(-) \times (-) = -$

$$(-18) + (-10) + (-8)$$

Combine like terms.

$$-36$$

Good work—each of the terms inside the parentheses were multiplied by -2. Then, you were able to combine like terms.

TOOLS FOR SUCCESS

When using distribution, it's important to remember the following:

- The number in front of the parentheses multiplies the terms in the parentheses.

- If the number being distributed is negative, it must be multiplied with that negative.

- It's helpful to use arrows to organize the distribution.

YOUR TURN!

Perform the distribution for these expressions below.

Try out a few examples:

1. 3(6 + 5)

2. –2(6.25 + 9.5 + 17)

3. You're making sandwiches for you and three friends. Use the setup below to figure out how many portions of each ingredient you will need in total.

   4(2 pieces of bread + 3 slices of turkey + 3 pieces of cheese + 1 squirt of mustard)

4. Use distribution to write an equivalent expression for 9(1 + 3 + 16).

5. Which of the following is equivalent to 7(10 + 4 + 7)? Select all that apply.

   a. (7 × 10) + (7 × 4) + (7 × 7)

   b. 7(21)

   c. 147

   d. 70 + 4 + 7

SIMPLIFYING WITH ORDER OF OPERATIONS

Performing a series of operations can be complicated. In math, when you've mixed operations, the order in which they need to get done is key.

> order of operations: the flow of operations to simplify a numerical expression into an equivalent expression, also known as PEMDAS (see opposite page)

For example, let's say you're totaling up some grocery items:

1 carton of milk + 2 boxes of cereal + 1 box of raisins − $1 off coupon

The costs are

$$\$5 + (2 \times \$4) + \$3 - \$1$$

You need the result of the cereal multiplication in order to move on. So, you have to multiply first:

$\$5 + (2 \times \$4) + \$3 - \$1$ *Multiplication before addition.*

$\$5 + \$8 + \$3 - \$1$ *Add/Subtract terms from left to right.*

$\$13 + \$3 - \$1$

$\$16 - \$1$

$\$15$

You can think of multiplication as being more powerful than addition. So, you needed to multiply the cost of the 2 boxes of cereal first.

TAKE A CLOSER LOOK

As you can see, the concept of order of operations is very important. When dealing with big expressions, keep PEMDAS in mind. PEMDAS stands for:

PARENTHESES

P: Parentheses ( )

Perform operations within parentheses and/or other grouping symbols.

$$25 - 5 \times (4 - 1) + 3^2 \div 3$$

$$25 - 5 \times 3 + 3^2 \div 3$$

EXPONENTS

E: Exponents

Find the value of all exponential expressions.

$$25 - 5 \times 3 + 3^2 \div 3$$

$$25 - 5 \times 3 + 9 \div 3$$

MULTIPLICATION AND DIVISION

M/D: Multiplication/Division (from left to right)

Perform all multiplication and division in order from left to right.

$$25 - 5 \times 3 + 9 \div 3$$

$$25 - 15 + 3$$

ADDITION AND SUBTRACTION

A/S: Addition/Subtraction (from left to right)

Perform all addition and subtraction in order from left to right.

$$25 - 15 + 3$$

$$10 + 3$$

$$13$$

A great way to help you remember the order of operations is the acronym

PLEASE EXCUSE MY DEAR AUNT SALLY

Based on the order of operations, look inside the parentheses first. The exponents go next, followed by multiplication or division, from left to right. Finally, add or subtract from left to right.

See if you can evaluate the expression below.

$(-15 + 2) - 10 \times 2 \div 4 - 21$

$(-15 + 2) - 10 \times 2 \div 4 - 21$ *Do the operations in parentheses first.*

$-13 - 10 \times 2 \div 4 - 21$ *No exponents, so multiply then divide (from left to right).*

$-13 - 20 \div 4 - 21$

$-13 - 5 - 21$ *Add or subtract (from left to right).*

$-18 - 21$ *Here, subtraction comes first!*

-39

Good job!

Evaluating expressions like this may seem overwhelming at first. Take it one step at a time and remember PEMDAS. Come up with your own acronym to remember it!

YOUR TURN!

Use Order of Operations to evaluate the expressions below.

1. $3 + 4 \times 10 - 24 \div 6$

2. $\frac{1}{2} \times 10 + 21 - (2 \times 3)$

3. $2(10.5 - 7.5) - 12 \div 2$

CHAPTER SUMMARY

ADDING AND SUBTRACTING RATIONAL NUMBERS

For solving problems that involve operations with integers, you can use different models: number lines (double or single), integer chips, and expressions or equations.

- **Zero Pair:** When you add –1 to +1, it equals 0, which "cancels" out the pair.

- **Adding Same-Signed Numbers**

    - Positive plus positive always equals positive.

    - Negative plus negative always equals negative.

- **Adding Different-Signed Numbers**

HOW IT ADDS UP	
+ + − = +	A larger positive number combined with a smaller negative number is a *positive*.
+ + − = −	A smaller positive number combined with a larger negative number is a *negative*.
− + + = −	A larger negative number combined with a smaller positive number is a *negative*.
− + + = +	A smaller negative number combined with a larger positive number is a *positive*.

- **Subtracting Negative Numbers**

SUBTRACTING NEGATIVE NUMBERS		
+ − −	*becomes*	+ + +
− − −	*becomes*	− + +

MULTIPLYING & DIVIDING RATIONAL NUMBERS

MULTIPLYING OR DIVIDING SIGNED NUMBERS				
+	× or ÷	+	=	+
+	× or ÷	−	=	−
−	× or ÷	+	=	−
−	× or ÷	−	=	+

THE DISTRIBUTIVE PROPERTY

When using distribution remember the following.

- The number in front of the parentheses multiplies the terms in the parentheses.

- If the number being distributed is negative, it must be multiplied with that negative.

- It's helpful to use arrows to organize the distribution.

SIMPLIFYING WITH ORDER OF OPERATIONS

When dealing with big expressions, remember you can simplify them using PEMDAS:

- **P:** Parentheses ( )

- **E:** Exponents

- **M/D:** Multiplication/ Division (from left to right)

- **A/S:** Addition/Subtraction (from left to right)

CHAPTER 5 VOCABULARY

distributive property: holds that multiplying a number (a) by a group of numbers added together (b + c) is equivalent to multiplying that number by each number separately. a(b + c) = ab + ac. This also holds true for subtraction: a(b − c) = ab − ac

equivalent expressions: two or more expressions that are equal in value. An expression is a letter and/or number sentence

like terms: variables with the same exponent or constants

order of operations: the flow of operations to simplify a numerical expression into an equivalent expression, also known as PEMDAS

CHAPTER 5 ANSWER KEY

ADDING/SUBTRACTING RATIONAL NUMBERS (P. 156)

1. –5 + –2 = –7

2. 10 + –4 = 6

3. –9 + 3 = –6

4. –12 + 15 + –8 + 3 = –2

ADDING DIFFERENT-SIGNED NUMBERS (P. 159)

1. –10 inches

2. 59.7 feet

SUBTRACTING RATIONAL NUMBERS (P. 162)

1. –5 – (–2) = –3

2. 10 – (–4) = 14

3. –9 – (–3) = –6

4. The temperature will drop 19 degrees. 27°F –19°F = 8°F

MULTIPLYING/DIVIDING RATIONAL NUMBERS (P. 168)

1a. –25 inches

b. 24.8 inches; No, it's not enough dirt to refill the hole!

2. Approximately –4.83 pounds each

THE DISTRIBUTIVE PROPERTY (P. 173)

1. 33

2. –65.5

3. 8 pieces of bread + 12 slices of turkey + 12 pieces of cheese + 4 squirts of mustard

4. (9 × 1) + (9 × 3) + (9 × 16)

5. a, b, and c are equivalent.

SIMPLIFYING WITH ORDER OF OPERATIONS (P. 176)

1. 39

2. 20

3. 0

EXPRESSIONS AND EQUATIONS: PART 1

As the weather gets colder and people move more indoors, you realize that your DIY s'mores kit isn't quite as fun when prepared over the stove. What if you sold something that people wanted all year long? A new business idea pops up: smoothies! Before you start a new business on a whim, you begin to think that maybe you should track the sales of smoothies first. How can your understanding of expressions and equations help you plan your new business idea?

EXPONENTS

A FORMULA FOR GROWTH

After figuring out your ingredients and supplies, you start selling. The sales are slow at first but then pick up as word-of-mouth gets going! The first 4 days of sales are below.

DAY	CUPS OF SMOOTHIES
1	2
2	4
3	8
4	16

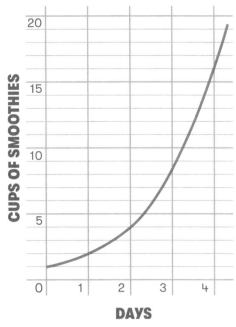

Boom. Your sales are growing at a shockingly fast rate!

After the fourth day, you consider the pattern. You take a close look to see that it doesn't appear to be a linear change, because the dependent variables are not growing by addition or subtraction. *So, how are your sales changing? (Hint: What's the pattern from 2 to 4 to 8 to 16?)*

🔍 TAKE A CLOSER LOOK

Over 4 days, your number of cup sales went from 2 to 4 to 8 and then to 16. Each day your sales are doubling, or multiplied by 2.

DAY	CUPS	EXPANDED FORM
1	2	2
2	4	2 × 2
3	8	2 × 2 × 2
4	16	2 × 2 × 2 × 2

$$(2 \times 2) \times 2 \times 2$$

$$(4 \times 2) \times 2$$

$$8 \times 2$$

$$16$$

That's an impressive rate of growth!

This repeated multiplication is a special feature of mathematics called exponents. Similar to how multiplication shows repeated addition, exponents show repeated multiplication.

For example, you can better represent the four days of sales 2 × 2 × 2 × 2 as 2^4.

exponent: the number of times
base multiplies itself

$$2^4 = 2 \times 2 \times 2 \times 2 = 16$$

base

4 times

Because each day's sales are multiplied by 2, the base is 2. The exponent, 4, is also called a power. It says 2 will multiply itself 4 times. Each day can be expressed in exponential form, as a base *raised* to a power.

The **square root** of a number is the value that, when multiplied by itself, gives you that number. For example, 3 × 3 (or 3^2) = 9, so we can say that 3 is the square root of 9.

exponent (power): a number that tells you the number of times to multiply a base number by itself

base: a number that is being multiplied by itself (according to the exponent)

square root: the base number for the exponent n^2. For example, $3^2 = 9$, so we can say that 3 is the square root of 9.

EXPONENTIAL FORM	EXPANDED FORM	STANDARD FORM
2^4	2 × 2 × 2 × 2	16

Look at each equivalent expression (in bold):

	CUPS OF SMOOTHIES	CUPS OF SMOOTHIES SOLD	
day	standard form	exponential	expanded forms
1	2	**2**	**2**
2	4	$\mathbf{2^2}$	**2 × 2**
3	8	$\mathbf{2^3}$	**2 × 2 × 2**
4	16	$\mathbf{2^4}$	**2 × 2 × 2 × 2**
5	?	?	?

You may notice there is a relationship between the number of days and the exponent for that day. For example, on Day 3 the exponent is 3 with the base of 2. If this continues, how would the fifth day's sales look in exponential form?

If you evaluate this expression, how many cups would then be sold on the fifth day?

$$2^5 = \underbrace{(2 \times 2)} \times 2 \times 2 \times 2$$

$$2^5 = \underbrace{(4 \times 2)} \times 2 \times 2$$

$$2^5 = \underbrace{(8 \times 2)} \times 2$$

$$2^5 = \underbrace{(16 \times 2)}$$

$$2^5 = 32$$

With this exponential pattern, Day 5 sales will be 32 cups of smoothies!

YOUR TURN!

Here is some practice with exponential form.

> 1. Write each expression in exponential form.
>   a. $5 \times 5 \times 5 =$
>   b. $4 \times 4 \times 4 \times 4 \times 4 =$
>
> 2. Identify the base and exponents for each.
>   a. 6^3
>   b. 9^5
>
> 3. Write in expanded form.
>   a. $2^6 =$
>   b. $6^2 =$
>
> 4. If the hiking trail that you're on is 100 miles, what is the exponential form equivalent of that distance?

EVALUATING NUMERICAL EXPRESSIONS

PRIOR KNOWLEDGE

As with other operations, exponents can be a part of a larger expression. Do you remember the order of operations?

When evaluating numerical expressions, you must begin by evaluating any operations in parentheses. Next, you have to apply exponents. Then you can multiply/divide (from left to right), and finally add/subtract (from left to right).

> numerical expression: a number sentence containing numbers and operations only

PEMDAS: A REFRESHER

1. **PARENTHESES**   ( )
2. **EXPONENTS** $\square^{\square}$
3. **MULTIPLICATION OR DIVISION**   × OR ÷
   (left to right)
4. **ADDITION OR SUBTRACTION**   + OR −
   (left to right)

For example, on the fifth day of sales, you gave away four free cups to friends and family. So, your actual sales could be expressed as

$$2^5 - 4$$

This means you start by evaluating 2^5 and then subtract the 4 freebies.

$$2^5 - 4$$
$$2 \times 2 \times 2 \times 2 \times 2 - 4$$
$$32 - 4$$
$$28$$

No parentheses, so exponents first then subtraction.

It makes sense that 28 cups were actually sold. Of the 32 cups, 4 were given away, so they were subtracted from your sales.

Now, look at a more complex problem: $12 - 8 \div 4 + 3\,[(6 + 2) - 3]^2$.

EXPRESSION	PROCESS EXPLAINED
$12 - 8 \div 4 + 3[(6 + 2) - 3]^2$	Using the order of operations, parentheses/groupings must go first. Within the grouping [ ], there is a set of parentheses; this must go first, so add 6 and 2.
$12 - 8 \div 4 + 3[(8) - 3]^2 = 12 - 8 \div 4 + 3[5]^2$	Within the grouping, you'll need to subtract 3 from 8, which results in 5.

$12 - 8 \div 4 + 3[25] = 12 - 8 \div 4 + 3[25]$	Complete multiplication and division from left to right. In this case, you'll need to divide 8 by 4 and then multiply 3 times 25.
$12 - 2 + 75 = 10 + 75 = 85$	Move onto adding and subtracting from left to right. In this case, you'll need to subtract 2 from 12 and then add 10 and 75.
$12 - 8 \div 4 + 3 [[6 + 2] - 3]^2 = 85$	The final answer is 85.

YOUR TURN!

Evaluate each expression into an equivalent expression.

1. $8^1 + 5$

2. $3^4 - (4 - 2)$

3. $(11 - 2)^3$

4. $9 + 4^2$

5. $(5 - 2)^3 - 1$

WRITING ALGEBRAIC EXPRESSIONS

With a better ability to read expressions, you can write and evaluate them as well. It is super helpful when real-life situations can be converted into math symbols.

PRIOR KNOWLEDGE

For example, you realize that—oops—you give away four free smoothies every day to friends and family. If you want to write an expression for the number of drinks sold each day, what could that be?

Need to represent an unknown number? Use a variable, such as c, for cups! Then, you can subtract four. You've expressed the number of cups sold as an algebraic expression—nice job!

In the language of math,

$$c - 4$$

c: the number of cups sold ⁐⁐⁐ *subtracted by 4 giveaways*

- What if 4 of your friends made and brought one smoothie each to sell in addition to the cups you are selling (c)? *How would you write that expression?*

$$c + 4$$

c: the number of cups sold ⁐⁐⁐ *additional 4 cups from friends*

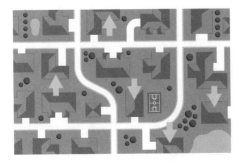

- There are 5 families on your block and you wanted to give each family the same number of smoothies. So, you should divide the number of cups, c, evenly among the families. *How would you write that expression?*

$$\text{c: the number of cups sold} \longrightarrow \frac{c}{5} \text{ or } c \div 5$$
$$\text{5 families splitting smoothies} \longrightarrow$$

- Since you're selling the same number of smoothies every day for 7 days a week, *how can you represent the expression for the number of beverages sold per week?*

$$7c \text{ or } 7 \times c$$

7 days per week / \ c: the number of cups sold per day

TAKE A CLOSER LOOK

Here are some other key phrases used in writing expressions.

PHRASES	SYMBOL
added to, more than, increased by, the sum of, total, plus	+
subtracted by, less than, fewer than, decreased by, the difference between, minus	−
multiplied by, the product of, times, per	✕
divided by, the quotient of, for every, ratio of	÷
some number, a value	variable
the quantity of, a group, groups of	( )
is, is the same as, is equivalent to, the result is	=

EXAMPLES

See if you can write expressions for the following. **Tip:** Try to identify the keywords first and then rewrite each with math symbols.

	VERBAL EXPRESSIONS	ALGEBRAIC EXPRESSIONS
a	The sum of 2 times a number and 18	
b	2 less than the quotient of 15 and a number	
c	3 times the difference of a number and 4	

Compare your answers to the ones below:

    a. $18 + 2x$

    b. $(15 \div n) - 2$

    c. $3(b - 4)$

Using other letters as variables (besides x) is okay!

YOUR TURN!

Turn each of the following verbal expressions into algebraic expressions.

	VERBAL EXPRESSIONS	ALGEBRAIC EXPRESSIONS
a	The sum of 7 times a number and 4	
b	−9 times the quotient of a number and 2	

EVALUATING ALGEBRAIC EXPRESSIONS

PRIOR KNOWLEDGE

As you saw earlier, completing operations in the correct order is important. Be sure to keep the order in mind when you **evaluate algebraic expressions** (see p. 196).

> **evaluate:** to complete the operations given in an expression

BIG OL' BATCHES OF SMOOTHIES

You know from experience that you won't sell every smoothie you make. Let's assume that you'll give away 4, as you did last time. This time, you only make 27 cups of smoothies, so the expression becomes:

$c - 4$	*27 is substituted in place of c.*
$(27) - 4$	*Use parentheses when substituting.*
23	*Perform operation to evaluate.*

If you make 27 smoothies, you can expect to actually sell 23 of them.

MULTIPLE SUBSTITUTIONS

Sometimes the expression's variable will appear more than once. If this happens, substitute the given value wherever you see the variable.

For example, evaluate the algebraic expression $x^2 + 8x$ for $x = 3$.

$x^2 + 8x$	*3 is substituted in place of all x's.*
$(3)^2 + 8(3)$	*Use parentheses when substituting.*
$9 + 8(3)$	*Perform exponent.*
$9 + 24$	*Multiply next.*
33	*Add to finish.*

YOUR TURN!

Evaluate the following algebraic expressions for their given variable values.

1. $2 + 3(b - 1)$ when $b = 9$

2. $2(x - 6)^2 + 2x$ when $x = 7$

Challenge: $(y - 3) \times 4 \times 10^2 \div \frac{1}{2} + 6 + 17y$ when $y = 2$

> **algebraic expression:** numerical and variable sentence (including numbers and/or variables)

EXPRESSIONS: ALGEBRAIC LANGUAGE

Now that you've worked with some algebraic expressions (yep, that's what you've been doing!), let's break down some of the key terms used in algebra.

 ## TAKE A CLOSER LOOK

Look at the algebraic expression $2x + 5y - 7$ and its key vocabulary:

$$2x + 5y - 7$$
terms

Terms in an expression can include a single number, a single variable, or a number and variable multiplied together. There are 3 terms above: $2x$, $5y$, and -7.

$$2x + 5y - 7$$
variables

Variables are a key part of algebraic expressions. Variables are single letters used in place of unknown numbers. The word *variable* says the letter's value isn't set—it can vary. The variables above are: x and y.

$$2x + 5y - 7$$
coefficients

Coefficients are numbers written in front of a variable or open parentheses. Like you saw in distribution, coefficients multiply the variable and/or the terms inside the parentheses. The coefficients above are 2 and 5.

$$2x + 5y - 7$$

$$\uparrow$$

constant

Constants are fixed numbers that stand alone as terms. The constant above is 7.

YOUR TURN!

See if you can identify the key parts of the expression below.

$$-7a + 3b - c + 15$$

Terms: _____   Variables: _____

Coefficients: _____   Constants: _____

EQUIVALENT EXPRESSIONS

Let's practice making equivalent expressions by combining like terms.

> **Tip:** It's helpful if you have a highlighter or colored pencil to identify like terms.

We'll be using different forms of expressions: expanded form (stretched out) and simplified form (after combining like terms).

Reminder example: $4x = x + x + x + x$.

> **like terms:** terms with the same variable and exponent on that variable or constants are "like"

ORIGINAL EXPRESSION	EXPANDED FORM (EQUIVALENT)	SIMPLIFIED EXPRESSION
$2x + 7x$	$\underbrace{(x + x) + (x + x + x + x + x + x + x)}_{9 \times x}$	$9x$
$-4a + 9a + 3b$	$(-a - a - a - a)$ $+ (a + a + a + a + a + a + a + a + a)$ $+ (b + b + b)$ $(\cancel{a}\,\cancel{a}\,\cancel{a}\,\cancel{a})$ $+ (\cancel{a} + \cancel{a} + \cancel{a} + \cancel{a} + \boxed{a + a + a + a + a})$ $+ (b + b + b)$	$5a + 3b$
$6m - 2n + 6n - 8m$	$(\cancel{m} + \cancel{m} + \cancel{m} + \cancel{m} + \cancel{m} + \cancel{m})$ $+ (-\cancel{m} - \cancel{m} - \cancel{m} - \cancel{m} - \cancel{m} - \cancel{m} - m - m)$ $-m - m = -2m$ $6m - 8m = -2m$ $-\cancel{n} - \cancel{n} + \cancel{n} + \cancel{n} + n + n + n + n = +4n$ $-2n + 6n = +4n$	$-2m + 4n$
$3[x + 2] - x$	$\underbrace{(x + 2) + (x + 2) + (x + 2) - x}$ 3 groups of $(x + 2)$ $x + x + \cancel{x} - \cancel{x} = 2x$ combine the x terms $2 + 2 + 2 = 6$ combine the constant terms	$2x + 6$

YOUR TURN!

Write an equivalent expression for each.

1. $2x - 3b + 4x$

2. $5y - 6 + 2 - 2y$

3. $2(c - 4) + 3c$

CHALLENGE: HOW TO USE EXPRESSIONS WITH PERCENTAGES

Your smoothie business seems to be doing pretty well, so you decide to add some snacks to your menu. You pull out an old trail mix recipe, and you realize it uses percentages instead of measurements. The total weight is broken up as

40% almonds
20% dried cranberries
27% peanuts
13% chocolate chips

Let's write an expression for each of these with w as total weight.

Hint: When percentages are used in calculations, they can be converted into decimals.

Starting with almonds, let's express 40% of weight (w).

$$0.4w$$

40% as a decimal is 0.4. The term "of" says to multiply, so 0.4 is a coefficient of the variable w.

Now, let's translate the other percentages of ingredients.

For dried cranberries: $0.2w$

For peanuts: $0.27w$

For chocolate chips: $0.13w$

Each ingredient is now an algebraic expression as a percentage of the total weight.

Using substitution and decimal multiplication, see if you can evaluate the weight of each ingredient given a total weight, w.

TOTAL WEIGHT (W)	ALMONDS 0.4W	DRIED CRANBERRIES 0.2W	PEANUTS 0.27W	CHOCOLATE CHIPS 0.13W
w= 10 pounds				

Compare your answers to the ones below.

TOTAL WEIGHT (W)	ALMONDS 0.4W	DRIED CRANBERRIES 0.2W	PEANUTS 0.27W	CHOCOLATE CHIPS 0.13W
w= 10 pounds	0.4 (10) = 4 pounds	0.2 (10) = 2 pounds	0.27 (10) = 2.7 pounds	0.13 (10) = 1.3 pounds

TAKE A CLOSER LOOK

What if you created a total for this expression? Creating a total is a process of adding. So, the weight of your trail mix ingredients would be

$$0.4w + 0.2w + 0.27w + 0.13w$$

Note: *All four terms have the same variable with the same exponent. This means they're like terms and can be combined. (When no exponent is present, it is assumed to be 1.)*

When you combine like terms with variables, their coefficients combine, and the variable stays the same:

$0.4w + 0.2w + 0.27w + 0.13w$

$\underbrace{(0.4 + 0.2 + 0.27 + 0.13)}\ w$

$\underbrace{1w}$

Combine coefficients of like terms.
0.4 + 0.2 + 0.27 + 0.13 = 1.00

Why do you think it makes sense that these terms added to 1.00?

Well, 1.00 represents 100%. Adding together these partial weights gets you the 100% of total weight! So, 1w could be written as just w. A variable by itself (like w) is equivalent to 1 whole variable (1w).

CHAPTER SUMMARY

EXPONENTS

This is a repeated multiplication, but in short form.

$$a^b = a \times a \times a \times a \ldots (b \text{ times})$$

$$\text{base}^{\text{exponent}} = \text{value}$$

EXPONENTIAL FORM	EXPANDED FORM	STANDARD FORM
2^4	$2 \times 2 \times 2 \times 2$	16

WRITING ALGEBRAIC EXPRESSIONS

Simplify examples and contexts into expressions based on key words and the relationships between values. The table below can help you translate words into algebraic expressions.

PHRASES	SYMBOL
added to, more than, increased by, the sum of, total, plus	+
subtracted by, less than, fewer than, decreased by, the difference between, minus	−
multiplied by, the product of, times, per	✖
divided by, the quotient of, for every, ratio of	÷
some number, a value	variable
the quantity of, a group, groups of	( )
is, the same as, equivalent to, the result is	=

EVALUATING ALGEBRAIC EXPRESSIONS

For evaluating algebraic expressions, first substitute the given value into the place of the variable. Once you've completed that step, follow the order of operations throughout the expression.

- **Order of Operations:** use the order of operations to evaluate expressions with grouping symbols (parentheses and brackets) and exponents.

  ① **PARENTHESES** $(\ )$

  ② **EXPONENTS** $\square^{\square}$

  ③ **MULTIPLICATION OR DIVISION** $\times$ OR $\div$
  (left to right)

  ④ **ADDITION OR SUBTRACTION** $+$ OR $-$
  (left to right)

EXPRESSIONS: ALGEBRAIC LANGUAGE

You can use vocabulary words to describe parts of expressions and/or equations.

- **Term:** a part of an expression.
- **Variable:** unknown value or a place holder for changing values.
- **Constant:** a known value that doesn't change. A regular ol' number!
- **Coefficient:** a number that multiples a variable or grouping.

COMBINING LIKE TERMS

This a process of simplifying expressions by combining terms together that have the same attributes (variable and exponents OR constants).

CHAPTER 6 VOCABULARY

algebraic expression: numerical and variable sentence (including numbers and/or variables)

base: a number that is being multiplied by itself (according to the exponent)

coefficient: a number that multiplies a variable (or base)

constant: a number that is unchanging

evaluate: to complete the operations given in an expression

exponent (power): a number that tells you the number of times to multiply a base number by itself

like terms: terms with the same variable and exponent on that variable or constants are "like"

numerical expression: a number sentence containing numbers and operations only

square root: the base number for the exponent n^2. For example, $3^2 = 9$, so we can say that 3 is the square root of 9

term: a part of an expression

variable: an unknown or varying value

CHAPTER 6 ANSWER KEY

EXPONENTS (P. 189)

1. a. 5^3

   b. 4^5

2. a. base: 6, exponent: 3

   b. base: 9, exponent: 5

3. a. $2 \times 2 \times 2 \times 2 \times 2 \times 2$

   b. 6×6

4. 10×10, or 10^2

EVALUATING NUMERICAL EXPRESSIONS (P. 191)

1. $8^1 + 5 = 13$

2. $3^4 - (4 - 2) = 3 \times 3 \times 3 \times 3 - 2 = 79$

3. $(11 - 2)^3 = 9^3 = 9 \times 9 \times 9 = 729$

4. $9 + 4^2 = 9 + 16 = 25$

5. $(5 - 2)^3 - 1 = 3^3 - 1 = 27 - 1 = 26$

WRITING ALGEBRAIC EXPRESSIONS FROM WORDS (P. 194)

a. $7c + 4$

b. $-9\left(\frac{m}{2}\right)$ or $-9(m \div 2)$

EVALUATING ALGEBRAIC EXPRESSIONS (P. 196)

a. 26

b. 16

Challenge: Follow PEMDAS!

$(y-3) \times 4 \times 10^2 \div \frac{1}{2} + 6 + 17y$

$-1 \times 4 \times 100 \div \frac{1}{2} + 6 + 34$

$-400 \div \frac{1}{2} + 6 + 34$

$-800 + 6 + 34$

$-794 + 34 = -760$

EXPRESSIONS: ALGEBRAIC LANGUAGE (P. 198)

Terms: $-7a$, $+3b$, $-1c$, $+15$

Variables: a, b, c

Coefficients: -7, $+3$, -1

Constants: $+15$

EQUIVALENT EXPRESSIONS (P. 199)

1. $6x - 3b$

2. $3y - 4$

3. $2c - 8 + 3c$ or $5c - 8$

7 EXPRESSIONS AND EQUATIONS: PART 2

You're hungry, so you head out to the corner store to buy some bags of popcorn. Your favorite brand costs $3 per bag. (It's a family-size bag. And you love popcorn.) If you want to purchase four bags, what's the best way to calculate the total cost? Let's see how we can use this simple multiplication problem to learn how to set up and solve even really complicated equations!

CHAPTER CONTENTS

CANDY   CANDY

WRITING AND INTERPRETING ONE-STEP EQUATIONS

To solve this problem, you could use repeated addition, or you could multiply 4 bags by $3 (or the reverse order) to find this result in one step. If you wrote this verbal expression with math symbols, it would look like this: **4** bags × $**3**.

TAKE A CLOSER LOOK

Although the expression 4 × 3 gives you the price you're looking for ($12), this isn't an equation. To make an equation, you need an equals sign and the result (if it's known). Or you can use a variable to represent an unknown quantity.

> **equation:** a numerical and/or algebraic sentence where one side of the equals sign has the same value as the other side of the equals sign

4 × 3 = 12	*One-step numerical equation*
or	
4 × 3 = c	*One-step algebraic equation*

It's important to note that by simply adding an equals sign, you create two sides of an equation.

For an equation to be true, the mathematical expression on one side of the equals sign must have the same value as the expression on the other.

expression on the left $4 \times 3 = 12$ expression on the right

must be equal to

$4 \times 3 = 12$

$12 = 12$

True!

So, are you ready to transition to equations? Well, practice makes better— so let's practice these key ideas. First, see if you can identify each example below as an expression or an equation.

EXPRESSION OR EQUATION		
$\dfrac{2x}{5} = 10$	$-5b$	$4c = 9$
$t - 3 = 7$	$-4(t - 3)$	$y = x^2$

Remember, the key difference between expressions and equations is the equals sign. Keep this in mind as you investigate each example.

EXPRESSION OR EQUATION?			
$-5b$	Expression	$\dfrac{2x}{5} = 10$	Equation
$-4(t - 3)$	Expression	$t - 3 = 7$	Equation
		$4c = 9$	Equation
		$y = x^2$	Equation

If an equation is true, the expression on the left equals the expression on the right.

EXAMPLE	TRUE OR FALSE	WHY?
$4 \times 3 = 12$	true	$4 \times 3 = 12$ $12 = 12$
$10 - 7 = 2$	false	$10 - 7 = 2$ $3 \neq 2$
$2 + (-6) = -8$	false	$2 + (-6) = -8$ $-4 \neq -8$
$\dfrac{16}{x} = 8$ when $x = 2$	true	$\dfrac{16}{x} = 8$ $\dfrac{16}{(2)} = 8$ $8 = 8$

It's also important to know that you can switch the expression on the left and right sides of these equations and they will still be true.

EXAMPLE	TRUE OR FALSE	WHY?
$12 = 4 \times 3$	true	$12 = 4 \times 3$ $12 = 12$
$8 = \dfrac{16}{x}$ when $x = 2$	true	$8 = \dfrac{16}{x}$ $8 = \dfrac{16}{(2)}$ $8 = 8$

Remember how you translated earlier? Well, equations can also be written in words represented with math symbols. For example,

4 bags of popcorn times **3** dollars per bag is 12 dollars
$$4 \times 3 = 12$$

There are some new keywords to add to your math vocabulary. Phrases like **is, are, will be,** and **results in** are some of the ways you can say *equals.* These help you know you're setting up an equation!

TOOLS FOR SUCCESS

Remember the list of keywords from chapter 6? Refer back to page 202 to help you translate from words to symbols.

Let's practice translating equations.

   a. You biked 7 miles, which is 3 more than the number of miles your friend biked.

   b. The difference between your older sister's age and your age, 12, is 4.

   c. Some number times $3 per bag is $18 of gummies.

   d. When a number of eggs is divided by 2, the result is 6.

As you did with expressions, read closely, identify each keyword, and translate as you go.

   a. You biked 7 miles, which is 3 more than the number of miles your friend biked.
   $$7 = m + 3$$

   b. The difference between your older sister's age and your age, 12, is 4.
   $$a - 12 = 4$$

   $$a - 12 = 4$$ Note: difference between the two numbers means the minus sign goes between.

   c. Some number times $3 per bag is $18 of gummies.
   b ×   3   = 18
   $$3b = 18$$ Note: 3 can be written as a coefficient.

   d. When a number of eggs is divided by 2, the result is 6.
   n ÷   2   = 6
   $$n \div 2 = 6$$

Now let's solve for those variables!

SOLVING ONE-STEP EQUATIONS

Think back to your playground days. You and your friends probably remember the seesaw. *How many people need to sit on either side to balance it horizontally? Is it possible that you would need more people on one side than the other? Why or why not?* These are the types of questions that you can solve using an equation. Equations are about balance.

You've already solved some equations in your life adventures so far—you just might not have realized it! Like dividing up food among friends, or figuring out how long it will take you to bike home from somewhere based on distance. And now, you're ready to make the jump to solving equations, one of the skills needed to be successful in math and in life.

TAKE A CLOSER LOOK

When you're trying to solve an equation, you're really looking for the value(s) that make it true! Your ultimate goal is to have your variable on one side, and a single number (constant) on the other.

In example (a), you biked 7 miles, which is 3 more than the number of miles your friend biked. The number of miles, m, that your friend biked is what you need to know. Look at the equation and its visual representation with the variable on the left side:

a. $m + 3 = 7$

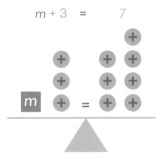

The scale *must* stay balanced, or it will not be an equation anymore. If you perform an operation on one side of the equation, you must do exactly the same thing to the other. To isolate m (to get it by itself), you need to take away 3 from the left side, so you must also take away 3 from the right side to stay balanced.

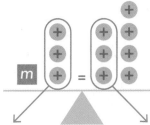

Subtracting 3 on the left side will isolate m.

Subtract 3.

After subtracting 3 from both sides, you can now see that $m = 4$. This means your friend biked 4 miles!

PRIOR KNOWLEDGE

As you learned above, what you do to one side of an equation you must do to the other side. This is also called using **inverse operations** to isolate a variable. What is the opposite of adding? It's subtracting! How about the opposite of multiplying? It's dividing! Inverse operations refer to what operation can "undo" parts of an equation to solve for a variable. As you saw with example (a), you subtracted 3 from both sides to isolate m because −3 is the inverse of +3.

inverse operation: the opposite operation to "undo" an operation

TOOLS FOR SUCCESS

Here are the common inverse operations:

OPERATION	INVERSE
✚	➖
➖	✚
✖	➗
➗	✖

Remember, an operation is undone by using its inverse (opposite).

Look at the solution process for example (a) written with math symbols:

a. m + 3 = 7

$$m + \cancel{3} = 7$$
$$\underline{\cancel{-}3 - 3}$$
$$m = 4$$

The inverse of + 3 is − 3.
Subtract 3 *from both sides to get m is equal to 4.*

A very useful fact about solving equations is that you can actually check your solution! Substitute the answer into the original equation and see if it makes the equation true

a. $m + 3 = 7$

$(4) + 3 = 7$ *Substitute 4 for m and simplify.*

$\overline{}$

$7 = 7$ *True, so m = 4 is correct!*

Checking your work can definitely give you some peace of mind when solving equations.

Let's try out example (b).

The difference between your older sister's age and your age, 12, is 4. How old is your sister? How can you set up a model of the equation?

b. $a - 12 = 4$

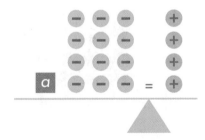

How will you isolate the variable, a?

The inverse of –12 is +12; you need to add 12 to both sides of the equation.

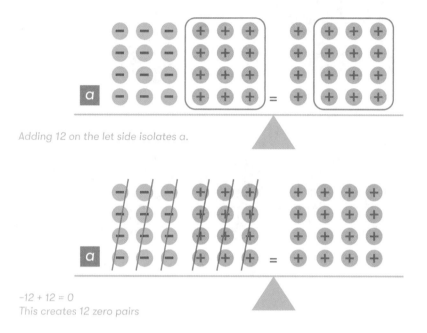

Adding 12 on the let side isolates a.

–12 + 12 = 0
This creates 12 zero pairs

Now you have *a* all by itself on the left side. By adding, the result will be +16 on the right. This means your older sister is 16 years old!

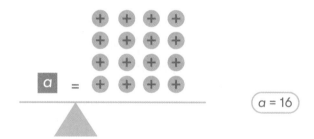

$a = 16$

Excellent! You kept the balance by using the inverse operations, –12 and +12, to isolate *a*. Look at the solution process for example (b) written with math symbols.

b. $a - 12 = 4$

$$a - \cancel{12} = 4$$
$$\underline{+\,12 + 12}$$
$$a = 16$$

Add 12 to both sides.
a is equal to 16.

Now, let's check that answer to make sure it's correct. Substitute $a = 16$ into the original equation for example (b):

b. $a - 12 = 4$

$$(16) - 12 = 4$$
$$\overline{}$$
$$4 = 4$$

Substitute 16 for a and simplify.
True, so a = 16 is correct!

Great job!

In example (c), you have some number times $3 per bag is $18 of gummies. So, how many bags of gummies at $3 per bag can you buy for $18?

Here is the equation and its visual representation:

c. $3b = 18$

Since the expression $3b$ means 3 times b, the left side of the equation needs the inverse of multiplication to be undone. Dividing by 3 will isolate b, and to maintain balance in the equation, you must divide by 3 on the right side as well.

c. $3b = 18$

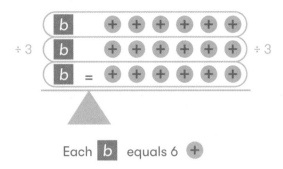

Each **b** equals 6 ⊕

Through division, you got *b* all by itself on the left side and 6 on the right. This means you can buy 6 bags of gummies!

Look at the solution process for example (c) written with math symbols:

c. $3b = 18$

$$\frac{\cancel{3}b}{\cancel{3}} = 18 \div 3 \qquad \textit{Divide by 3 on both sides.}$$

_____ *b is equal to 6.*

$$1b = 6$$

To check your answer, substitute $b = 6$ into the original equation:

c. $3b = 18$

$$3(6) = 18 \qquad \textit{Subsitute 6 for b and simplify.}$$

_____ *True, so b = 6 is correct!*

$$18 = 18$$

Nice work!

Finally, in example (d), the number of eggs is divided by 2 and the result is 6. So, how many eggs were there? Division can sometimes be difficult to represent visually, but this is where your fraction skills come in handy!

Remember, when a number is cut in half, it can be represented with a fraction: $n \div 2 = \dfrac{n}{2}$

d. $n \div 2 = 6$

To undo n being divided by 2, you need the inverse operation, multiplication. Multiply by 2.

d. $n \div 2 = 6$

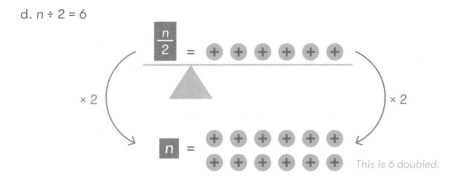

This is 6 doubled.

So, there would be 12 eggs in total!

Here is the solution process for example (d), written with math symbols:

$$d.\ n \div 2 = 6$$
$$\times 2 \times 2$$
$$\overline{\qquad\qquad}$$
$$n = 12$$

Multiply by 2 on both sides.

n is equal to 12.

To check your answer, substitute n = 12 into the original equation:

$$d.\ n \div 2 = 6$$
$$(12) \div 2 = 6$$
$$\overline{\qquad\qquad}$$
$$6 = 6$$

Substitute 12 for n and simplify.

True, so n = 12 is correct!

Fantastic!

YOUR TURN!

For each example, translate the scenario into an equation and then solve it.

1. You currently have $80. How much more would you need to reach $150?

2. If each step you take measures 2 feet, how many steps will you take to walk 200 feet?

3. 5 people shared the total bill for camping. If each person owes $22, how much was the bill?

4. Your family ate 15 packs of your favorite spiced nuts, and now you only have 22 packs left. How many packs did you have before your family dug in?

SOLVING TWO-STEP EQUATIONS

You decide you're going to get in shape for summer by doing some trail running. One week you run 4 short trails and one long 6-mile trail. If you run 14 miles altogether, how far are the short trails?

🔍 TAKE A CLOSER LOOK

The combination of the short and long trails means this equation will have two terms. Take a moment to translate:

4 short trails and the 6-mile trail equal 14 miles all together.

$$4s + 6 = 14$$

Here is the visual representation of 4s + 6 = 14:

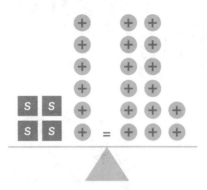

Just like with one-step equations, the goal of two-step equations is to isolate the variable and maintain balance. With two-step equations, move any constants first.

So, to isolate s, you would need to subtract 6 on the left side and subtract 6 on the right side.

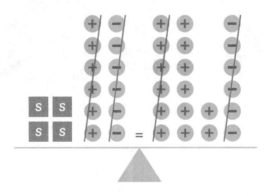

+6 − 6 = 0
This creates 6 zero pairs on each side of the equals sign.

Subtract 6 on both sides and simplify.

Result: 4s = 8

With 4s isolated on the left, you can now solve for the short-trail length, s.

4s = 8

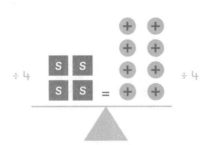

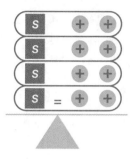

Each **s** equals 2 ➕

$$s = 2$$

This means your short trail runs were 2 miles each!

PRIOR KNOWLEDGE

Using your math symbol skills, you can solve the two-step equation:

a. $4s + 6 = 14$
　　$-\ 6\ -\ 6$　　　*Subtract 6 on both sides and simplify.*

$4s\ \ \ = 8$
$\div 4\ \ \ \div 4$　　　*Divide by 4 on both sides and simplify.*

$s\ \ \ = 2$　　　*s is equal to 2.*

Good job! Next, just like with one-step equations, you can check your answer in two-step equations. Substitute the answer into the original equation and see if it makes the equation true:

a. $4s + 6 = 14$　　　*Substitute 2 for s and use the order of*
$4(2) + 6 = 14$　　　*operations to simplify.*

$8 + 6 = 14$

$14 = 14$　　　*True, so s = 2 is correct!*

Consider this situation: One day, you buy 3 bags worth of candy and your friend buys 2 bags worth. All of your bags appear to be about the same size. *If the total weight of the candy combined is 20 pounds, how many pounds does each bag weigh?*

Take a moment to translate:

3 bags of candy plus 2 more bags results in a total weight of 20 pounds.

$$3c + 2c = 20$$

Here is the visual representation of $3c + 2c = 20$:

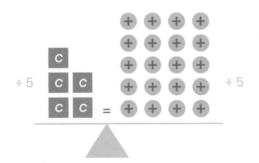

Terms with the same variable and exponent on that variable are "like." As you can see, there will be $5c$ in total. So, c can be isolated after dividing by 5: $5c = 20$.

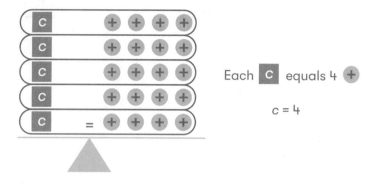

Each c equals 4 +

$c = 4$

This means each bag of candy weighs 4 pounds!

PRIOR KNOWLEDGE

Also with math symbols, you can solve this two-step equation:

b. $3c + 2c = 20$ *3c and 2c are **like terms.***

$5c = 20$ *Combine like terms*

$\div 5 \quad \div 5$ *Divide by 5 on both sides.*

$c = 4$ *c is equal to 4.*

Be careful when you check your answer in this two-step equation.
The answer ($c = 4$) should be substituted into each of the variables in the original equation:

b. $3c + 2c = 20$

$3(4) + 2(4) = 20$ *Substitue 4 for <u>both</u> c variables and simplify using the order of operations.*

$12 + 8 = 20$

$20 = 20$ *True, so c = 4 is correct!*

Excellent!

TOOLS FOR SUCCESS

When solving a two-step equation, it's important to remember that even though you're looking to isolate a variable, you might need to undo more than one operation or combine like terms first.

Here by subtracting 6.

$$4s + 6 = 14$$
$$\underline{-6 \quad -6}$$
$$4s \quad = 8$$
$$\div 4 \quad \div 4$$
$$\overline{}$$
$$s \quad = 2$$

First, isolate the term with the variable...

Then, isolate the variable

EXAMPLE B

Here by combining like terms.

$$3c + 2c = 20$$
$$5c \quad = 20$$
$$\div 5 \quad \div 5$$
$$\overline{}$$
$$c \quad = 4$$

First, isolate the term with the variable...

Then, isolate the variable

Inverse operations are the key!

YOUR TURN!

Solve each two-step equation.

1. $3w - w = 18$

2. $\dfrac{k}{6} = 3$

3. $-2y + 8y = 24$

UNDERSTANDING AND SOLVING INEQUALITIES

GRAPHING ON A NUMBER LINE

Imagine it's a perfect Saturday afternoon in the summer. Not a cloud in the sky. You and your friends want to spend time on the water, so you decide to use the free kayaks offered by the parks department. Life jackets are required to use the kayaks. As everyone is adjusting their life jackets, you realize that they all look the same. Why is it that you can each wear the same size life jacket even though you're all different heights and weights? It's because this type of item has a weight and size limit. A life jacket can hold up to a certain weight limit, or it's designed to fit someone with a maximum height. The stylish life jackets that you and your friends are wearing can hold a maximum of 150 pounds, which begs the question: What is the most a person can weigh if they want to use this type of life jacket?

PRIOR KNOWLEDGE

When a situation has a type of maximum or minimum value, it can be represented with an **inequality**. Here are the inequality symbols you may remember (comparing values from left to right of the symbol):

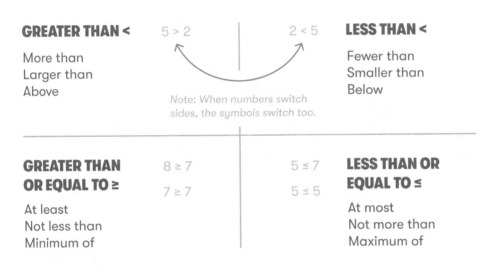

GREATER THAN <

5 > 2

More than
Larger than
Above

2 < 5

LESS THAN <

Fewer than
Smaller than
Below

Note: When numbers switch sides, the symbols switch too.

GREATER THAN OR EQUAL TO ≥

8 ≥ 7

7 ≥ 7

5 ≤ 7

5 ≤ 5

LESS THAN OR EQUAL TO ≤

At least
Not less than
Minimum of

At most
Not more than
Maximum of

How much can a person weigh if they want to use a life jacket with a maximum weight of 150 pounds? You can set this up with a variable and an inequality:

weight of users ⟵———— $w ≤ 150$ ————⟶ maximum weight
↓
can be equal to but must not be more than

> **inequality:** a numerical or algebraic sentence where one side is not equal to the other side; it can be *greater than, greater than or equal to, less than, or less than or equal to*

This represents all of the unknown weights a person could have and still be able to use this size life jacket.

Let's represent this on a number line.

⌕ TAKE A CLOSER LOOK

When you graph an exact solution on a number line, only one number is highlighted or shaded. For example, let's say the instructor weighs 150 pounds:

$w = 150$

For inequalities, there are a lot of possible solutions. Since the language of inequalities can be a little tricky, it helps to visualize them. A maximum of 150 pounds looks like this:

$w \le 150$

- 150 is the "starting value"

- Since the symbol is ≤, the circle should be closed because it will include 150 in the solution.

- The arrow should go to the left since you're looking for values that are less than or equal to 150.

GRAPHING INEQUALITIES ON A NUMBER LINE CHECKLIST

☐ Circle the key value on the number line.

☐ Determine if you fill in your circle or leave it open.

Fill it in if greater or less than AND equal to (≥, ≤)

Leave it open if greater or less than but NOT equal to (>, <)

☐ Determine if you highlight left or right based on the values needed.

Remember, you can always test solutions on the number line. The highlighted area of the inequality is where you want to be. So, let's test it out for numbers that are 150 or less.

- Will the life jacket work for someone with a weight of 95 pounds?

- How about 160 pounds?

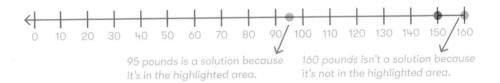

95 pounds is a solution because it's in the highlighted area.

160 pounds isn't a solution because it's not in the highlighted area.

When w = 95

(95) ≤ 150

95 ≤ 150

True! 95 pounds is a solution.

When w = 160

(160) ≤ 150

160 ≤ 150

False. 160 pounds isn't a solution.

Remember how an equation can be reversed and remain balanced?

$$4 + y = 10 \qquad \text{or} \qquad 10 = 4 + y$$

It's also true for inequalities, but you've got to pay close, special attention to the direction the inequality symbol is facing because it needs to match! For example:

$$95 \leq 150 \qquad \text{can become} \qquad 150 \geq 95$$

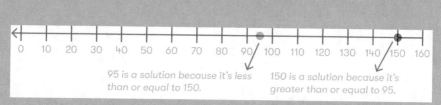

95 is a solution because it's less than or equal to 150.

150 is a solution because it's greater than or equal to 95.

YOUR TURN!

1. Write an inequality for the graph below using *k* as the unknown number.

2. Graph the inequality *r* > 10 on the number line below.

3. You have at least $9 you can use to buy lunch food. Write an inequality using *n* to represent how much you can spend on lunch. Give two possible prices you can pay for lunch.

SOLVING INEQUALITIES IN ONE OR MORE STEPS

All right, are you ready to combine your problem-solving skills with your knowledge of inequalities? Let's say the kayaking instructor took you and your friends out on a sailboat that can carry at most 8 people without knowing each passenger's weight. You and the instructor already count for 2 people. *How many more people can board the boat?*

TAKE A CLOSER LOOK

In this specific example, the "at most" part is saying you can have 8 people aboard the boat or fewer. Set up an inequality statement to represent the number of people the boat can hold including you and the instructor:

$$m + 2 \leq 8$$

$$\begin{array}{r} m + 2 \leq 8 \\ -2 \quad -2 \\ \hline m \leq 6 \end{array}$$

Subtract 2 from both sides.

You might notice that, similar to equations, you needed to subtract the 2 from both the left side and the right sides to keep the balance.

At most, 6 people or fewer can board the boat. Graph your solution:

Test some of the numbers from the solution area in the original inequality. For example, what if 4 more people boarded the boat? When $m = 4$, is 4 a solution?

4 is less than 6, so 4 *is* a solution.

A DOG TOY INEQUALITY

After enough fun in the sun, you and your friends decide to head somewhere with air conditioning and fun. As you walk through the entrance of your local dog rescue to visit the puppies, you overhear the staff chatting. Even though the shelter has a budget of $52 to purchase 6 new toys for the puppies, they want to try and have $10 or more leftover to buy other things. Set up this situation as an inequality:

Let p = price of each puppy toy:

$$\$52 - 6p \geq \$10$$

Now the question is: How much should they pay for each new dog toy to reach their goal? How can you solve for p?

TAKE A CLOSER LOOK

Just like solving an equation with more than one step, the term with the variable needs to be isolated. You require $10 to be left over from your $52 available balance of money. This means you need to first know the difference, and then divide that by the 6 toys:

$p \leq 7$	$52 - 6p \geq 10$	
Starting Number: 7	$\underline{-52 \qquad -52}$	Subtract 52 from both sides.
$\leq$: closed circle, includes 7	$-6p \geq -42$	
$\leq$: arrow to the left,	$\underline{\div -6 \quad \div -6}$	Divide by −6 on both sides.
values less than 7	$p \leq 7$	Switch the inequality symbol
Place a closed circle on 7		when you divide or multiply
and draw an arrow to the		by a negative.
left.		

Awesome! If the shelter can find where to buy each dog toy for $7 or less, they will have at least $10 remaining.

YOUR TURN!

Solve the following inequalities. Then, graph the solution and state a possible value.

1. $-3d \geq -18$

2. $7x + 3 > 31$

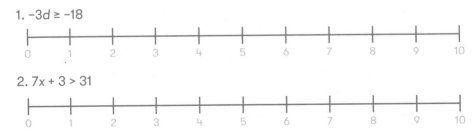

CHAPTER SUMMARY

WRITING AND INTERPRETING ONE-STEP EQUATIONS

You've explored the similarities and differences between expressions and equations. As a reminder, the one difference between the two is that equations must include an equals sign.

EQUATION	EXPRESSION
$2(a - 4) = 12$	$3b + 4$

SOLVING ONE- AND TWO-STEP EQUATIONS

When you solve equations, your goal is to solve for the value of the unknown value, the variable. Use inverse operations to "undo" the operations on the variable. You'll need to be mindful of using the inverse operations to isolate the variable, so that you can find the solution to the equation. This solution should satisfy the equation, meaning when substituted back into the equation, the left side of the equation is equal to the right side of the equation.

UNDERSTANDING AND SOLVING INEQUALITIES

• Graphing on a Number Line

Sometimes solutions will be a group of values, or a range of values; this is true in the case of inequalities. Here are some key ideas to remember when graphing inequalities on a number line:

DIRECTION	OPEN OR CLOSED CIRCLE
$<$ or $\leq$ Arrow to the LEFT	$<$ or $>$ OPEN Circle
$>$ or $\geq$ Arrow to the RIGHT	$\leq$ or $\geq$ CLOSED Circle

• Solving Inequalities in One or More Steps

You can apply the same strategies for solving equations to inequalities, but with one difference; when you divide using a negative number, you must swap the inequality symbol.

$$-6p \geq -42$$
$$\underline{\div -6p \div -6}$$
$$p \leq 7$$

CHAPTER 7 VOCABULARY

equation: a numerical or algebraic sentence where one side of the equals sign is equal in value to the other side of the equals sign

inequality: a numerical or algebraic sentence where one side is not equal to the other side; it can be greater than, greater than or equal to, less than, or less than or equal to

inverse operation: the opposite operation to "undo" an operation

CHAPTER 7 ANSWER KEY

SOLVING ONE-STEP EQUATIONS (P. 220)

1. $80 + x = 150$
   $x = 70$

2. $2s = 200$
   $s = 100$

3. $b \div 5 = 22$
   $b = 110$

4. $t - 15 = 22$
   $t = 37$

SOLVING TWO-STEP EQUATIONS (P. 226)

1. $w = 9$ 2. $k = 18$ 3. $y = 4$

GRAPHING ON A NUMBER LINE (P. 231)

1. $k \leq 25$

2.

3. $n \geq 9$; answers vary: $10 and $12 are two possible solutions.

SOLVING INEQUALITIES IN ONE OR MORE STEPS (P. 234)

1. $d \leq 6$

2. $x > 4$

NOTES

8 EXPRESSIONS AND EQUATIONS: PART 3

On lazy days without much to do, you've started to really enjoy walking along the beach by yourself and collecting starfish. You've begun to track how many of them you pick up based on the number of hours your walks last. You start to wonder what the relationship is between the amount of time you walk and the number of starfish you find. Without you even realizing it, your walk on the beach is getting you into the world of proportional relationships.

PROPORTIONAL RELATIONSHIPS

USING SLOPE TO INTERPRET RATE

NUMBER OF HOURS BEACH-WALKING, X	NUMBER OF STARFISH COLLECTED, y
0	0
0.5	1
1	2
1.5	3
2	4

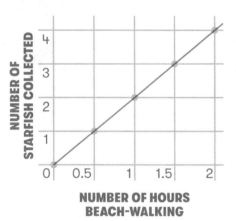

CALCULATING SLOPE/RATE OF CHANGE

In analyzing this table and graph, you notice that you've been collecting two starfish per hour. This is called the rate of change or slope of the line. The rate of change or slope tells you the growth pattern of the relationship between the independent (x) and dependent (y) variables.

$$\text{slope} = \text{rate of change} = \frac{(\text{change in } y)}{(\text{change in } x)}$$

rate of change/slope: the ratio of change in the dependent variable to the change in the independent variable—the steepness of the line that is formed by the ratio; the ratio can be negative (decreasing) or positive (increasing)

Let's discuss some strategies for finding the slope or rate of change of a relationship. Mathematicians use **Δ, delta**, as shorthand for change.

TABLE

Δx = change in x values

Δx = +1

NUMBER OF HOURS BEACH-WALKING, X	NUMBER OF STARFISH COLLECTED, Y
0	0
0.5	1
1	2
1.5	3
2	4

Δy = change in y values

Δy = +2

$$\text{rate of change} = \frac{\text{change in } y}{\text{change in } x} = \frac{\Delta y}{\Delta x} = \frac{2 \text{ starfish}}{1 \text{ hour}} = 2 \text{ starfish per hour}$$

When trying to calculate slope from a graph, you can use another version of the slope formula:

$$\text{slope} = \text{rate of change} = \frac{\text{rise } (\uparrow\downarrow)}{\text{run } (\leftarrow\rightarrow)} = \frac{\text{vertical change}}{\text{horizontal change}} = \frac{\Delta y}{\Delta x}$$

You can best use this version of the slope formula by choosing two "friendly" coordinates on the line. (These are coordinates that are easy to work with.) Once you choose your coordinates, you can then find the vertical and horizontal changes (or distances) between each coordinate.

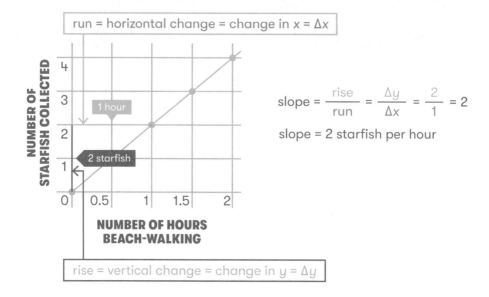

run = horizontal change = change in x = Δx

NUMBER OF STARFISH COLLECTED

1 hour

2 starfish

NUMBER OF HOURS
BEACH-WALKING

rise = vertical change = change in y = Δy

$$\text{slope} = \frac{\text{rise}}{\text{run}} = \frac{\Delta y}{\Delta x} = \frac{2}{1} = 2$$

slope = 2 starfish per hour

Let's say you were only given two coordinates (from a list, table, or graph) to calculate the slope or rate of change for a linear relationship. To solve, you would use the **slope formula**:

$$\text{slope} = \frac{\Delta y}{\Delta x} = \frac{y_2 - y_1}{x_2 - x_1}$$

Coordinate 1: (x_1, y_1)
Coordinate 2: (x_2, y_2)

Note: These coordinates can be ANY two coordinates on the line.

Using the starfish example from before, you can use two coordinates to find the slope of the line:

Coordinate 1: (0, 0)
Coordinate 2: (1, 2)

$$\text{slope} = \frac{y_2 - y_1}{x_2 - x_1} = \frac{2 - 0}{1 - 0}$$

slope = 2 starfish per hour

TYPES OF SLOPES

There are many different types of lines in math problems. Each line is connected to different types of slopes—and there are four different types of slopes.

POSITIVE	NEGATIVE	ZERO	UNDEFINED
Positive Slope: increasing rate of change: **up** on the right side.	Negative Slope: decreasing rate of change: **down** on the right side.	Zero Slope: a flat horizontal line; it occurs when there's no change in the y-values, y = #	Undefined Slope: a vertical line; it occurs when there's no change in the x-values, x = #

YOUR TURN!

1. Calculate slope of a line containing the following coordinates:

    a. (3, 7) and (6, 31)

    b. (5, 16) and (10, −2)

2. Find the slope (often represented by the symbol m) of the line showing the relationship between time and cost using the numbers in the table below:

TIME (MIN), X	5	10	20	30
COST ($), Y	40	60	100	140

COMPARING UNIT RATES

Let's say that one morning, you and your sister wake up and realize you forgot to get your mom something for her birthday. (It happens to the best of us!) Before she gets home from work, you both decide to go out and collect flowers for her, since you're on a budget and can't afford a fancier bouquet. Each of you has collected 15 flowers to use for your homemade flower arrangement, which smells and looks even better than a store-bought one!

PRIOR KNOWLEDGE

After an hour and a half, your sister needs to get back home to get ready for swim practice. While she heads home, you continue to gather flowers, which takes another half hour. On your way home, you think about the proportional relationship between the number of flowers each of you hand-picked and the time in which each of you spent looking for them:

You: 15 flowers in 2 hours

Your sister: 15 flowers in 1.5 hours

You want to convert these into unit rates so you can compare them. *So, how many flowers per hour were each of you gathering?*

Translating "flowers per hour" into the fraction $\frac{flowers}{hours}$, you calculate your rate:

You = $\frac{15}{2}$ = 7.5 flowers per hour   Your Sister = $\frac{15}{1.5}$ = 10 flowers per hour

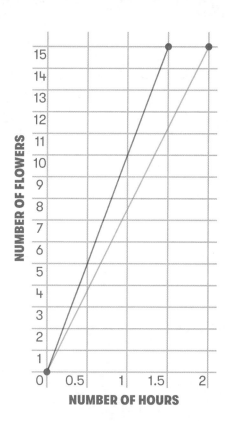

It makes sense that your sister's rate is greater than your rate since she finished picking her flowers before you did. When you get home, you decide to put these rates onto a graph to visually compare them.

You put a coordinate at (0, 0) since you both started at the same time.

For your line (in blue), you connected a second coordinate at (2, 15) to represent the 2 hours it took you to gather your 15 flowers.

For your sister's line (in red), you connected a second coordinate at (1.5, 15) for the 1.5 hours it took for her to gather her 15 flowers.

TAKE A CLOSER LOOK

The slope of each of these two lines is clearly different. Your sister's line is steeper because she gathered flowers at a faster rate than you. Your line is more gradual (not as steep) because you picked your flowers at a slower rate compared to your sister.

When comparing the slopes of multiple lines:

Steeper slopes show faster rates of change.
Gradual slopes show slower rates of change.

So, what is the slope for each of your lines? Good news—you already found that! On your way home, when you found the two rates of change for you and your sister, you were calculating the slope!

You = $\dfrac{15}{2}$ = 7.5 flowers per hour   Your Sister = $\dfrac{15}{1.5}$ = 10 flowers per hour

YOUR TURN!

Compare the graphs of the three relationships below.

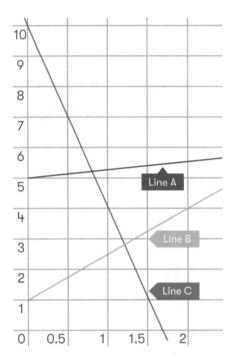

a. Which has the steepest positive slope?

b. Which has the steepest negative slope?

c. Which has the most gradual (least steep) slope?

LINEAR RELATIONSHIPS

When discussing linear relationships, you can use four different models to represent the same relationship: table, graph, verbal, and equation. In this section, we'll examine how to write **linear equations**. The general form of a linear equation is $y = mx + b$.

slope

$$y = mx + b$$

y-intercept

m = rate of change = slope
b = y-intercept, when $x = 0$

---

linear equation: an equation that includes a relationship between two variables that results in a straight line; must include a constant rate of change (slope)

WRITING AN EQUATION FROM A VERBAL DESCRIPTION

You can create an equation based on your flower bouquet. For this example, x represents the number of hours gathering flowers (independent variable) and y represents the number of total collected flowers (dependent variable). To write the equation, you need two pieces of information:

slope, m **and** y-intercept, b

EQUATION	INFORMATION
$y = 7.5x + 0$ $y = 7.5x$ where x = the number of hours and y = total number of flowers picked	• For the slope or the rate of change, we use the 7.5 flowers per hour. • For the y-intercept/when x = 0, we use 0 because at 0 hours, you've picked 0 flowers, (0, 0).

In situations where the y-intercept is (0, 0), the linear equation can be written in two ways, like the above example:

$$y = 7.5x + 0$$

$$y = 7.5x$$

You can include the "+0" or write the equation without it since the equations are still equivalent.

WRITING AN EQUATION FROM A TABLE OR GRAPH

TABLE	
NUMBER OF HOURS GATHERING FLOWERS, X	**NUMBER OF FLOWERS COLLECTED, Y**
0	0
1	7.5
2	15
3	22.5
4	30

$\Delta x = 1$ $\Delta y = 7.5$

$$m = \text{slope} = \frac{\Delta y}{\Delta x} = \frac{7.5}{1} = 7.5 \text{ flowers per hour } \textbf{(average)}$$

$$b = y\text{-intercept} = 0$$

$$y = 7.5x + 0$$

OR

$$y = 7.5x$$

GRAPH	EQUATION

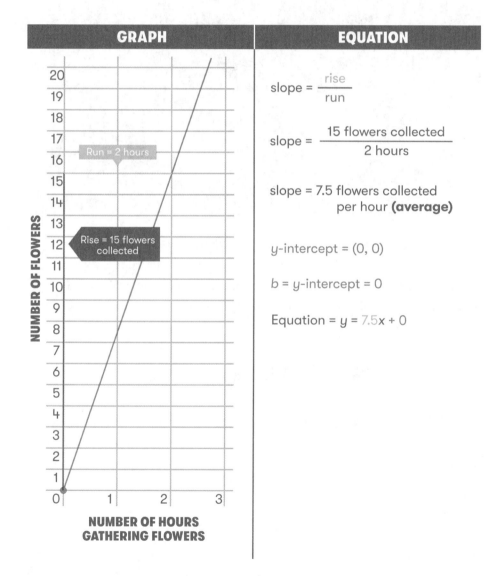

slope = $\dfrac{\text{rise}}{\text{run}}$

slope = $\dfrac{15 \text{ flowers collected}}{2 \text{ hours}}$

slope = 7.5 flowers collected per hour **(average)**

y-intercept = (0, 0)

$b = y$-intercept = 0

Equation = $y = 7.5x + 0$

Graph labels:
- NUMBER OF FLOWERS
- Run = 2 hours
- Rise = 15 flowers collected
- NUMBER OF HOURS GATHERING FLOWERS

LET'S PUT THOSE SKILLS TO WORK!

The next day, you realize the bouquet is looking a little thin, and you want to fill it out with 30 more flowers to add to the ones you collected yesterday. Like a flower blooming, a question springs into your head: *Based on my rate of collection yesterday, how many hours will it take to collect 30 additional flowers?*

PRIOR KNOWLEDGE

Yesterday you gathered 7.5 flowers per hour. Assuming your rate is the same, you could take the number of flowers you need, 30, and subtract 7.5 repeatedly to find your answer:

After hour #1: 30 − 7.5 = 22.5 flowers

After hour #2: 22.5 − 7.5 = 15 flowers

You realize you could continue this process, but it would be better to represent repeatedly subtracting 7.5 through multiplication. You look back at the equation you created, $y = 7.5x$, and decide since using 7.5 flowers per hour decreases your total amount of flowers that are unaccounted for, you should make the 7.5 negative. So, you create a new equation:

$y = 30 - 7.5x$

y = number of flowers to gather

x = number of hours spent collecting

You can also write the equation as $y = -7.5x + 30$.

So, the question remains: *How many hours will you spend gathering what you need at the rate of 7.5 flowers per hour?*

TAKE A CLOSER LOOK

If you graph the equation, $y = 30 - 7.5x$, you can find out.

NUMBER OF HOURS GATHERING FLOWERS, X	NUMBER OF FLOWERS REMAINING, Y
0	30
1	22.5
2	15
3	7.5
4	0

Note: *Since this relationship doesn't include (0, 0), it's a nonproportional relationship.*

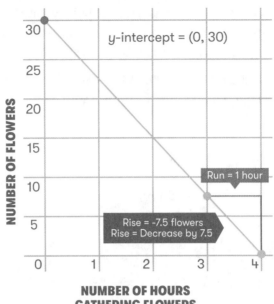

y-intercept = (0, 30)

NUMBER OF FLOWERS

Run = 1 hour

Rise = -7.5 flowers
Rise = Decrease by 7.5

NUMBER OF HOURS
GATHERING FLOWERS

For every 1 hour spent gathering, the total number of flowers you need to gather decreases by 7.5 flowers, which is your slope!

HOW TO CREATE THE GRAPH OF A LINE FROM SLOPE-INTERCEPT FORM

Take a look at how you would graph the equation $y = 6 - 3x$.

1. Start the line by making a coordinate point at the y-intercept

2. After plotting the y-intercept, use the slope $\frac{\text{rise} (\uparrow\downarrow)}{\text{run} (\leftarrow\rightarrow)}$ to plot at least one other coordinate.

3. Use a straight-edged object (like a ruler or side of a book) to connect the coordinates.

4. Draw the line as far as the graph allows and use arrows at the end(s) if the line should continue.

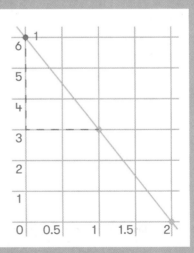

YOUR TURN!

Complete the slope-intercept challenge for the scenario below:

You and a friend are planning on hiking a 9-mile hiking trail at a rate of $2\frac{1}{4}$ miles per hour.

1. Create an equation in slope-intercept form for the miles remaining after each hour of hiking.
   miles remaining =
   _____ – _____ per hour

2. Using this equation, create a realistic graph of the line, remembering to scale your x- and y-axis appropriately.

3. How many hours will it take you to finish the 9-mile trail?

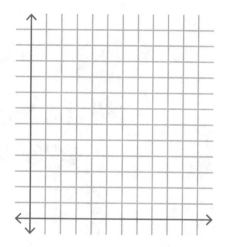

SOLVING AND GRAPHING SYSTEMS OF LINEAR EQUATIONS

One weekend, you're all set to meet up with your friend at the intersection of Main Street and Birch Lane. This is your usual meet-up spot, since you live on Main Street and he lives on Birch Lane. Finding each other at the intersection of these two streets is an example of solving a **system of linear equations**. It's the point where two equations cross. Taking a look at the graphs that follow, can you identify the coordinate representing the solution of each system?

system of linear equations: two or more linear equations that include the same variables

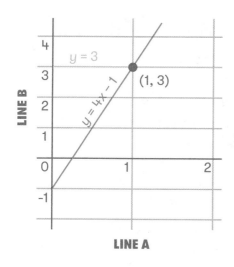

LINE A

Line A and Line B intersect at point (1, 3). Although Line A and Line B are made up of an infinite number of coordinates, they only share one point: (1, 3), which is considered their solution.

If you consider the point where you and your friend meet up, the intersection of Main Street and Birch Lane is the only place where these two roads cross. So, it's your solution!

TAKE A CLOSER LOOK

$$y = 3$$

$$y = 4x - 1$$

These two equations, the system of linear equations, created the first graph. Do you think you could solve for their intersection point without graphing?

There are two general methods for solving systems algebraically: the substitution method and the combination/elimination method.

In order to solve this system algebraically, remember that the solution, (1, 3), came from the intersection of the two lines on the graph. This intersection (*solution*) is where both equations have the same x- and y-values, where they're equal.

> **intersection/solution:** the location where two or more linear equations intersect and have the same value for both variables

SOLVING SYSTEMS BY SUBSTITUTION METHOD

So, when working with equations in the form "y =", you can set the two equations equal to each other by substituting the second y with the value from the first equation.

Equation 1: $y = 3$
Equation 2: $y = 4x - 1$

$3 = 4x - 1$ *Replace the "y" with the "3."*

$3 = 4x - 1$
$+1 \qquad +1$ *Use inverse operations to isolate the constants to one side of the equation by adding 1 to both sides of the equation.*

$4 = 4x$
$\dfrac{4}{4} \quad \dfrac{4}{4}$ *Use inverse operations to isolate the variable to one side of the equation by dividing by 4 on both sides of the equation.*
$1 = x$

You found the value of x = 1. So, why isn't this the final step?

> Remember from the graphs, the solution to a system of equations will be coordinates, (x, y), because they're intersection points.

So, the value you just found, x = 1, is only the x-value of the coordinate, so let's use that to find the y-value.

$y = 4 (1) - 1$ *You can find the y-value by substituting, x = 1*
$y = 4 - 1$ *into the second equation and evaluating.*
$y = 3$

Now that you have both values, the final solution is confirmed, x = 1 and y = 3. You can also write it as a **coordinate pair**, (1, 3).

> **coordinate pair (ordered pair):** a set of numbers that define the location of a point on a coordinate grid

CHECK YOUR SOLUTION(S)!

$$y = 3$$

$$y = 4x - 1$$

Let's say you didn't know from the graph that (1, 3) is the correct solution to the system.

How could you check your answer (besides graphing it)?

If you substitute the x- and y-values from your solution into either original equation, it should create a true statement, meaning the left side of the equation equals the right side of the equation.

Equation 1: $y = 3$
Equation 2: $y = 4x - 1$

CHECK THE SOLUTION (1,3)	
$y = 3$	$y = 4x - 1$
$3 = 3$	$3 = 4(1) - 1$
Note: There's no x variable in the equation, so you only substitute the y-value.	$3 = 4 - 1$
	$3 = 3$
	True Statement

You've successfully checked (1, 3) for the second equation and proven it's the solution to the system. Ready to give the second set of equations a try? Take a look at the system below:

$$y = -x + 1$$

$$y = 3x + 5$$

First, combine the two equations by substituting the statement −x + 1 in for the y in the bottom equation:

$y = -x + 1$ $y = 3x + 5$ ___ $-x + 1 = 3x + 5$	Substitute "y" with "-x+ 1."
$-x + 1 = 3x + 5$ $\quad -1 \qquad -1$ ___ $-x = 3x + 4$	Use inverse operations to isolate the constants to one side of the equation by subtracting 1 from both sides of the equation.
$-x = 3x + 4$ $-3x \;\; -3x$ ___ $-4x = 4$	Use inverse operations to isolate the terms with variables to one side of the equation by subtracting 3x from both sides of the equation.
$\dfrac{-4x = 4}{-4 \quad -4}$ $x = -1$	Use inverse operations to isolate the variable to one side of the equation by dividing by -4 on both sides of the equation.

Are you done? Not yet! Time to check your solution.

Use x = -1 to substitute back into both of the original equations and solve for y. You can use either equation,

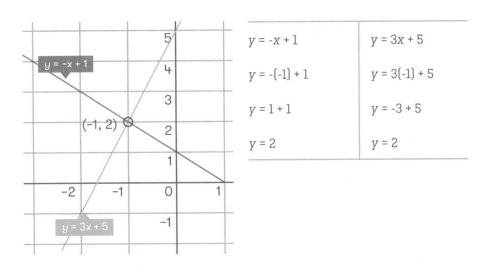

$y = -x + 1$	$y = 3x + 5$
$y = -(-1) + 1$	$y = 3(-1) + 5$
$y = 1 + 1$	$y = -3 + 5$
$y = 2$	$y = 2$

So, the solution to this system of equations is (-1, 2), or x = -1 and y = 2. As you can see, both equations have an output of 2 when the input is -1, or the coordinate pair (-1, 2).

Good work!

YOUR TURN!

Use your skills to solve the system of linear equations below.

- Make sure you find the full solution, the values of x and y.

- After finding your answer, check to make sure you're correct by substituting x and y back into both of the original equations.

$$y = 1.5x + 3$$

$$y = -4x - 2.5$$

DIFFERENT FORMS OF LINEAR EQUATIONS

Most of the situations we have been discussing are about **independent** and **dependent variables**, where one variable directly affects the other variable. Sometimes, you'll encounter situations called co-dependent, where the two variables "negotiate" for one fixed value. The two forms of linear equations are as follows:

SLOPE-INTERCEPT FORM	STANDARD FORM
$y = mx + b$	$Ax + By = C$
This form is mostly used for situations where there's one rate related to the independent variable and one constant (fixed) value that will directly change the dependent variable value.	This form is used when you have two variable quantities that combine to a third fixed quantity (constant).
Example: $y = -x + 1$	Example: $2x + 5y = 42$

SOLVING SYSTEMS WITH ELIMINATION

As you check the weather before a camping trip, you see that you need to buy some rain ponchos and some tarps to make rain shelters. You estimate that you'll need a total of 10 ponchos and tarps. Once at the store, you find out that the ponchos cost 5 dollars each and the tarps cost 10 dollars each. Your parents said you can spend no more than 75 dollars on your gear. *How many ponchos and tarps can you buy, assuming you want to spend the full amount?* For this situation, writing a system would be helpful.

SLOPE-INTERCEPT FORM	STANDARD FORM
$x + y = 10$	The number of ponchos and tarps is 10 items in total.
$5x + 10y = 75$	5 dollars per poncho and 10 dollars per tarp must equal 75 dollars.

Note: Both equations are in standard form.

For the elimination method, first ask: Which variable would you like to eliminate?

Start by trying to eliminate the x's. This can only happen if the coefficients and variables are equal. You don't have that now, but you can make it so by using multiplication.

> **standard form:** an equation form for linear relationships where there are two variables that are co-dependent and combine to a third fixed amount, $Ax + By = C$

TRY IT ON ANOTHER EXAMPLE

Let's solve this system of equations using elimination.

$x + y = 10$ $5x + 10y = 75$	To change 1x into 5x, multiply the first (top) equation by 5.
$5(x + y = 10)$ $5x + 10y = 75$	By multiplying the first equation by 5, you will get a new equation that is equivalent.
$5x + 5y = 50$ $5x + 10y = 75$	Now, you have the two 5x's, which you can eliminate by subtracting the two equations.
$5x + 5y = 50$ $-(5x + 10y = 75)$ _____ $-5y = -25$ $\dfrac{-5y}{-5} = \dfrac{-25}{-5}$ $y = 5$	After you subtract the second equation from the first equation, you can then begin to solve the equation for the variable that is remaining. This is combination by subtraction.
$x + y = 10$ $x + (5) = 10$ $-5 \quad -5$ _____ $x = 5$	Substitute the value of the variable from the previous step, $y = 5$, into one of the equations; the first one is the simplest. Then solve for the other variable, x.
Solution: (5, 5)	Check your final solution in both equations to make sure it produces a true statement for both. This solution means that with 75 dollars, you can buy 5 ponchos and 5 tarps.

YOUR TURN!

Solve this system using elimination.

$3x - y = 7$

$2x - 3y = 7$

SOLUTIONS TO SYSTEMS OF LINEAR EQUATIONS: TYPES

All of the problems that we have already completed in this chapter are "one solution" systems because there was only one intersection between the two lines.

Systems of linear equations have three different types of solutions: one solution, no solution, and infinitely many solutions.

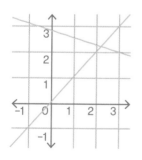

one solution

one intersection

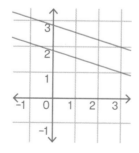

no solution

no intersection

parallel lines

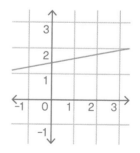

infinitely many solutions

infinitely many intersections

same line, equivalent lines

NO SOLUTIONS

Below is an example of a system that has no solution.

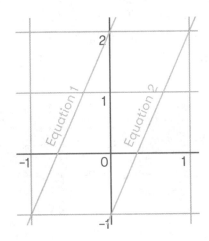

Do you notice anything about the two equations?

Equation 1: $y = 3x + 2$

Equation 2: $y = 3x - 1$

The two equations have the same slope, 3, but different y-intercepts. This means they will change at the same constant rate, but they will cross the y-axis at different points.

Because linear equations have constant rates of change, these two lines will continue forever in their directions without ever intersecting.

PRIOR KNOWLEDGE

How do you think you could prove these two equations have no solution without graphing (algebraically)? Take a moment and try to solve their system:

> *Spoiler alert—you'll create a mathematical statement that isn't true!*

Equation 1: $y = 3x + 2$
Equation 2: $y = 3x - 1$

$y = 3x + 2$
$y = 3x - 1$

Using substitution, you can set the equations equal to one another.

$3x + 2 = 3x - 1$

$3x + 2 = 3x - 1$
$-3x \quad\quad -3x$
_____

But, when you attempt to isolate the variable, you run into a problem.

$2 = -1$

$2 \neq -1$

Is this a true statement? Does 2 equal -1? No!

You can say this is equation is "solved," but the actual answer to this system is that there's **no solution**. This proves what you saw in the graph—these lines will never cross.

INFINITELY MANY SOLUTIONS

What about two lines that are on top of each other? If you and a friend are on the same street and traveling in the same direction, in how many places could you cross/intersect?

The answer is there are an infinite number of times you could intersect.

When two equations overlap, there are infinite solutions to that system.

infinite solutions: when two equations for a system represent the same relationship, they will intersect infinitely since they are the same line

TAKE A CLOSER LOOK

The graph below contains two equations that are labeled.

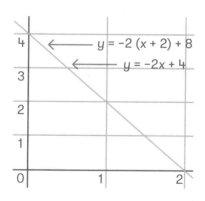

What is going on here?! Both lines are graphed, but you can only see them as one. The coordinates for the first equation are the same as the coordinates for the second equation!

That's odd, the equations seem to be different, but are they? One way to figure this out is to solve the system algebraically:

$y = -2x + 4$ $y = -2(x + 2) + 8$ ———————————— $-2x + 4 = -2(x + 2) + 8$	Using substitution, you can make one equation from the two.
$-2x + 4 = -2(x + 2) + 8$ $-2x + 4 = -2x - 4 + 8$ $-2x + 4 = -2x + 4$	Before you can isolate the variable, you must simplify the right side of the equation: Use the distributive property to simplify the right side of the equation. Combine -4 and 8 to continue to simplify the right side of the equation.
$-2x + 4 = -2x + 4$	Next, you might want to isolate the variable—but wait! Do you notice anything about the two sides of the equation?

They're equal! The second original equation, $y = -2(x + 2) + 8$, simplified to the same equation as the first one, $y = -2x + 4$. So, because the two equations are equal, they create the same graph and have infinite solutions.

$$-2x + 4 = -2x + 4$$

This system has infinite solutions.

What do you think would happen if you finished solving the system instead of stopping at $-2x + 4 = -2x + 4$?

Let's see!

$$\begin{array}{c} -2x + 4 = -2x + 4 \\ +2x \qquad +2x \\ \hline 4 = 4 \end{array}$$

This is another "forever true" statement! This system does, in fact, have an infinite number of solutions.

This is a true statement, $4 = 4$, and will be forever true because there's no variable to change the values.

YOUR TURN!

Using the algebraic method, solve each system of linear equations. Then state the type of solution: one solution, no solution, or infinite solutions.

1. $y = 2x - 3$
   $y = 5 + 4(x - 2)$

2. $y = -0.5(x - 2)$
   $y = -0.5x + 7$

3. $y = 6x + 6$
   $y = 2(3x + 3)$

DEFINING AND IDENTIFYING FUNCTIONS

Using coordinate pairs and tables of values, you can determine if a relationship is a **function**. By describing inputs and outputs as *x*'s and *y*'s, you can say:

A function's **input**, *x*, will have only one **output**, *y*.

Mathematicians call the input values or independent variable values the **domain**. They also have a name for the output values or dependent variable values, the **range**.

We'll first look at a function and non-function through a method called mapping, where the relationship between one value in the domain is linked, or mapped, to a value in the range by a rule or arrow.

function: a type of mathematical relationship in which every input results in one, and only one, output

independent variable (input): an unknown or varying value that stands alone and isn't changed by the other variables in a relationship or equation (i.e., time passed, items bought)

dependent variable (output): an unknown or varying value based on the value of the independent variable and the relationship given (i.e., money paid per hour, cost for total items)

domain: the values for the independent variable

range: the values for the dependent variable

mapping: a visual representation of the correspondence between the inputs and outputs of two sets of numbers

That's a lot of terms to remember, but you'll get the hang of it as you look at the next few examples.

RELATION A:

(−5, −2) (−1, −8) (9, −8) (4, 8)

Domain: −5, −1, 9, 4
Range: −2, −8, 8

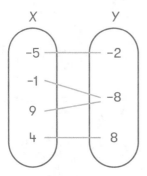

mapping A
FUNCTION!

Notice EVERY x-value goes to exactly one y-value. Therefore it's a function.

RELATION B:

(−5, −8) (4, 8) (−5, −2)

Domain: −5, 4
Range: −8, 8, −2

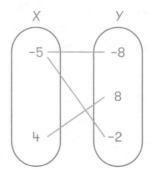

mapping B
NOT A FUNCTION!

Notice that −5 maps to two different y-values. Therefore it is NOT a function.

We can look at the above relations using a table of values, list of coordinates, or graphs. How can you determine if a relation is a function through these representations?

SET A			

(−1, 4) (1, 4) (2, 8) (3, 12)

INPUT (X)	−1	1	2	3
OUTPUT (Y)	−4	4	8	12

Set A is a function because each of its inputs result in only one output.

(−1, 4) (1, 4) (2, 8) (3, 12)

INPUT (X)	−1	1	2	3
OUTPUT (Y)	−4	4	8	12

SET B			

(9, 3) (25, 5) (9, −3) (16, 4)

INPUT (X)	9	25	9	16
OUTPUT (Y)	3	5	-3	4

Set B isn't a function because one of its inputs, 9, has more than one output.

(9, 3) (9, −3) (16, 4) (25, 5)

INPUT (X)	9	9	16	25
OUTPUT (Y)	3	-3	4	5

You can also test if a relation is a function by using the **vertical line test**. If you can draw a vertical line that goes through *more than one* coordinate in the relation, then it's NOT a function.

SET A

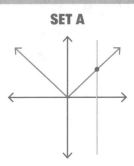

This is a function because the vertical line goes through **one** point.

SET B

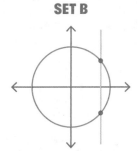

This isn't a function because the vertical line goes through **two** points.

vertical line test: a method for determining whether a graphed relation is a function; if the "vertical line" touches the graph more than one time, the relation is not a function

YOUR TURN!

Find the domain and range for each relation and determine whether the relation is a function.

1.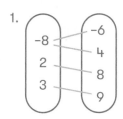

2.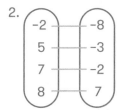

3.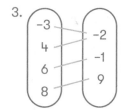

4.

INPUT (X)	-2	-1	0	1	2
OUTPUT (Y)	4	1	0	1	4

5. (-4, 2); (-2, 4); (0, 6); (-4, -2); (-2, -4)

CHAPTER SUMMARY

PROPORTIONAL RELATIONSHIPS

• **Linear Equation** ($y = mx + b$): This equation allows us to make predictions about the path of the relationship based on the rate of change and y-intercept.

• **Slope, m**: Rate of change or steepness of a line.

USING SLOPE TO INTERPRET RATE

TABLE

$$\text{slope} = \text{rate of change} = \frac{\text{change in } y}{\text{change in } x} = \frac{\Delta y}{\Delta x}$$

GRAPH

$$\text{slope} = \text{rate of change} = \frac{\text{rise } (\uparrow\downarrow)}{\text{run } (\leftarrow\rightarrow)} = \frac{\text{vertical change}}{\text{horizontal change}} = \frac{\Delta y}{\Delta x}$$

TWO COORDINATES

$$\text{slope} = \frac{\Delta y}{\Delta x} = \frac{y_2 - y_1}{x_2 - x_1}$$

TYPES OF SLOPE

• Positive Slope ↗   • Zero Slope →

• Undefined Slope ↑   • Negative Slope ↘

y-intercept, b: Value of y when $x = 0$, or the initial value.

LINEAR RELATIONSHIPS

There are three different types of solutions:

   • One solution: Solution (x, y). The intersection point of two lines.

   • No solution: Same slope, different y-intercept, parallel lines.

- The equations will have equal slopes but different y-intercepts.

- Their graphs will be parallel lines that will never intersect.

- The solution process will result in a false statement (like 2 ≠ −1).

- A conclusion must be made at the end of your process ("this system has no solutions").

- Infinitely many solutions: Same exact line.

  - In slope-intercept form, they will have equal slopes and equal y-intercepts. Each equation will represent the same operations (when simplified).

  - The graph of the system will be two identical lines that overlap each other.

  - The algebraic solution will result in a statement that is forever true (like 4 = 4).

  - A conclusion must be made at the end of your process ("this system has infinite solutions").

SOLVING AND GRAPHING SYSTEMS OF LINEAR EQUATIONS

- Substitution method

- Elimination method

DEFINING AND IDENTIFYING FUNCTIONS

- **Domain**: x-values

- **Range**: y-values

- A function's input, x, will have only one output, y.

- **Vertical line test**: Use vertical lines on a graph of a relation to figure out if a relation is a function. If you can draw more than one through the relation, it's not a function.

CHAPTER 8 VOCABULARY

coordinate pair (ordered pair): a set of numbers that define the location of a point on a coordinate grid

dependent variable (output): an unknown or varying value based on the value of the independent variable and the relationship given (i.e., money paid per hour, cost for total items)

domain: the values for the independent variable

function: a type of mathematical relationship in which every input results in one, and only one, output

independent variable (input): an unknown or varying value that stands alone and isn't changed by the other variables in a relationship or equation (i.e., time passed, items bought)

infinite solutions: when two equations for a system represent the same relationship, they will intersect infinitely since they are the same line

intersection/solution: the location where two or more linear equations intersect and have the same value for both variables

linear equation: an equation that includes a relationship between two variables that results in a straight line; must include a constant rate of change (slope)

mapping: a visual representation of the correspondence between the inputs and outputs of two sets of numbers

range: the values for the dependent variable

rate of change/slope: the ratio of change in the dependent variable to the change in the independent variable—the steepness of the line that is formed by the ratio; the ratio can be negative (decreasing) or positive (increasing)

slope-intercept form/linear equation: an equation that represents a linear relationship with a slope and y-intercept, $y = mx + b$

standard form: an equation form for linear relationships where there are two variables that are co-dependent and combine to a third fixed amount, $Ax + By = C$

system of linear equations: two or more linear equations that include the same variables

vertical line test: a method for determining whether a graphed relation is a function; if the "vertical line" touches the graph more than one time, the relation is not a function

y-intercept: when $x = 0$, the location in the coordinate plane where the relationship intersects the y-axis

CHAPTER 8 ANSWER KEY

PROPORTIONAL RELATIONSHIPS

TYPES OF SLOPES (P. 245)

1. a. $m = \dfrac{24}{3} = 8$

   b. $m = \dfrac{-18}{5} = -3.6$

2.

TIME (MIN), x	5	10	20	30
COST ($), y	40	60	100	140

$$\text{slope} = \frac{\text{change in cost}}{\text{change in time}} = \frac{\$20}{5 \text{ minutes}} = \frac{\$4}{1 \text{ minute}} = \$4 \text{ per minute}$$

COMPARING UNIT RATES (P. 248)

a. Line B   b. Line C   c. Line A

WRITING AN EQUATION FROM A TABLE OR GRAPH (P. 255)

1. $y = 9 - 2.25x$

where y = miles remaining and x = hours passed

2.

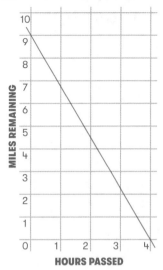

HOURS PASSED

3. It will take 4 hours to finish the trail.

SOLVING SYSTEMS BY SUBSTITUTION METHOD (P. 261)

FINDING X:

$y = 1.5x + 3$

$y = -4x - 2.5$

$1.5x + 3 = -4x - 2.5$

$-3 -3$

$1.5x = -4x - 5.5$

$+4x +4x$

$5.5x = -5.5$

$$\frac{5.5x}{5.5} = \frac{-5.5}{5.5}$$

$x = -1$

FINDING Y:

$y = 1.5x + 3$

$y = 1.5 (-1) + 3$

$y = -1.5 + 3$

$y = 1.5$

Solution: $(-1, 1.5)$

Checking solution in $y = 1.5x + 3$:

$(1.5) = 1.5 (-1) + 3$

$1.5 = -1.5 + 3$

$1.5 = 1.5$

Checking solution in $y = -4x - 2.5$:

$(1.5) = -4 (-1) -2.5$

$1.5 = 4 - 2.5$

$1.5 = 1.5$

SOLVING SYSTEMS USING ELIMINATION (P. 264)

$3x - y = 7$

$3(3x - y = 7)$

$9x - 3y = 21$

Subtract the two equations.

$9x - 3y = 21$

$-(2x - 3y = 7)$

_____

$7x = 14$

$x = 2$

$3x - y = 7$

$3(2) - y = 7$

$6 - y = 7$

$-y = 1$

Divide both sides by -1

$y = -1$

Solution = (2, –1)

SOLUTIONS TO SYSTEMS OF LINEAR EQUATIONS (P. 269)

1. $y = 2x - 3$

   $y = 5 + 4(x - 2)$

   $2x - 3 = 5 + 4(x - 2)$

   $2x - 3 = 5 + 4x - 8$

   $2x - 3 = 4x - 3$

   $-3 = 2x - 3$

   $0 = 2x$

   $0 = x$

   $y = 2x - 3$

   $y = 2(0) - 3$

   $y = 0 - 3$

   $y = -3$

   There is **one solution**:

   (0, –3)

2. $y = -0.5(x - 2)$

   $y = -0.5x + 7$

   Equation 1:

   $y = -0.5(x - 2)$

   $y = -0.5x + 1$

   Notice that each of the equations has the same slope (-0.5 or $-\frac{1}{2}$). Therefore, they will be parallel lines and never intersect, leading to **no solution**.

3. $y = 6x + 6$

   $y = 2(3x + 3)$

   $6x + 6 = 2(3x + 3)$

   $6x + 6 = 6x + 6$

   Notice when we compare the two equations that they are equal. They will result in two of the exact same line. Therefore, they will always intersect, leading to **infinitely many solutions.**

DEFINING AND IDENTIFYING FUNCTIONS (P. 273)

1. Domain: −8, 2, 3
   Range: −6, 4, 8, 9
   Not a Function

2. Domain: −2, 5, 7, 8
   Range: −8, −3, −2, 7
   Function

3. Domain: −3, 4, 6, 8
   Range: −2, −1, 9
   Function

4. This is a function because each input results in only one output (no inputs go to more than more output).

INPUT (X)	−2	−1	0	1	2
OUTPUT (Y)	4	1	0	1	4

   Domain: -2, -1, 0, 1, 2; Range: 0, 1, 4

5. (−4, 2); (−2, 4); (0, 6); (−4, −2); (−2, −4)

   This isn't a function because the inputs of −4 and −2 each have more than one output. The input of −4 has both 2 and 4 as outputs. The input of −2 has both 4 and −4 as outputs.

   Domain: -4, -2, 0; Range: -4, -2, 2, 4, 6

9 AREA, VOLUME, AND SURFACE AREA

Have you ever stopped to look at most of the objects you come across in your daily life? If you look closely, you'll notice that almost all of them are shapes or are made from shapes. Take a paper airplane, for example. That started as a rectangular or square piece of paper. Then you folded it so that it formed other rectangles, squares, diamonds, and triangles. In this chapter, you'll learn ways to see and measure shapes that will help in all kinds of ways—from planting a garden to building a tree house!

AREA

Measurements of one dimension can have names like length, width, or height. If you have an object in front of you, you can use a ruler or measuring tape to determine these measurements. Triangles, squares, and circles are examples of objects that have two dimensions, such as width and length, and no thickness. The space inside a triangle, square, or circle is known as its area. The area of a closed figure can be measured in square units, such as square feet.

area: the amount of space occupied by a two-dimensional shape

DIMENSIONS

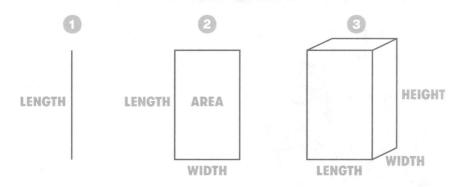

① LENGTH

② LENGTH | AREA | WIDTH

③ HEIGHT | WIDTH | LENGTH

PRIOR KNOWLEDGE

For a rectangle, opposite sides are equal. You can find a rectangle's area by multiplying its length and its width. The rectangle below has a length of 7 units and a width of 5 units.

1	2	3	4	5	6	7
8	9	10	11	12	13	14
15	16	17	18	19	20	21
22	23	24	25	26	27	28
29	30	31	32	33	34	35

width = 5 units

length = 7 units

The rectangle has an area of 7 units × 5 units, or 35 square units. If you were to count each of the units in the rectangle, you'd be able to count 35 square units.

IRREGULAR SHAPES

Look at the shape below.

This shape is called **irregular** because it doesn't look like the ones you'd think of as regular shapes: squares, rectangles, and triangles. The good news is that an irregular shape can be **decomposed** (broken apart) into recognizable shapes in order to find its area.

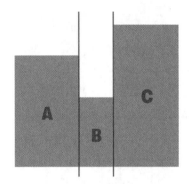

Here's some exciting news: there's no right or wrong way to decompose a shape. It's totally up to you how you want to decompose it! Here are two ways you can decompose this shape:

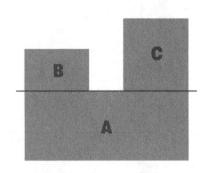

See? Kinda cool that there's room for multiple solutions.

irregular shapes: shapes that do not conform to the features of regular shapes

decomposing shapes: dividing irregular shapes into simpler regular shapes such as a rectangle, square, circle, or triangle

YOUR TURN!

Draw lines on the shapes to show how they can be decomposed.

TAKE A CLOSER LOOK

Let's say there's a big tree in your backyard that would make a great place for a tree house. You and your friends draw a scaled-down diagram on a piece of paper to show where the entrance will be. This will help you figure out how much wood you'll need for the floor. Taking a look at the irregular shape below, how could you find its area?

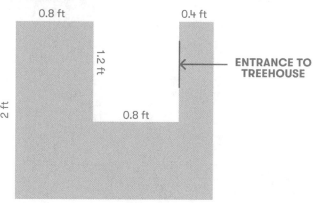

0.8 ft

0.4 ft

1.2 ft

ENTRANCE TO TREEHOUSE

2 ft

0.8 ft

By decomposing it into smaller shapes, you can find the smaller areas that make up the total.

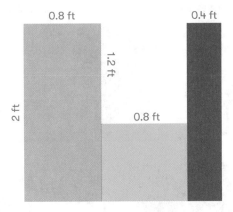

The blue rectangle has a short side of 0.8 ft and a long side of 2 ft. So, its area is 0.8 × 2 = 1.6 ft².

Area = Length × width
Area = 0.8 ft × 2 ft
Area = 1.6 ft²

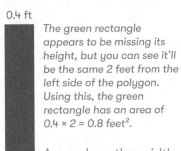

The green rectangle appears to be missing its height, but you can see it'll be the same 2 feet from the left side of the polygon. Using this, the green rectangle has an area of 0.4 × 2 = 0.8 feet².

Area = Length × width
Area = 0.4 ft × 2 ft
Area = 0.8 ft²

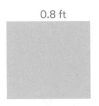

When you look at the yellow shape, it appears you're missing the length of a side. How could you find it?

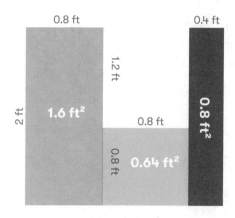

The entire height of the shape is 2 ft. Part of the inside height is given as 1.2 ft, so you can subtract that to find the missing piece.

2 ft – 1.2 ft = 0.8 ft

Did you notice that the yellow shape is a square?

It has an area of 0.8 ft × 0.8 ft = 0.64 ft².

Putting the smaller areas together, the entire shape has a total area of 1.6 ft² + 0.64 ft² + 0.8 ft² = 3.04 ft²

ANOTHER PATH

Surprise! There's actually a fourth space that's kind of part of this shape. Can you see it? It's the cutout for the entrance to the tree house!

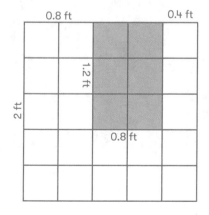

How could this empty space help you? Well, if you find the area of the whole shape—including this part—then you can subtract the empty space!

Total space – empty space = irregular shape space

EMPTY SPACE

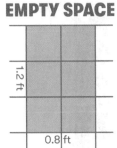

Area = Length × width
Area = 1.2 ft × 0.8 ft
Area = 0.96 ft²

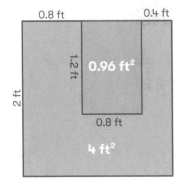

0.8 ft   0.4 ft

1.2 ft

0.96 ft²

2 ft

0.8 ft

4 ft²

Using the earlier idea, you can subtract the shaded region (the empty space from the total space) to find the area of the irregular figure.

Total space – empty space = irregular shape space
4 ft² – 0.96 ft² = 3.04 ft²

YOUR TURN!

Have you ever grown vegetables in a community garden or do you know someone who has? Because more than one person shares the space, each gardener is given a specific area to plant.

Below is a diagram of a garden plot (shown in green) with some measurements in feet. There's a big tree in the middle that takes up 2 square feet. What is the total area of the garden that you can plant?

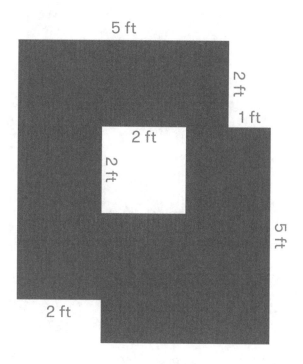

![Tools for Success icon] **TOOLS FOR SUCCESS**

Remember, when finding the area of an irregular shape, it's important to:

1. Decompose shapes into squares and/or rectangles and find the area of each shape.

2. Then, add all the areas together for the total area.

3. Figure out missing lengths by adding or subtracting the length of other parts that are already given.

IRREGULAR SHAPES WITH TRIANGLES

So, what would you do to find the area of an arrow's shape?

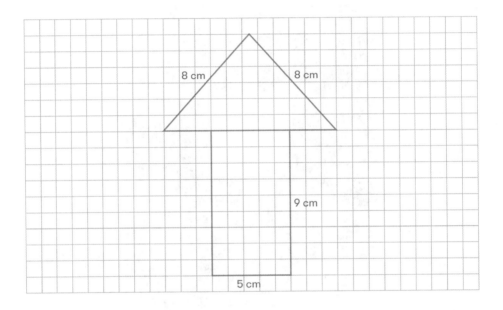

The arrow shape can be decomposed into two shapes: a triangle and a rectangle. However, the triangle is a shape that doesn't have a clear number of whole units that fit inside.

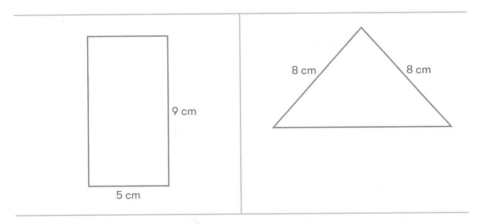

Rectangle	Triangle
Area = length × width Area = 9 × 5 Area = 45 cm²	Area = ?

One way to find the area of the triangle is to use the formula below.

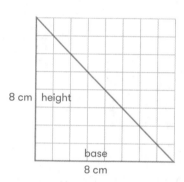

The triangle (which happens to be a right triangle—more about those in Chapter 11) has a base measuring 8 centimeters and a height measuring 8 centimeters. What's its area?

If you try to put square units inside the triangle and then count them, it can't be done. That's because the units would get cut off.

This is when a formula is extremely helpful. The area of a triangle is found using

$$A = \frac{1}{2} \times \text{base} \times \text{height}$$

To obtain the area, A, you multiply the base by the height of the triangle and divide by 2.

For this example, you can substitute the measurements of base and height into the formula and then calculate.

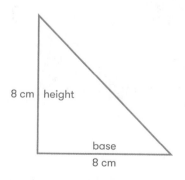

$$A = \frac{1}{2} \times 8 \text{ cm} \times 8 \text{ cm}$$

$$A = \frac{1}{2} \times 64 \text{ cm}^2$$

$$A = \frac{64 \text{ cm}^2}{2}$$

So, this triangle has an area of 32 square centimeters, or 32 cm².

You might be thinking whoa, back up a minute—where did this triangle area formula even come from? Thanks for bringing it up! In the last example, what if there were two of those triangles instead of one? And, what if you composed the two triangles into a familiar shape? Look:

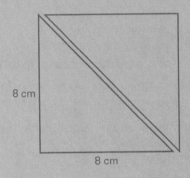

Two triangles placed together in this way form a square. What's the area of this new square? Recall that the area of the square = *base* × *height* (you can also say the area of the square or rectangle equals *length* × *width*. In the case of the square, of course, the sides are always equal).

Area = 8 centimeters × 8 centimeters. Put the measurements of base and height into the formula and then calculate.

The square has an area of 64 square centimeters, or 64 cm².

Now, how could you find the area of just one of these triangles if you wanted to? Simple! Since the diagonal splits it into two triangles, you can divide the area of the square by 2. This will get you the area of one triangle:

$$\text{Area}_\Delta = \frac{1}{2} \times 64 \text{ cm}^2 = 32 \text{ cm}^2$$

That's all there is to it. Now, you, too, know how mathematicians discovered the formula for the area of a triangle:

$$\text{Area}_\Delta = \frac{1}{2} \times \text{base} \times \text{height}$$

TAKE A CLOSER LOOK

You can find the area of a triangle using the formula
$A = \frac{1}{2} \times base \times height$.

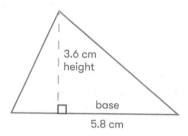

3.6 cm
height

base

5.8 cm

$A = \frac{1}{2} \times base \times height$

$A = \frac{1}{2} (5.8 \text{ cm})(3.6 \text{ cm})$

$A = 10.44 \text{ cm}^2$

Let's go back to calculate the total area of the arrow shape.

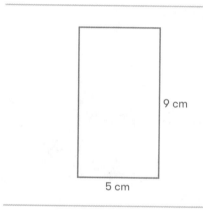

9 cm

5 cm

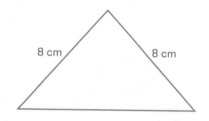

8 cm   8 cm

Area = length × width

Area = 9 × 5

Area = 45 cm²

Area = $\frac{1}{2}$ × base × height

Area = $\frac{1}{2}$ × 8 × 8

Area = 32 cm²

Putting the rectangle and the triangle areas together, the polygon (arrow shape) has a total area of

$$45 \text{ cm}^2 + 32 \text{ cm}^2 = 77 \text{ cm}^2$$

TOOLS FOR SUCCESS

When finding the area of an irregular shape, it's important to remember:

1. For a square or rectangle, the area will be the length × height.

2. For a triangle, the area will be half of the base × height

3. For irregular shapes, decompose the shapes into squares, rectangles, or triangles. Find the area for each shape, and then add all the amounts together to find the total area.

YOUR TURN!

Part 1: Find the area of the following regular figures.

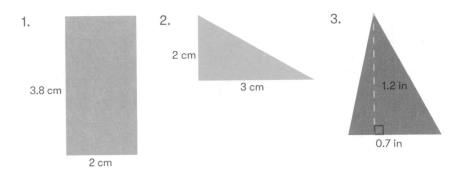

1. 3.8 cm, 2 cm

2. 2 cm, 3 cm

3. 1.2 in, 0.7 in

Part 2: Find the area of the irregular shapes below. Be sure to write the correct units.

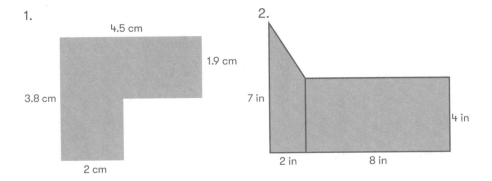

1. 4.5 cm, 1.9 cm, 3.8 cm, 2 cm

2. 7 in, 2 in, 8 in, 4 in

SPECIAL QUADRILATERALS

Let's get into quads! No, not your thigh muscles. We're talking about quadrilaterals. What are they? You'll be happy to hear that you already know some examples: squares and rectangles. Any two-dimensional shape that's enclosed with four sides is a quadrilateral. Special quadrilaterals like kites have areas that may seem a little tricky to find.

quadrilateral: a four-sided figure

TAKE A CLOSER LOOK

See if you can decompose the kite into triangles and/or rectangles.

There are a couple of different ways you can do it. But no matter how you slice it, you'll end up with two triangles—look at the illustrations on the next page and you'll see.

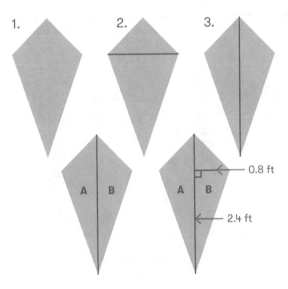

$$\text{Area (triangle A or B)} = \frac{1}{2} \times \text{base} \times \text{height}$$

$$\text{base} = 2.4 \text{ feet}$$

$$\text{height} = 0.8 \text{ feet}$$

$$\text{Area (triangle A or B)} = \frac{1}{2} \times 2.4 \text{ feet} \times 0.8 \text{ feet} = 0.96 \text{ sq. feet}$$

Putting the two triangle areas together, the kite has a total area of

$$\text{Area (kite)} = 0.96 \text{ square feet} + 0.96 \text{ square feet} = 1.92 \text{ square feet}$$

TOOLS FOR SUCCESS

When finding the area of a special quadrilateral like a kite, it's important to remember:

1. The shape can be decomposed into two or more triangles.

2. Key lengths like base and height of the triangles are required.

3. For a triangle, the area will be half of the base × height.

4. The areas of the triangles that make up the decomposed quadrilateral need to be added up to find the total area of the kite.

YOUR TURN!

Summer might not feel complete without at least one day of kite flying! So, you decide to make your own and test it out. You find two sticks for the frame, measuring 20 inches and 24 inches. You create two diagrams to find the area for the kite's fabric. How much fabric do you need for your kite? Here is a diagram of the kite's measurements to help you with your calculations:

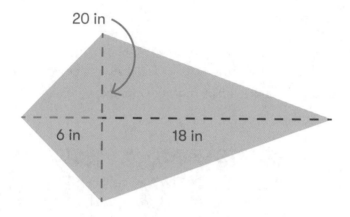

POLYGONS IN THE COORDINATE PLANE

Polygons like the red square on the opposite page can be created when you connect points, (x, y), on the coordinate plane. The sides of the polygons will be the **line segments** between the vertices. **Vertices** are points where two or more line segments meet.

Using the coordinate plane, you can find the length of a polygon's sides by counting the units between the vertices. The distance between the points A and B (opposite) is 13 units, which mathematicians write as $\overline{AB}$ = 13 units.

Reminder: A grid has a horizontal x-axis and a vertical y-axis. The point where the axes meet is the point of origin (0, 0). All points on a grid can be identified by two numbers or a set of ordered pairs written as (x, y). x is the x-coordinate, which shows where the point is located on the x-axis. y is the y-coordinate that shows where the point is located on the y-axis. Points with positive coordinates (x, y) are in the first quadrant, points with negative and positive coordinates (-x, y) are in the second quadrant, points with negative coordinates (-x, -y) are in the third quadrant, and points with positive and negative coordinates (x, -y) are in the fourth quadrant.

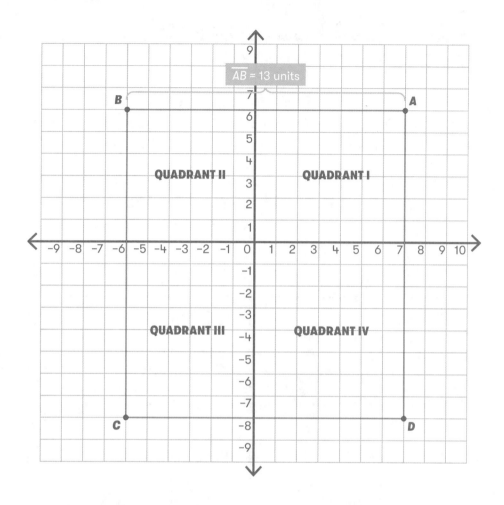

polygon: a closed shape with three or more sides. The term is more general than *triangle* or *rectangle*, which must have three or four sides, respectively

line segment: a line with two endpoints

vertex (plural, vertices): the intersection of two or more endpoints of a line segment

IRREGULAR POLYGONS IN THE COORDINATE PLANE

Your math class is going on a field trip to one of your local state parks. For incentive, there's treasure to be found! You and your classmates are using a map to find your way around. Each unit on the map equals two miles.

MAP OF THE STATE PARK

1. What is the distance between the campsite and the picnic area?

2. The treasure hunt starts at the entrance and leads first to the lake. What is the distance between the park entrance and the lake?

3. How far is the campsite from the visitor center?

Next, how do you think you could find the perimeter of the entire state park, in units and miles?

 TAKE A CLOSER LOOK

Let's break it down using the map on the opposite page. We can look at the distances between each feature of the park, and then calculate the distance around the perimeter of the entire park.

LOCATION TO LOCATION	LENGTH
Picnic Area (−4, 4) to Lake (3, 4)	7 units = 14 miles
Lake (3, 4) to Park Entrance (3, −5)	9 units = 18 miles
Park Entrance (3, −5) to Parking Lot (2, −5)	1 unit = 2 miles
Parking Lot (2, −5) to Visitor Center (2, −3)	2 units = 4 miles
Visitor Center (2, −3) to Campsite (−4, −3)	6 units = 12 miles
Campsite (−4, −3) to Picnic Area (−4, 4)	7 units = 14 miles
Park perimeter	**32 units = 64 miles**

TOOLS FOR SUCCESS

When drawing polygons in the coordinate plane, it's important to remember:

1. You can find the length of a polygon's vertical or horizontal line segment sides by counting the distance between the x- or y-coordinates.

2. Once you have the lengths of the sides, you can find the area of the polygon.

YOUR TURN!

Using the grid below, plot the coordinates of the school, the library, the town hall, and the sports stadium to create a map of the town. Draw the polygon between the different locations and find the length of each of their horizontal and vertical sides or distances between them.

Each unit on the map equals 1 mile.

Sports Stadium Point Q: (−3, 2)

School Point R: (4, 2)

Library Point S: (4, −3)

Town Hall Point T: (−3, −3)

What is the distance between the sports stadium and the school?

What is the distance between the school and the library?

What is the distance between the library and the town hall?

What is the distance between the sports stadium and the town hall?

DISTANCE
$\overline{QR}$ =
$\overline{RS}$ =
$\overline{ST}$ =
$\overline{QT}$ =

VOLUME

RECTANGULAR PRISMS

As you help prepare for your summer camp's end-of-the-season party, you've been put in charge of making sure there's enough ice for all the coolers. You need to store a bunch of individual ice cubes. Each cube has a **volume** of 1 in³, which means its length, width, and height all measure 1 inch.

rectangular prism: a three-dimensional figure where the base is a regular rectangle

volume: the space inside a three-dimensional figure

7 in | **CONTAINER BASE**

5 in

ICE CUBE

1 in
1 in
1 in

Each cooler you're storing the ice cubes in measures 7 in × 5 in × 10 in. *How many ice cubes will fit in each cooler?*

PRIOR KNOWLEDGE

Start with something you already know how to do: finding the area of the base of the cooler. If you place the cubes in an 7 × 5 array, how many will there be?

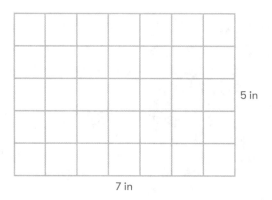

5 in

7 in

Since each cube is 1 in × 1 in, there will be 35 ice cubes (7 × 5).

$$\text{Area of the base} = 7 \text{ in} \times 5 \text{ in} = 35 \text{ in}^2$$

For the total cooler, how many ice cubes would fit if there were 10 layers?

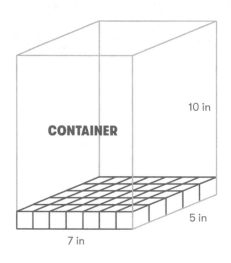

CONTAINER

10 in

7 in

5 in

For the third dimension of height, you could add the number of cubes (35) in the base layer 10 times (35 × 10 = 350) to get your answer. Therefore, 350 ice cubes fit into the 7 in × 5 in × 10 in container.

Note: This also means the cooler has a volume of 350 cubed centimeters (cm³). A solid figure's volume is measured in cubic units that fit within the boundaries of the figure.

You can use the formula, V = length × width × height = lwh to find the volume V of a rectangular prism.

So, 7 in × 5 in × 10 in = 350 in³ gives you the number of ice cubes that fit into it, since each cube is 1 in³ in volume.

The dimensions are in units cubed (units³) because the object is a three-dimensional object and because you're multiplying the numbers and the three dimension's units when you find the volume.

TAKE A CLOSER LOOK

Think back to the three calculations you just made. First, you found the area of the base:

$$\text{Base Area} = \text{length} \times \text{width}$$

$$\text{Base Area} = 7 \text{ in} \times 5 \text{ in}$$

$$\text{Base Area} = 35 \text{ in}^2$$

Then, you multiplied by the total height to find the volume:

$$\text{Volume} = \text{base area} \times \text{height}$$

$$\text{Volume} = 7 \text{ in} \times 5 \text{ in} \times 10 \text{ in}$$

$$\text{Volume} = 350 \text{ in}^3$$

TOOLS FOR SUCCESS

When finding the volume of a right rectangular prism, remember:

1. A solid figure is a figure that has three dimensions.

2. Volume is measured by the space inside the figure.

3. For rectangular prisms, the formula for volume is:
   Volume = length × width × height

4. The units for volume are cubed, as in cubed centimeters, or cm³.

YOUR TURN!

1. Find the volume of the right rectangular prism below.

8 ft

13 ft

3.5 ft

2. A rectangular freezer has a volume of 30 cubic feet, a length of 5 feet, and a width of 3 feet. What's the height?

3. A family is renting a truck that's 20 ft long, 8 ft wide, and 9 ft high to move their belongings to another town. How many boxes with a volume of 20 ft³ can fit inside the truck?

4. You're helping make over a neighborhood garden. One of its features is a wooden planter box in the shape of a right rectangular prism.

   a. You decide to paint the outside of the planter. How much surface area will you need to cover if you leave the bottom unpainted and it's open at the top? The paint cans tell you how many square feet each can will cover, so convert your answer from square inches to square feet.

   b. What's the amount of soil (volume) that will be required if the planter box is to be filled to the top?

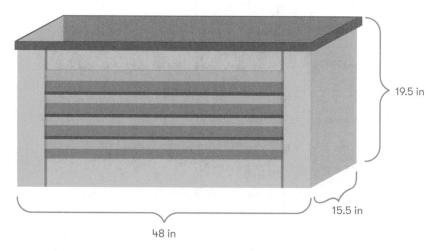

19.5 in

15.5 in

48 in

COMPOSITE SHAPES

You've been asked to help plan for the community pool. The blueprint for the pool is a composite shape. This means it can be seen as multiple, three-dimensional figures put together. You've worked with composite shapes before—but those were only two dimensions.

🔍 TAKE A CLOSER LOOK

The pool is 12 feet wide and 22 feet long. It starts in the shallow end at a depth of 3 feet. The shallow end continues for half of the pool's total length. The floor then drops down to a depth of 10 feet.

Your job is to figure out how many cubic feet of water you're going to need to fill up the pool.

👢 PRIOR KNOWLEDGE

You know filling up a three-dimensional shape means you need volume. So, it's time to use your stellar decomposition skills! How do you think you could break down the pool into smaller shapes?

Take a minute to think about the different possible options. You use your best drawing skills to sketch out a 3-dimensional diagram of the pool, which looks something like this:

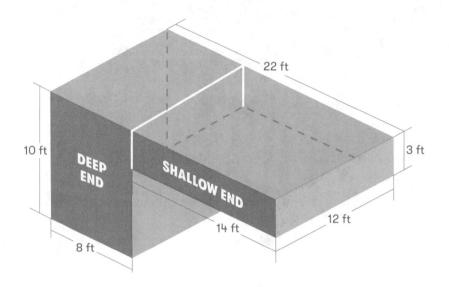

Calculate the measurements of each rectangular prism:

Shallow end: Volume = (12 ft) × (14 ft) × (3 ft) = 504 ft³

Deep end: Volume = (12 ft) × (8 ft) × (10 ft) = 960 ft³

Next, you can add together the volume of the two shapes to find the total:

Total Volume = 504 ft³ + 960 ft³

Total Volume = 1,464 ft³

The pool will need 1,464 cubic feet of water.

Large amounts of water are typically measured in gallons. So, how many gallons of water will it take to fill this pool? To convert cubic feet into gallons, you can multiply the number of cubic feet by 7.5, because each cubic foot takes 7.5 gallons to fill.

1,464 × 7.5 gallons = 10,980 gallons of water

YOUR TURN!

The community is considering a second pool option. Below is its blueprint.

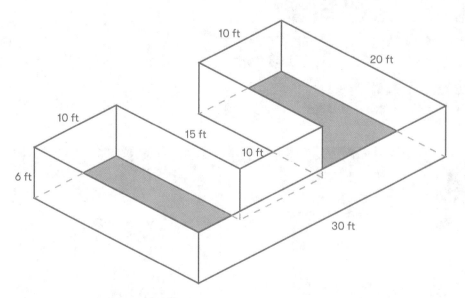

Determine the pool's volume in cubic feet.

VOLUME OF SHAPE 1	VOLUME OF SHAPE 2	VOLUME OF SHAPE 3

Which community pool option requires more water? Explain your reasoning.

_____

_____

_____

_____

_____

SURFACE AREA OF RIGHT RECTANGULAR PRISMS

You're giving a friend a birthday gift. Let's make sure you have enough paper to wrap the box!

TAKE A CLOSER LOOK

The gift box measures 12 in × 5 in × 8 in. How can you figure out the amount of wrapping paper needed to cover this box?

You can trace each side of the box and then find the area of each side. When you add the areas of the top, bottom, and sides together, you get the total amount of wrapping paper needed.

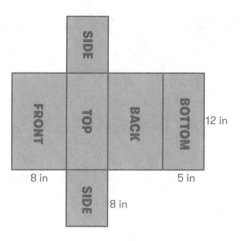

The box is a right rectangular prism. You can picture the box broken down into a flat **net**. It has 6 faces: top, bottom, front, back, and left- and right-side ends.

You can now see that the surface area of the box is the sum of the areas of all the faces. Let's find the total surface area.

Start with the top and bottom of the box.

Each measure 12 in × 5 in and the two have an area of:

$$\text{Area of top} = 12 \text{ in} \times 5 \text{ in} = 60 \text{ in}^2$$
$$\text{Area of top and bottom} = 2(12 \text{ in} \times 5 \text{ in})$$
$$\text{Area of top and bottom} = 2(60 \text{ in}^2)$$
$$\text{Area of top and bottom} = 120 \text{ in}^2$$

Next, the left and right sides that measure 5 in × 8 in have an area of:

$$\text{Area of one side} = 5 \text{ in} \times 8 \text{ in} = 40 \text{ in}^2$$
$$\text{Area of sides} = 2(5 \text{ in} \times 8 \text{ in})$$
$$\text{Area of sides} = 2(40 \text{ in}^2)$$
$$\text{Area of sides} = 80 \text{ in}^2$$

Finally, the front and back measure 12 in × 8 in each and have an area of:

$$\text{Area of front} = 12 \text{ in} \times 8 \text{ in} = 96 \text{in}^2$$
$$\text{Area of front and back} = 2(96 \text{ in}^2)$$
$$\text{Area of front and back} = 192 \text{ in}^2$$

net: a two-dimensional diagram used to represent a three-dimensional figure that is opened and flat to show the different faces of the figure

Putting it all together, this box has a surface area of:

Surface Area (top and bottom) + Surface Area (front and back) + Surface Area (sides) =

Area (sides) = 120 in² + 80 in² + 192 in² = 292 in²

So, your gift will need 292 in² of wrapping paper.

ANOTHER PATH

All right rectangular prisms have two sides that have an area of length × width, two sides that have an area of width × height, and two sides that have an area of length × height.

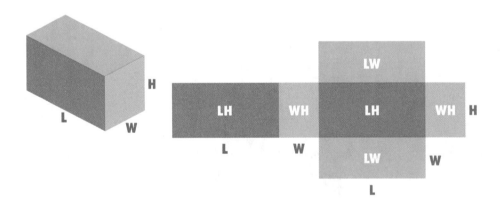

So, their surface area can also be found by the general formula:

Surface Area = 2 [(length × width) + (width × height) + (length × height)]

TOOLS FOR SUCCESS

When finding the surface area of a rectangular prism, it's important to remember:

1. A geometric net can be used to flatten the figure.

2. Find the area of each side from the net. Then combine the areas to find the total surface area.

YOUR TURN!

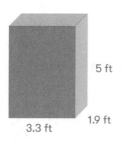

5 ft

1.9 ft

3.3 ft

You're building a new doghouse for your puppy. The house is in the shape of a rectangular prism, and will measure 5 ft × 1.9 ft × 3.3 ft. How much material will you need to build it?

• Create and label a net to represent its 6 separate sides.

• Find the total surface area.

CHAPTER SUMMARY

AREA: THE TWO-DIMENSIONAL SPACE OF A SHAPE

- **Rectangle**: The area of a rectangle is length × width.
- **Triangles**: The area of a triangle is $\frac{1}{2}$ × base × height.
- **Area of Irregular Shapes**: When you try to find the area of irregular shapes, you can decompose shapes into smaller shapes such as rectangles, squares, and triangles.
- **Polygons in the Coordinate Plane**: You can also find the area of figures in the coordinate plane by counting the vertical and horizontal distances (dimensions). You can also count the unit squares that are inside the figure to help find the area.
- **Irregular Polygons in the Coordinate Plane**: The same way that you can decompose figures when they're not in the plane, you can decompose large irregular figures into smaller figures in the coordinate plane.

VOLUME

- Volume is the amount of space inside a three-dimensional figure.
- You can find the volume of a rectangular prism by using the formula: Volume = length × width × height

SURFACE AREA OF RIGHT RECTANGULAR PRISMS

The surface area is the total area of all the faces of a figure. To find the surface area of a rectangular prism, you can create a net to lay out all the faces and find the sum of all the areas. Alternatively, you can use the formula:

Surface Area = 2 [(length × width) + (width × height) + (length × height)]

CHAPTER 9 VOCABULARY

area: the amount of space occupied by a two-dimensional object

decomposing shapes: dividing irregular shapes into simpler regular shapes such as a rectangle, square, circle, or triangle

irregular shapes: shapes that do not conform to the features of regular shapes

line segment: a line with two endpoints

net: a two-dimensional diagram used to represent a three-dimensional figure that is opened and flat to show the different faces of the figure

polygon: a closed shape with three or more sides. The term is more general than triangle or rectangle, which must have three or four sides, respectively

quadrilateral: a four-sided figure

right rectangular prism: a three-dimensional figure where the base is a regular rectangle

vertex (plural, vertices): the intersection of two or more endpoints of a line segment

volume: the space inside a three-dimensional figure

CHAPTER 9
ANSWER KEY

AREA (P. 287)

Here are some possible solutions:.

IRREGULAR SHAPES (PP. 290–291)

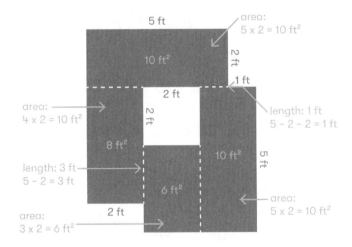

Allowing for the tree in the center, you'll be able to plant a total area of

10 ft^2 + 10 ft^2 + 6 ft^2 + 8 ft^2 = 34 square feet

IRREGULAR SHAPES WITH TRIANGLES (P. 296)

PART 1

1. A = 3.8 cm × 2 cm = 7.6 cm²

2. A = $\frac{1}{2}$ (2 cm) (3 cm) = 3 cm²

3. A = $\frac{1}{2}$ (0.7 in) (1.2 in) = .42 cm²

PART 2

1. Area of Rectangle 1 + Area of Rectangle 2 =
   Total Area: 7.6cm² + 4.75cm² = 12.35cm²

2. Decompose the shape into two rectangles and a triangle.

   Rectangle 1: 8 in × 4 in = 32 in²   *Rectangle 2*: 2 in × 4 in = 8 in²

   Triangle: $\frac{1}{2}$ (2 in × 3 in) = 3 in²

   Total Area = Area of Rectangle 1 + Area of Rectangle 2 +
   Area of the Triangle

   Total Area = 32 in² + 8 in² + 3 in²   Total Area = 43 in²

SPECIAL QUADRILATERALS (P. 299)

You can decompose the kite to find its dimensions as follows:

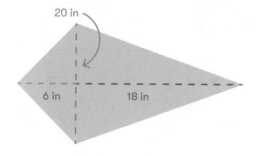

Area Left Triangle = $\frac{1}{2}$ × 20 in × 6 in = 60 in²

Area Right Triangle = $\frac{1}{2}$ × 20 in × 18 in = 180 in²

Area of kite = 60 in² + 180 in² = 240 in²

POLYGONS IN THE COORDINATE PLANE (P. 304)

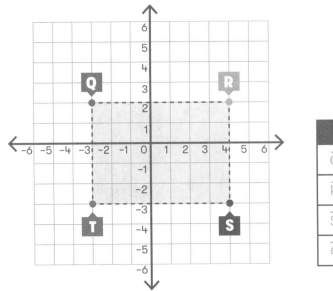

DISTANCE
$\overline{QR}$ = 7 miles
$\overline{RS}$ = 5 miles
$\overline{ST}$ = 7 miles
$\overline{QT}$ = 5 miles

VOLUME: RIGHT RECTANGULAR PRISMS (P. 308)

1. Volume of the rectangular prism (length × width × height):
   13 × 3.5 × 8 = 364 ft³

2. 30 ft³ = 5 ft × 3 ft × height
   30 ft³ = 15 ft² × height
   30 ft³/15 ft² = height
   2 ft = height

3. Volume of truck: V = 20 ft × 8 ft × 9 ft = 1,440 ft³
   Volume of each box: 20 ft³
   1,440 ft³ ÷ 20 ft³ = 72 boxes can fit into the truck

4a. Each end panel: 15.5 in × 19.5 in = 302.25 in²
   Each side panel: 48 in x 19.5 in = 936 in²
   302.25 in² × 2 end panels = 604.5 in²
   936 in² × 2 side panels = 1,872 in²
   Surface area = 2,476.5 in² (206 ft²)
   You'll need enough paint to cover 2,476.5 in² (206 ft²) of
   surface area.

4b. Volume = 48 in × 15.5 in × 19.5 in = 14,508 in³ (1,209 ft³)

You'll need 14,508 in³ (1,209 ft³) of soil to fill the planter box to the top.

COMPOSITE SHAPES (P. 311)

1.

VOLUME OF SHAPE 1	VOLUME OF SHAPE 2	VOLUME OF SHAPE 3
10 ft × 20 ft × 6 ft = 1,200 ft³	10 ft × 5 ft × 6 ft = 300 ft³	10 ft × 20 ft × 6 ft = 1,200 ft³

1,200 ft³ + 300 ft³ + 1,200 ft³ = 2,700 ft³; 7.5 gallons × 2,700 = 20,250 gallons of water; the second option requires more water.

SURFACE AREA OF RECTANGULAR PRISMS (P. 315)

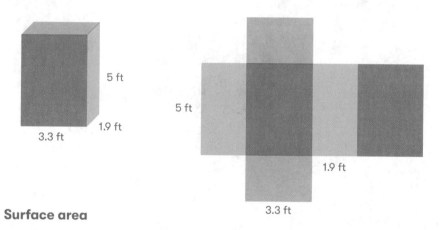

Surface area

RED		BLUE		YELLOW
2 (3.3 × 5 ft)		2 (3.3 × 1.9 ft)		2 (5 × 1.9 ft)
= 2 (16.5 ft²)	+	= 2 (6.27 ft²)	+	= 2 (9.5 ft²)
= 33 ft²		= 12.54 ft²		= 19 ft²

Total Surface Area = 64.54 ft²

10

CROSS SECTIONS, CIRCLES, VOLUME, AND ANGLES

Geometry is a branch of math that focuses on shapes, sizes, dimensions, angles, and much more. You use geometry a lot in your everyday life. How many items can you fit into your backpack? How many ways can you arrange the furniture in your room? All of these everyday challenges are connected to geometry—even slicing a block of cheese for a grilled cheese sandwich!

CHAPTER CONTENTS

CROSS SECTIONS OF SOLIDS

Solid, right rectangular prisms (see the previous chapter if you're unsure what that is) can be cut into thin, three-dimensional slices called **cross sections** or **planes**. You can think of them like individual slices from a block of cheese. The shape of the "slice" will depend on where the cut starts and where it finishes on the cheese block. Look at this example:

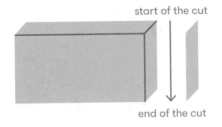

start of the cut

end of the cut

When you turn the slice toward you, the shape matches that of the right face of the block. To put it simply: it's a rectangle. Do you think this will always be the case? Is there another way you could slice the cheese to make another rectangle? Or other shapes?

🔍 TAKE A CLOSER LOOK

If you were to cut a slice from the left side and continue horizontally as well as parallel to the base, what would the slice look like? Draw the slice below.

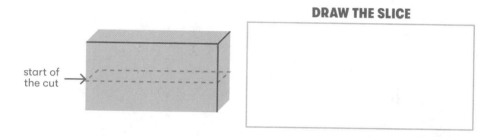

DRAW THE SLICE

start of the cut →

Try cutting the block diagonally, starting from the upper left edge. What would the slice look like now? Draw the slice below.

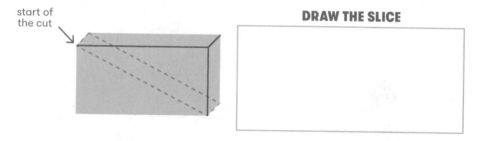

start of the cut

DRAW THE SLICE

As you can see, all three slices are different in shape and size, even though each slice came from the same block of cheese.

cross section: a "slice" of a shape from a 3-dimensional object

plane: a 2-dimensional shape or surface

PRIOR KNOWLEDGE

You're probably familiar with moldable clay, which can be used to create tons of different three-dimensional (3-D) shapes. Let's say you have a neon yellow lump of clay that you mold into a rectangular pyramid. Then, you cut it vertically. *What would the shape of the slice look like?*

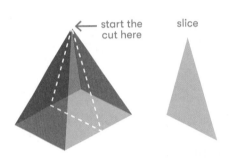

Starting at the top of the pyramid, if you're cutting vertically from top to bottom, you'll create a triangular slice.

Now, let's get experimental: put the pieces back together and cut in a different direction. *What would the slice look like if you cut horizontally and parallel to the base?*

Draw the slice below.

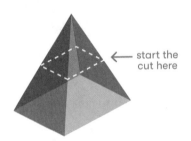

DRAW THE SLICE

And one more: *What would the slice look like if the pyramid was cut diagonally?* Draw the slice below.

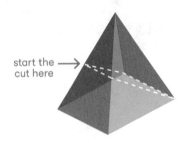

DRAW THE SLICE

It's all about the direction in which you choose to cut the figure. That decision gives you clues about what the slice will look like. Remember to pay attention to the direction you cut.

TOOLS FOR SUCCESS

When cross sections are taken from rectangular prisms or rectangular pyramids, it's important to remember:

1. Cross sections can be called slices or planes.

2. A parallel cut to a prism or pyramid's base will look like that face.

3. Diagonal slices will often look like parallelograms, but it depends on where the cut starts and stops.

YOUR TURN!

Connect the points IJKL in each figure to create a cross section. Circle the type of cut and the shape of the slice.

1.

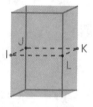

TYPE OF CUT	SLICE SHAPE
horizontal	triangle
vertical	rectangle
diagonal	parallelogram

2.

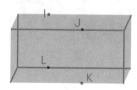

TYPE OF CUT	SLICE SHAPE
horizontal	triangle
vertical	rectangle
diagonal	parallelogram

3.

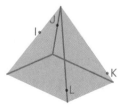

TYPE OF CUT	SLICE SHAPE
horizontal	triangle
vertical	rectangle
diagonal	parallelogram

CIRCLES: FINDING CIRCUMFERENCE AND AREA

Have you ever ridden in a car through the countryside and counted all the farms you pass? If you have, you've most likely seen a structure with a cylindrical shape that extends from the ground up, with a roof that looks like a cone. These are called silos—a building commonly used on farms to hold grain. Now, let's say you and a bunch of friends stop and visit that farm. If you decided to run around the base of this building, *what type of shape would you be tracing? What information would this give you?*

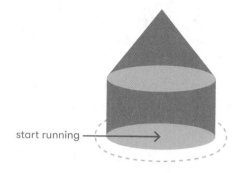

start running

Running around the base of this silo (cylinder base) follows the path of a circle. The length around a circle is its **circumference**.

You'd be running in a circle, of course. If you know the circumference of a circle, you can use it to find the circle's area. Why would a farmer want to know this? Well, maybe that farmer has more wheat than she can store, and needs to build another silo.

THE UNIQUE PROPERTIES OF A CIRCLE

Suppose you count your steps all the way around the silo and find out that the circumference is about 63 ft. You also use steps to see how wide the silo is, finding its **diameter** to be about 20 ft. How is the diameter related to the circumference? You're about to learn one of the qualities that makes a circle so unique. Since we're using approximate values, we're going to use the curvy equals sign ($\approx$), which means "approximately equal to."

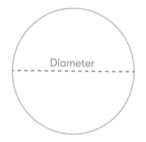

Diameter

Circumference $\approx$ 63 ft
Diameter $\approx$ 20 ft
63 = 20 × _____
If you divide, $\frac{63}{20} \approx 3.14$

circumference: the length around a circle

> **diameter:** the distance from one edge of a circle to another through the center of the circle

Have you heard of the shortened number, 3.14, before? It's a very special number called **pi**, the Greek letter **π**. The value of π (pi) comes from dividing a circle's circumference by its diameter.

$$\pi = \frac{\text{circumference}}{\text{diameter}} = 3.14$$

Every single time you divide any circle's circumference by its diameter, you'll get π. . . every single time!

> **pi:** an irrational number, approximately 3.14
>
> **irrational number:** any real number that cannot be turned into a simple fraction

TAKE A CLOSER LOOK

From the previous silo example, you can now write an equation for calculating a circle's circumference.

$$\text{circumference} = \pi \times \text{diameter}$$

Rewrite this equation with variables for circumference and diameter:

$$C = \pi d$$

Nice work! You now have a way to calculate the circumference of any circle.

A HANDY TRICK

Since a radius is half the diameter, you can also replace diameter with 2 × radius:

$$C = \pi \times 2r \quad \text{or} \quad C = 2\pi r$$

Just as there's a special relationship between the diameter and the circumference of a circle, there's a unique formula for the area of a circle:

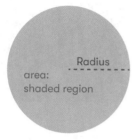

area:
shaded region

$$\text{Area} = \pi \, (\text{radius})^2$$
$$\text{Area} = \pi r^2$$

Ready to put these formulas to use? The farmer with the silo tells you about friends in Idaho who discovered crop circles in their corn field. Some people think aliens made the pattern—the shapes seem too perfect to be made by human-controlled machines—yet others are sure it's a convincing hoax.

Both of the two larger circles had a reported diameter of 40 feet, and the smaller circle's diameter was 10 feet. That's a lot of flattened corn! How much corn is now ruined in one of the large circles? And how much in the smaller circle?

For the larger, let's start by finding its area. Use the approximate value of 3.14 for π.

First, divide the diameter by 2 to find the radius:

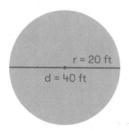

r = 20 ft
d = 40 ft

$$r = \frac{\text{diameter}}{2} = \frac{40 \text{ ft}}{2} = 20 \text{ ft}$$

Now, let's plug the radius and 3.14 into the area formula:

Large Circle Area: $A = \pi r^2$

$\approx 3.14(20 \text{ ft})^2$

$\approx 1{,}256 \text{ ft}^2$

All the corn covering 1,256 ft² for one of the larger circles is now unusable. Thanks, aliens.

REMINDER

The units for area are in square feet because they represent two dimensions—length × width.

You can simply repeat this process for the smaller circle:

Smaller Circle Area: $A = \pi r^2$

$A \approx 3.14(5 \text{ ft})^2$

$A \approx 78.5 \text{ ft}^2$

The corn covering 78.5 ft² for the smaller circle is now unusable, too.

Remember, the radius of the smaller circle is half its diameter:

$$r = \frac{10 \text{ ft}}{2} = 5 \text{ ft}$$

TOOLS FOR SUCCESS

When finding the area or circumference of a circle, it's important to remember:

1. The diameter is the distance from edge to edge through the center of a circle.

2. The radius is the distance from the center of the circle to the edge of the circle.

3. Either radius or diameter must be known.

4. The formula for circumference is C = πd or C = 2πr.

5. The formula for area is A = πr².

YOUR TURN!

Find the circumference and area of the circles below. Use 3.14 for the value of π, and be sure to include the units in your final answer. Round your answer to the nearest tenth of the appropriate unit.

CIRCLE	CIRCUMFERENCE	AREA
23 cm		
$1\frac{1}{2}$ m		

PROBLEM SOLVING: STANDARD SHAPES

12 ft

18 ft

The farmer tells you that there's going to be a surplus of wheat this year, and she'll need extra space to store the grain. She asks you and your friends to help figure out if another silo could fit next to the current one, given the space available.

You determine that the space available is a rectangle with dimensions of 18 feet by 12 feet. The existing silo goes right up to the borders of the 12-foot side. *Could another silo of the same size fit next to it? Or would a second silo need to be smaller?*

TAKE A CLOSER LOOK

If the silo's diameter is 12 ft, where could you start?

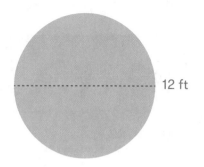

Remember, the radius is always half of the diameter:

$$r = \frac{12 \text{ ft}}{2} = 6 \text{ ft}$$

Since you're trying to find out what size silo will fit in the remaining space, this is the area you'll take away from the rectangular space:

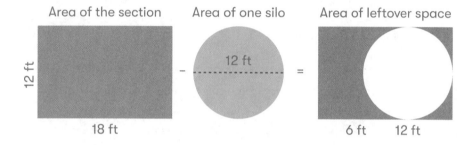

| Area of the section | Area of one silo | Area of leftover space |

PRIOR KNOWLEDGE

Start by finding the area of each shape

AREA OF THE SECTION (LENGTH × WIDTH)	AREA OF THE SILO πR²
18 ft × 12 ft = 216 ft²	π(6 feet)² ≈ 113 ft²

Next, subtract out the area of the silo from the area of the section:

Area of the Section - Area of the Silo = leftover area

216 ft² – 113 ft² = 103 ft²

leftover area = 103 ft²

The leftover space can fit another silo up to 103 square feet, so it would need to be a silo with a much smaller diameter.

VOLUME: CYLINDERS, CONES, AND SPHERES

After you determine the maximum diameter of the new silo, you and the farmer wonder just how much grain the new silo can hold. What is the volume of the new silo?

VOLUME OF A CYLINDER

Let's use what we already know—how to calculate the volume of a prism—to figure out what we don't: how to calculate the volume of a cylinder.

VOLUME OF A PRISM	VOLUME OF A CYLINDER
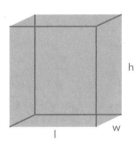	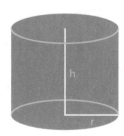
V = length × width × height V = area of base × height	V = area of base × height

TAKE A CLOSER LOOK

The new silo is a right cylinder measuring 64.5 feet high with a diameter of 41.5 feet.

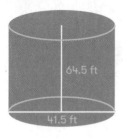

> **Volume of a Cylinder:**
> $V = \text{Area}_{\bigcirc} \times \text{height}$
> $V = \pi \, \text{radius}^2 \times \text{height}$
> $V = \pi r^2 h$

To find the radius of the silo: $\text{radius} = \dfrac{\text{diameter}}{2}$

$$\text{radius} = \dfrac{41.5 \text{ ft}}{2} = 20.75 \text{ ft}$$

To find the area of the circular base, use $A = \pi r^2$:

$A = 3.14 \times 20.75 \text{ ft}^2 \approx 1{,}351.97$ cubic feet

If you enter the radius of 20.75 feet and the height, 64.5 feet, into the formula, you get:

$$V = \pi (20.75 \text{ ft})^2 \times (64.5 \text{ feet})$$

$$V = 87{,}201.82 \text{ ft}^3$$

The new silo will contain 87,201.82 ft^3 of grain.

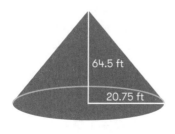

VOLUME OF A CONE

Let's say there's a cone funnel that you will use to pour grain into the silo. How many times would you need to use the funnel to fill the silo if the cone is the same height and has the same radius? The formula for volume of a cone is $V = \dfrac{\pi r^2 h}{3}$.

You may notice that the formula is the cylinder formula divided by 3, so you can say that the 3 cones of the same height and radius will equal one cylinder. Let's try out the formula for the cone funnel.

$$V = \frac{\pi r^2 h}{3} = \frac{\pi (20.75)^2(64.5)}{3} = \frac{\pi(430.56)(64.5)}{3}$$

$$V = \frac{\pi(27{,}771.12)}{3} = \frac{(3.14)(27{,}771.12)}{3} = \frac{(87{,}201.32)}{3} = 29{,}067.11 \nwarrow$$

Note: This number is the volume of the cylinder from the earlier example.

VOLUME OF A SPHERE

Your next task is to find out how much water a spherical bulb used to slowly feed plants can hold. If the radius of the sphere is 4 inches, how much water does the feeder hold?

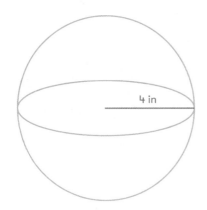

4 in

Volume of a Sphere = $\frac{4}{3}\pi r^3$

$V = \frac{4}{3}\pi \times 4\ in^3$

$V = \frac{4}{3}\ 3.14 \times 4\ in^3$

$V = 267.9$ cubic inches

There are 1,728 cubic inches in 1 cubic foot. You do a quick internet search and find that a cubic foot holds about 7.5 gallons of water. So, the amount of water that the bulb can hold is $\frac{267.9\ in^3}{1728\ in^3} \times 7.5 = 1.16$ gallons of water.

TOOLS FOR SUCCESS

Along with the right cylinder, there are formulas for the volume of a right circular cone and a sphere. Note: they all require the radius.

RIGHT CYLINDER

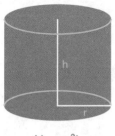

$$V = \pi r^2 h$$

RIGHT CIRULAR CONE

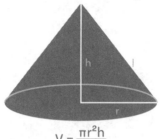

$$V = \frac{\pi r^2 h}{3}$$

SPHERE

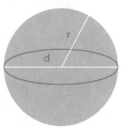

$$V = \frac{4}{3} \pi r^3$$

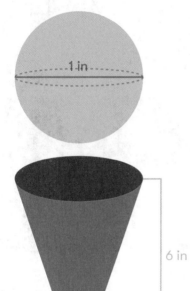

YOUR TURN!

Even the things we love most—like ice cream—involve math. At your local ice cream shop, you order a cone with one scoop of vanilla and one scoop of chocolate. As you watch it being assembled, you wonder what the total volume of ice cream will be. You assume all the space in the cone is full of ice cream (hey, it's our hypothetical fantasy) and the scoop is a perfect sphere. If both shapes have a diameter of 1 inch and the cone's height is 6 inches, how much ice cream is there altogether? Use 3.14 for π and round your answer to the nearest tenth.

ANGLES

ANGLE TYPES

Let's begin with a math fact that will impress your friends and family: a straight line is also an angle! An **angle**, as you know, is the shape that's formed when two lines meet at a common endpoint. Usually we think of them as "crooked" shapes, like the letter "V." But straight lines can also be called angles: "straight angles." All straight angles measure 180 degrees— half of a circle—a useful fact, as you'll see.

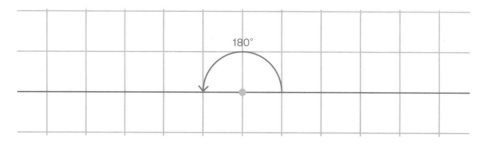

TAKE A CLOSER LOOK

Look at the diagrams below to see the different types of relationships that can exist between angles.

Complementary angles are two angles that add up to 90°. When the angles are next to each other (adjacent), as seen below, they'll always form a right angle.

52° + 38° = 90°

Supplementary angles are two angles that add up to 180°. When the angles are next to each other (adjacent) as seen below, they'll always form a straight line.

52° + 128° = 180°

---

angle: a shape that is formed when two **rays** or line segments meet at a common endpoint

ray: a line that extends infinitely in one direction from an endpoint

complementary angles: angles that add up to 90 degrees

supplementary angles: angles that add up to 180 degrees

FINDING UNKNOWN ANGLE MEASURES

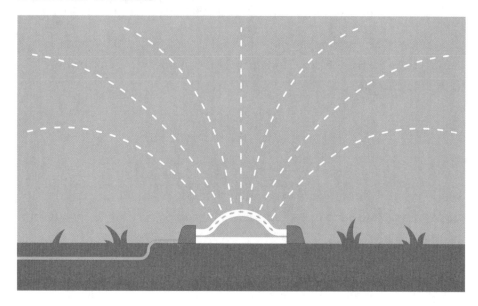

Watering the lawn is one of your summer chores. But when you set up the sprinkler, you realize it is only covering 45 degrees of the yard.

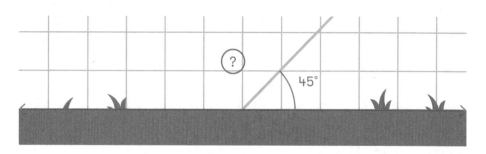

What angle measurement is the sprinkler missing?

PRIOR KNOWLEDGE

Together, the two angles from the sprinkler form a supplementary angle. Setting up the equation to equal 180°, you create the following equation.

$$?° + 45° = 180°$$

$$?° + 45° = 180°$$
$$\underline{\ -45°\ \ -45°\ }$$ *Subtract 45 from both sides.*
$$?° = 135°$$

Excellent! The sprinkler needs to move another 135° in order to cover the entire lawn.

YOUR TURN!

a. The corner of a bookcase is divided into two angles to form complementary angles. If one of the angles is 31°, what's the other?

b. A cooling fan can rotate a total of 180°. If it's unplugged after making an 86° rotation, how much of the turn is incomplete?

MORE ABOUT ANGLES

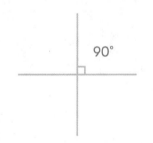

If you love angles, you're in luck! There are plenty more relationships between angles to cover.

Vertical angles are two angles that are across from each other when two lines intersect. They're equal in measurement. Lines that intersect at a 90-degree angle form two sets of 90-degree vertical angles. These lines are called **perpendicular**.

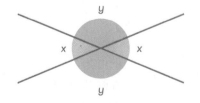

If one angle, x, measures 76°, then the opposite angle—the vertical angle, y—must equal 76° also.

Angle x and angle y are supplementary angles (meaning they add up to 180°); if y is 76°, then x must equal 104°, since 180 − 76 = 104.

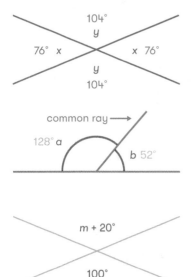

Since x and y are vertical angles, if x is 76°, then y must be 104°.

Since angle a and angle b share a common vertex and a common ray, angle a and angle b are adjacent angles.

Since the angle measuring 100° is opposite the angle measuring $m + 20°$, you know that they're vertical angles, so they're equal. Therefore, $m + 20° = 100°$.

If you want to find the value of m, you can use inverse operations to help you out.

$$\begin{array}{r} m + 20° = 100° \\ \underline{- 20° \quad - 20°} \\ m = 80° \end{array}$$

vertical angles: congruent/equal angles that are opposite an intersection point of two lines

perpendicular: describes two lines or line segments that form right angles at their intersection (meeting point)

adjacent angles: angles that are next to one another

Let's practice using these angle relationships to help solve some problems. It's always fun to find stuff that's missing, so start by trying to find some missing angle measurements.

🔍 TAKE A CLOSER LOOK

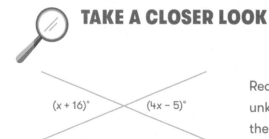

Ready for a challenge? Find the unknown angle measurements in the diagram on the left.

Since the angles are across from each other on two intersecting lines, they're vertical angles and equal in measure. So, you can use an equation to help you find the value of x, and then use that to find the measure of each angle. You can set each expression equal to one another since you know the angles are equal.

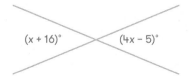

$$x + 16 = 4x - 5$$
$$\underline{-4x \quad\quad -4x}$$
$$-3x + 16 = -5$$
$$\underline{-16 \quad -16}$$
$$\underline{-3x = -21}$$
$$-3 \quad -3$$
$$x = 7$$

Step 1: Subtract 4x from both sides.

Step 2: Subtract 16 from both sides.

Step 3: Divide both sides by −3.

But wait! You're not done yet. You need to use this value of x to find the measure of the angles. The good news is that because they're equal, you only have to calculate one of the angles.

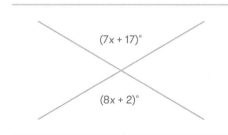

$(x + 16)^\circ = ?$

$(7 + 16)^\circ = ?$

$(7 + 16)^\circ = 23^\circ$

Since one angle is 23°, both angles are 23°.

YOUR TURN!

Find the values of the variables in each problem and the measure of each angle.

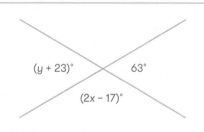

CHAPTER SUMMARY

CROSS SECTIONS OF SOLIDS

You can think of "cross sections" as 3-D figures of things that you would slice. Depending on the slice that you cut, the shape of the cross section will change. Pay close attention to how you're cutting into these figures.

CIRCLES: FINDING CIRCUMFERENCE AND AREA

Circumference is the curved length around a circle. The radius is the distance from the center of the circle to its perimeter (edge), and radius is always half the circle's diameter. Area, then, accounts for all the 2-D space that occupies the inside of a circle.

AREA OF A CIRCLE	CIRCUMFERENCE OF A CIRCLE
Area= $\pi \times \text{radius}^2$	$C = 2 \times \pi \times \text{radius}$
	OR
	$C = \pi \times \text{diameter}$

VOLUME: CYLINDERS, CONES, AND SPHERES

- You can find the volume of a cylinder by using the formula:

    Volume = Area of the Base × Height

    Volume = $A_{circle} \times h$

    $V = \pi r^2 h$

- A cone with the same height and base as a cylinder will have one-third the volume of the cylinder.

$$\text{Volume} = \frac{\text{Area of the base} \times \text{height}}{3}$$

$$\text{Volume} = \frac{\text{Area}_\bigcirc \times \text{height}}{3}$$

$$\text{Volume} = \frac{\pi r^2 h}{3} = \frac{1}{3} \times \pi r^2 h$$

- Since there's no actual height, you must use the diameter to act as the height of the sphere. This will be represented by 2r. There's also a relationship that a sphere is $\frac{2}{3}$ of the volume of a cylinder with the same radius. So, you can use the volume of a cylinder equation as the beginning for the formula.

$$V = 2 \times \frac{\pi r^2 2r}{3} = 4 \times \frac{\pi r^3}{3} = \frac{4}{3} \times \pi r^3$$

ANGLE TYPES

ANGLE RELATIONSHIP	DIAGRAM
COMPLEMENTARY ANGLES A pair of angles that add up to 90°	60° 30°
SUPPLEMENTARY ANGLES A pair of angles that add up to 180°	120° 60°
VERTICAL ANGLES Opposite angles of an intersection are equivalent.	B A A B

CHAPTER 10 VOCABULARY

adjacent angles: angles that are next to one another

angle: a shape that is formed when two **rays** or line segments meet at a common endpoint

circumference: the length around a circle

complementary angles: angles that add up to 90 degrees

cross section: a "slice" of a shape from a three-dimensional object

diameter: the distance between one edge of a circle to another through the center of the circle

irrational number: any real number that cannot be turned into a simple fraction

parallel: describes lines or line segments that have the same slope/rate of change and never meet

perpendicular: describes two lines or line segments that form right angles at their intersection (meeting point)

pi, or π: an irrational number, approximately 3.14

plane: a two-dimensional shape or surface

radius: the distance between the center of a circle and its edge; half the circle's diameter

ray: a line that extends infinitely in one direction from an endpoint

supplementary angles: angles that add up to 180 degrees

vertical angles: congruent/equal angles that are opposite an intersection point of two lines

CHAPTER 10 ANSWER KEY

CROSS SECTIONS OF SOLIDS (P. 327)

TYPE OF CUT	SLICE SHAPE
1. Horizontal	Rectangle
2. Vertical, Diagonal	Rectangle
3. Diagonal	Parallelogram

CIRCLES: FINDING CIRCUMFERENCE AND AREA (P. 333)

CIRCLE	CIRCUMFERENCE	AREA
23 cm	*Formula: C = π × diameter* C = π (23 cm) ≈ 72.2 cm	*Formula: A = π × radius²* $A = \pi \left(\frac{23 \text{ cm}}{2}\right)^2 \approx 415.3 \text{ cm}^2$
$1\frac{1}{2}$ m	*Formula C = 2 × π × radius* $C = 2\pi \left(1\frac{1}{2} \text{ m}\right) \approx 9.4 \text{ m}$	*Formula: A = π × radius²* $A = \pi \left(1\frac{1}{2} \text{ m}\right)^2 \approx 7.1 \text{ m}^2$

VOLUME: CYLINDERS, CONES, AND SPHERES (P. 339)

Formula for the volume of the cone use: $V = \pi r^2 \left(\frac{h}{3}\right)$ and for the scoop: $V = \frac{4}{3}\pi r^3$ since it's a sphere.

d = 1 in, r = 0.5 in, h = 6 in

Volume (cone) + Volume (sphere) = **Total Ice Cream**

Volume (cone) = $\frac{1}{3}\pi r^2 h$

Volume (cone) = $\frac{1}{3}\pi (0.5 \text{ in})^2 6 \text{ in}$

Volume (cone) = $\frac{1}{3}\pi (0.25 \text{ in}^2) 6 \text{ in}$

Volume (cone) = $\pi(0.5 \text{ in}^3)$

Volume (sphere) = $\frac{4}{3}\pi r^3$

Volume (sphere) = $\frac{4}{3}\pi (0.5 \text{ in})^3$

Volume (sphere) = $\frac{4}{3}\pi (0.125 \text{ in}^3)$

Volume (sphere) = $\pi(0.16 \text{ in}^3)$

$\pi(0.5 \text{ in}^3) + \pi(0.16 \text{ in}^3) = 0.66 \pi \text{ in}^3 = 2.0724 \text{ in}^3$

2.0724 in³ ~ 2.1 in³ total ice cream

YOUR TURN (P. 343)

a. Complementary angles add up to 90°, so subtract 31 from 90 to get the complementary angle.

$$90° - 31° = 59°$$

b. Supplementary angles add up to 180°, so subtract 86 from 180 to get the supplementary angle.

$$180° - 86° = 94°$$

MORE ABOUT ANGLES (P. 345)

(Problem on left)	(Problem on right)
$7x + 17 = 8x + 2$	$y + 23 = 63$
$7x + 15 = 8x$	$y = 40$
$15 = 1x$	$63 + 2x - 17 = 180$
$7x + 17 = 7(15) + 17 = 105 + 17 = 122°$	$2x + 46 = 180$
$8x + 2 = 8(15) + 2 = 120 + 2 = 122°$	$2x = 134$
$180 - 122 = 58°$	$x = 67$
The measurement for the two missing angles is 58°.	$180 - 63 = 117$
	The measurement for the missing vertical angle is 117°.

SIMILARITY, CONGRUENCE, AND ANGLE RELATIONSHIPS

Did you know that when you ride your bike or skateboard, your brain makes geometric calculations every time you turn a corner? Instinctively, your brain's been using geometry your whole life. Other applications of geometry in everyday life include construction work, astronomy, computer-aided design, and pretty much everything in between. Geometry is used for measuring the size, shape, and position of shapes and figures. Let's dive in!

CHAPTER CONTENTS

SCALE FACTOR, SIDES, AND AREA

Whether you're aware of it or not, you've benefited (directly or indirectly) from scaling, especially when it comes to things like models and maps. Creating smaller or larger versions of objects is both helpful and useful. By scaling up or scaling down, measurements can be gathered and made into more useful sizes.

PRIOR KNOWLEDGE

A **scale factor (k)** is a ratio that compares measurements such as the length of an object in a drawing to the length of the actual, physical object the drawing depicts. The scale factor, then, is the ratio of scale measurements to actual measurements, without regard to units. To find the actual measurements of an object, all you have to do is multiply the scale measurements by a scale factor.

The scale factor of ▱ABCD to ▱WXYZ is 4.

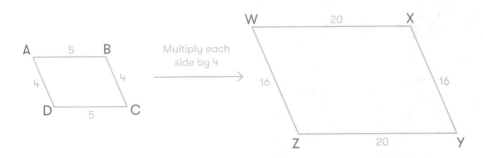

Multiply each side by 4

This relationship can be described as:

Actual measurement = scaled object measurement × scale factor

scale factor: the number by which all the components of an object are multiplied in order to create a proportional enlargement or reduction

TAKE A CLOSER LOOK

Your friend just texted you a picture of your favorite climbing tree. You know from experience in real life that this tree is much bigger than its scaled-down photo. The scale factor for this photo is 50, meaning the actual size of the tree is 50 times bigger in both width and length. So, how can you find the actual width and height of the tree?

Since you know the scale factor is 50, you can use multiplication to find the tree's actual width. On your phone, the tree's width is 0.8 inches.

Actual tree width = scaled object measurement × scale factor

Scaled object (Picture) width: 0.8 inches

Actual tree width = 0.8 inches × 50

Actual tree width = 40 inches

Now find the actual height of the tree. On your phone, the tree's height is 4.2 inches.

Actual tree height = scaled object measurement × scale factor

Actual tree height = _____ × 50

Actual tree height = _____ inches

So, the actual tree's height is 210 inches.

When scaling, it's often necessary to convert measurements. Since it would be better to have the tree's dimensions expressed in feet rather than inches, use your conversion skills to make it happen. With the conversion rate $\frac{1 \text{ foot}}{12 \text{ inches}}$ you can find:

$$\text{Width: } 40 \text{ inches} \times \frac{1 \text{ foot}}{12 \text{ inches}} = \frac{40}{12} \text{ feet} = 3.3 \text{ feet}$$

$$\text{Height: } 210 \text{ inches} \times \frac{1 \text{ foot}}{12 \text{ inches}} = \frac{210}{12} \text{ feet} = 17.5 \text{ feet}$$

Ta-da! Now you know that the small tree on your phone is actually 3.3 feet wide by 17.5 feet tall in reality!

USING A SCALE DRAWING

Now let's turn our focus to the dimensions of your bedroom. You've decided to redo your bedroom, but you want an idea of where you'll rearrange each piece of furniture before you begin moving things around. First, you draw a small scale of your room on a piece of paper.

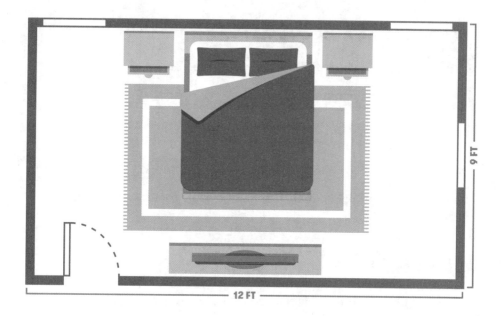

If the scale factor is $\frac{1}{48}$, what would be the dimensions, in inches, of this room on the scaled-down model?

Since the actual dimensions are given in feet but your paper's measurements are in inches, you'll have to convert to inches first:

Length: 12 feet × 12 inches per foot = 144 in

Width: 9 feet × 12 inches per foot = 108 in

Next, you can use the scale factor, $\frac{1}{48}$, to scale-down to the model size:

SCALE FACTOR = ¼₈	COMPUTATION	SCALE DRAWING
ACTUAL LENGTH 144 inches	$144 \text{ inches} \times \frac{1}{48}$	**LENGTH** 3 inches
ACTUAL WIDTH 108 inches	$108 \text{ inches} \times \frac{1}{48}$	**WIDTH** 2.25 inches

Nice! On your paper model, the room will be 3 inches × 2.25 inches.

TOOLS FOR SUCCESS

When scaling, it's important to remember:

1. Identify the scale factor on a legend, key, or using another method.

2. Scaling up will have a scale factor greater than 1.

3. Scaling down will have a scale factor between 0 and 1.

4. Multiply the original dimensions by the scale factor to convert the measurements.

YOUR TURN!

Look again at the furniture dimensions in your bedroom.

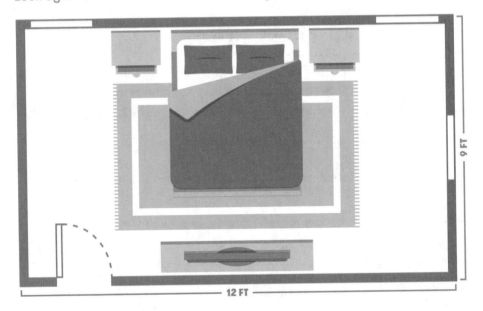

1. If the scale factor is $\frac{1}{48}$, what would be the length on the scaled-down drawing, in inches, of a bed that is 72 inches long?

2. What would be the width of the bed on the scaled-down drawing if the actual width of the bed is 36 inches long?

3. Could you fit a second bed of the same size in the room and place a dresser that's 60 inches wide between the two beds?

CONGRUENCE

In geometry, congruence means two objects have the same dimensions. In other words, their side-lengths and angles are the same.

CONGRUENT TRIANGLES

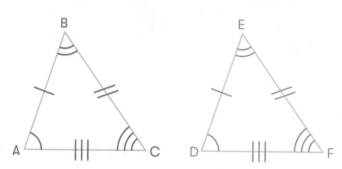

ROTATION, REFLECTION, AND TRANSLATION

Congruent shapes, however, are often drawn in different positions—so it can be tricky to see their congruence at first glance. For example, in the image below, the second triangle has been rotated to the left 90 degrees—but they have the same side-lengths and angle measurements.

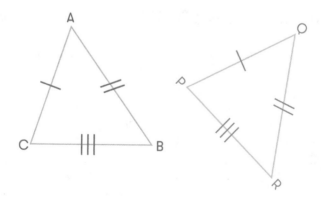

Congruent shapes can rotate, reflect, and/or translate. When this happens, we say the second image has been transformed.

congruence (symbol: ≅) : the quality of being equal in size and shape

transformation: a rigid motion that creates a similar or congruent figure

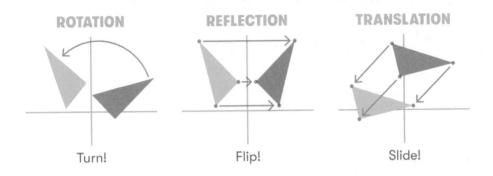

ROTATION	REFLECTION	TRANSLATION
Turn!	Flip!	Slide!

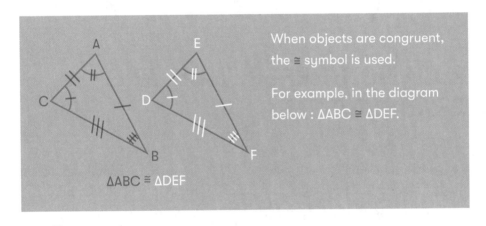

When objects are congruent, the ≅ symbol is used.

For example, in the diagram below : △ABC ≅ △DEF.

△ABC ≅ △DEF

TAKE A CLOSER LOOK

How do you think △ABC could be moved in order to land exactly on top of △GHI?

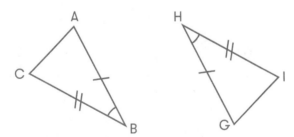

You can note that angle B and angle H are congruent based on their markings. You can also note that side AB and HG are congruent. And side BC and side HI are congruent too. You need to make sure that when you map one triangle onto the other, those sides and angles match up.

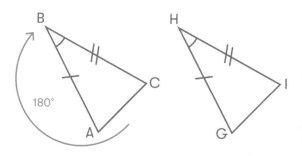

If you **rotate** the triangle about point B (using point B as the center) in a 90-degree fashion clockwise, you'll notice that point C is now the topmost angle.

If you were to continue rotating △ABC another 90 degrees clockwise, how would that align with △GHI? After this rotation, you'll find that △ABC aligns with △GHI. Altogether, this would be a 180-degree rotation.

> **rotation:** a turn of an object/figure; there will be a degree and direction of turn around the origin or any coordinate in the plane; it creates a congruent figure

 ## ANOTHER PATH

What about another way to move △ABC onto △GHI?

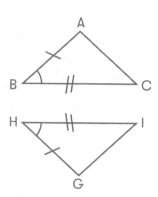

You can also try to reflect (mirror image) the triangle over a line made by vertex B. You may notice after this reflection, vertex A is in the topmost position. But we need vertex A to be in the bottommost position. How can that happen?

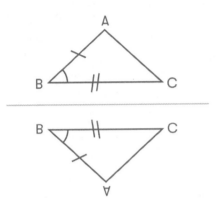

You can then **reflect** ΔABC over a line created by vertex C. This will place ΔABC in the same position as that of ΔGHI.

TRANSFORMATIONS IN THE COORDINATE PLANE

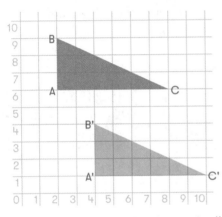

Let's examine a triangle in the coordinate plane, ΔABC and ΔA'B'C'. How can the blue triangle be moved from the location of the orange triangle?

Two shifts, or **translations**, on ΔABC could have shifted it to ΔA'B'C'. It could have been translated horizontally 2 units to the right and then 5 units vertically down to create ΔA'B'C'.

reflection: a turn of an object/figure; the reflection occurs over a reflection line; it creates a congruent figure

translation: a slide of an object/figure, a shift up, down, left, and/or right; it creates a congruent figure

Let's break that down into two clear steps.

STEP 1:	STEP 2:
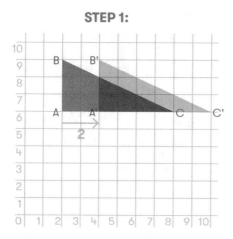	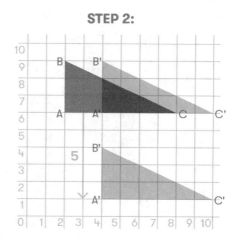

Step 1: The triangle is translated 2 units to the right.

Step 2: The triangle is translated 5 units down.

ANOTHER PATH

The order in which these two translations could've happened wouldn't change the congruence of ΔABC and ΔA'B'C'. This means you could translate *down first, then right and still maintain* ΔABC ≅ ΔA'B'C'.

TOOLS FOR SUCCESS

When working with congruent objects, it's important to remember:

1. The objects will have the same dimensions (side-lengths and angles).

2. The symbol to show congruency is ≅.

3. Congruent shapes can be rotated, reflected, or translated from the original shape.

YOUR TURN!

1. Describe the transformations in the shapes below. Be sure to use the terms rotation, reflection, or translation in your description.

a.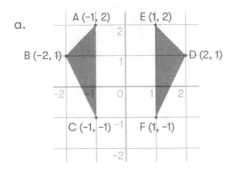

b.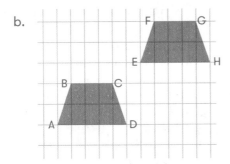

SIMILARITY

Are your bedroom scale drawing and your actual bedroom from earlier in the chapter congruent? Nope! Since the drawing and the actual room don't have the same length and width measurements, they're not congruent. Even though they aren't the same, it's fair to say that the two objects are similar. Objects that have the same shape and congruent, corresponding (matching) angles—but are different sizes—are called similar.

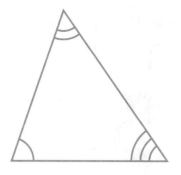

Similar triangles

TAKE A CLOSER LOOK

Since each of the corresponding sides of the room decreases by the same **scale factor** (see pages 354 through 358 if you need a refresher), the actual room and model are similar. This means they're the same shape—just in two different sizes. (As you'll recall since your model was made on a paper measured in inches, and your actual bedroom was measured in feet.)

DIMENSIONS	ACTUAL ROOM	SCALE FACTOR	MODEL ROOM
Length	144	$\frac{1}{48}$	3
Width	108	$\frac{1}{48}$	2.25

DILATIONS

Applying a scale factor is a special type of transformation called dilation. You can determine if two shapes are similar by applying a dilation. Look at the examples on the next page. Which of the rectangles do you think are similar to each other?

similar: a figure/object that is the same shape but a different size than the original (symbol: ~)

dilation: a transformation that creates similar figures by using the scale factor to increase the side-lengths or coordinates

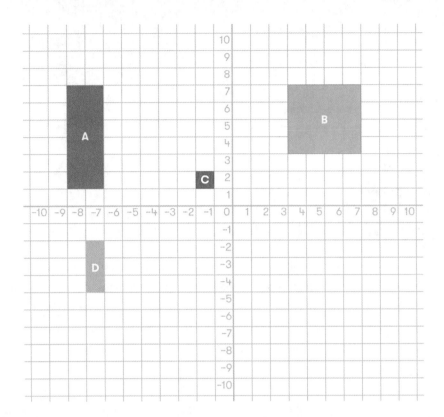

Rectangles *A* and *D* appear to be similar.

To be sure, check the scale factor of their corresponding sides:

DIMENSIONS	RECTANGLE D	RECTANGLE A	SCALE FACTOR
Length (longer side)	3	6	× 2
Width (shorter side)	1	2	× 2

If each side of Rectangle D is dilated by a factor of 2, it creates the dimensions of Rectangle A. So, these rectangles are similar since even though they're different sizes, they're still the same shape.

Rectangles B and C also appear to be similar. Again, you can check the scale factor of their corresponding sides:

DIMENSIONS	RECTANGLE B	RECTANGLE C	SCALE FACTOR
Length (horizontal sides)	1	4	× 4
Width (vertical sides)	1	4	× 4

As you might have noticed, each of these rectangles has equal sides. This means they're squares! Which also means they're similar! *What would be the scale factor applied from Square B to create Square C?* Square C is 4 times the size of Square B.

One more set to compare: *Could Rectangle B and Rectangle D be similar?* It seems like Rectangle B could be "stretched" horizontally to create Rectangle D.

Check out each set of corresponding sides to be sure:

DIMENSIONS	RECTANGLE B	RECTANGLE D	SCALE FACTOR
Length (horizontal sides)	1	3	× 3
Width (vertical sides)	1	1	× 1

When a shape is dilated, the scale factor must be applied to all sides. Since both the length and width don't have a common scale factor, Rectangles B and D are not similar.

 TOOLS FOR SUCCESS

To determine similarity between shapes:

1. Observe whether objects have the same shape but different sizes.

2. Dilate the shapes to see if congruent corresponding side-lengths can be made.

3. Apply the same scale factor to their corresponding sides to confirm similarity.

YOUR TURN!

1. Are figure B and C similar or congruent? Explain your reasoning. If they are similar, determine the scale factor.

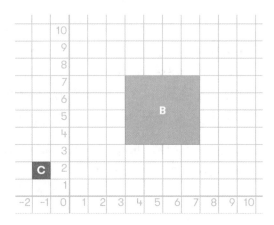

2. Verify that the trapezoids ABCD and A'B'C'D' are similar.

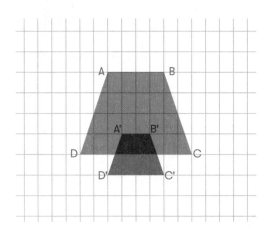

ANGLE RELATIONSHIPS

ANGLES CREATED BY PARALLEL LINES AND A TRANSVERSAL

One evening, you and your friend visit a zip line. As you glide down the cables, you're taken with the view of a stunning, fiery sunset. At a certain point, your friend speeds slightly in front of you, moving directly between you and the setting sun.

PRIOR KNOWLEDGE

The two zip lines are parallel to each other. If they weren't, you and your friend would probably crash into each other.

ZIP LINE A

ZIP LINE B

Your sight line connects you, your friend, and the Sun in the distance. This sight line is known as a transversal line.

This creates a set of **corresponding angles** that you and your friend share.

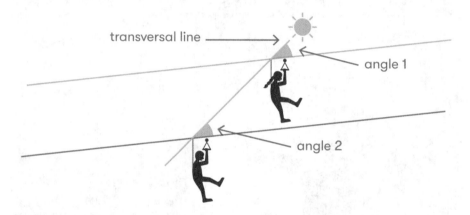

transversal line

angle 1

angle 2

transversal line: a line that intersects two parallel lines is called a transversal line

corresponding angles: angles that are at the same location of each intersection

Corresponding angles formed from parallel lines have the same measurement (congruent).

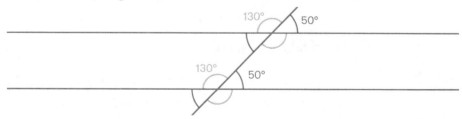

130° 50°

130° 50°

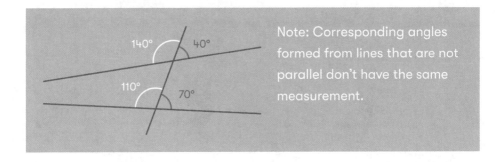

Note: Corresponding angles formed from lines that are not parallel don't have the same measurement.

ANGLE–ANGLE RELATIONSHIPS

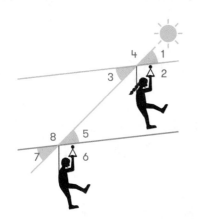

Look at some of the other important sets of angles in this system. Can you spot them?

 **TAKE A CLOSER LOOK**

That's right! We have vertical angles. You learned previously that vertical angles are on the opposite side of an intersection. You also know that vertical angles have the same measurements. Let's review:

ANGLE TYPE	ANGLES	MEASUREMENT
Corresponding	$\angle 1$ and $\angle 5$	Congruent (Equal)
Vertical	$\angle 1$ and $\angle 3$	Congruent (Equal)
Vertical	$\angle 5$ and $\angle 7$	Congruent (Equal)

It turns out a lot of the angle measurements are congruent. For fun, let's use what we've learned about transformations to prove it. The measures of $\angle 1$ and $\angle 3$ as well as $\angle 2$ and $\angle 4$ are congruent. Think about rotating $\angle 1$ or $\angle 3$ around the intersection point of the parallel line and the transversal.

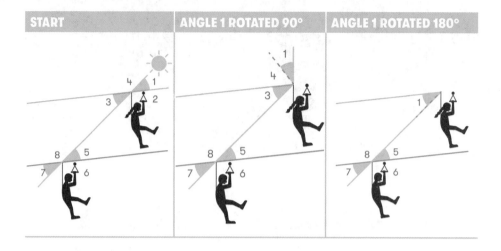

| START | ANGLE 1 ROTATED 90° | ANGLE 1 ROTATED 180° |

ALTERNATE INTERIOR ANGLES

With a 180° rotation of angle 1, you can see $\angle 1 \cong \angle 3$. The same can be seen for $\angle 2 \cong \angle 4$.

Now Let's look at the remaining angles. *Do you think any of these are congruent?*

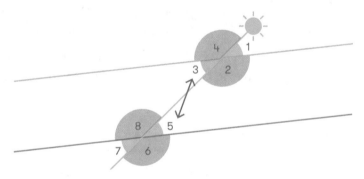

Yes! The measures of $\angle 3$ and $\angle 5$ are also congruent. They're called alternate interior angles. Let's break down the name's three parts:

- alternate: on *opposite* sides of the transversal
- interior: *inside* of the parallel lines
- angles: measures created between one of the parallel lines and the transversal

ALTERNATE EXTERIOR ANGLES

Let's apply the transformation to these angle relationships as well. Through a 180° rotation and a translation, you can see the congruence of ∠3 and ∠5.

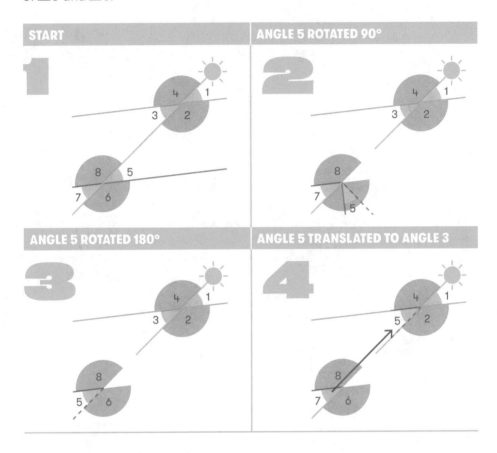

The measures of ∠1 and ∠7 are also congruent. Can you guess what they're called? **Alternate exterior angles**:

- alternate: on *opposite* sides of the transversal

- exterior: *outside* of the parallel lines

- angles: measures created between one of the parallel lines and the transversal

Through a 180° rotation and a translation, you can see the congruence of ∠1 and ∠7.

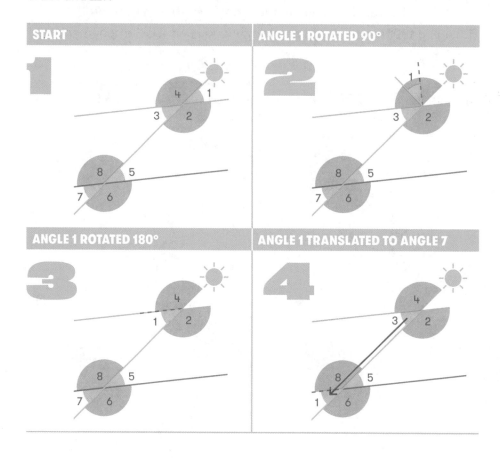

Can you identify the remaining sets of congruent angles?

Hint: They're supplementary.

Recall that supplementary angles form a straight line (and add up to 180°).

The zip lines and sight line (transversal line) make sets of supplementary angles along the parallel lines. Take a look at them in the "start" illustration at the top of page 374.

SUPPLEMENTARY ANGLE PAIRS	
∠1 and ∠4	∠5 and ∠8
∠3 and ∠4	∠7 and ∠6

There are other supplementary angles hiding in zip lines and sight lines, too. Study those diagrams of the zip lines. Can you see them?

SUPPLEMENTARY ANGLE PAIRS	
∠5 and ∠6	∠2 and ∠1
∠3 and ∠2	∠8 and ∠7

alternate interior angles: congruent angles that are on opposite sides of the transversal line, on the inside of two parallel lines

alternate exterior angles: congruent angles that are on opposite sides of the transversal line, on the outside of two parallel lines

YOUR TURN!

Using your understanding of these new types of angles, identify the measurement for each angle.

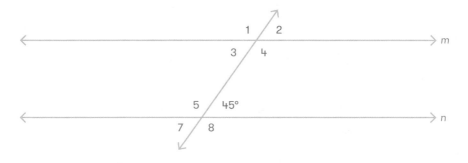

THE PYTHAGOREAN THEOREM

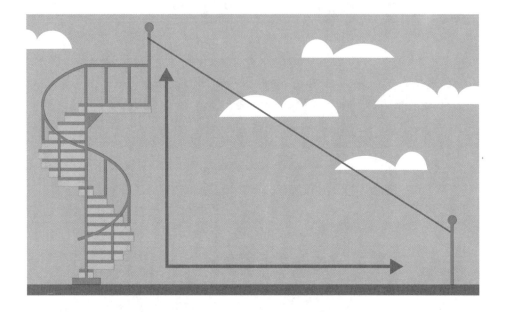

The **Pythagorean Theorem** is a relationship of the lengths of the sides of a **right triangle**.

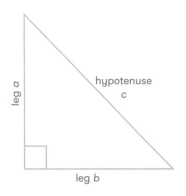

Pythagorean Theorem:
leg a^2 + leg b^2 = hypotenuse^2
$(a \cdot a) + (b \cdot b) = (c \cdot c)$
$a^2 + b^2 = c^2$

In a right triangle, adding the squares of the legs will equal the square of the hypotenuse.

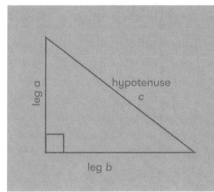

The sides must be labeled properly. Each leg can be "a" or "b," but the **hypotenuse** must be in the "c" position.

Pythagorean theorem: states that the sum of the squares of the legs of a right triangle are equal in value to the square of the hypotenuse

right triangle: a triangle in which one of the angles forms a 90-degree (right) angle

hypotenuse: the longest side of a right triangle, always across from the right angle

TAKE A CLOSER LOOK

Let's visualize the Pythagorean Theorem in action using the triangle below:

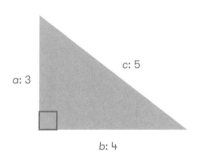

First, be sure to label each side of the triangle correctly. Remember: either leg can be a or b, but c must be the hypotenuse.

Next, enter these side-length values into the formula and evaluate— in this case, the values are 3, 4, and 5 (see illustration). Of course, be sure to follow the correct order of operations!

EXAMPLE WORK	EXPLANATION
$a^2 + b^2 = c^2$	Pythagorean Theorem
$(3)^2 + (4)^2 = (5)^2$	Enter side-lengths into the formula.
$9 + 16 = 25$	Evaluate each term. Then combine the terms.
$25 = 25$	Awesome—you've verified that the Pythagorean Theorem works!

Let's go one more step and look at each side-length visually "squared":

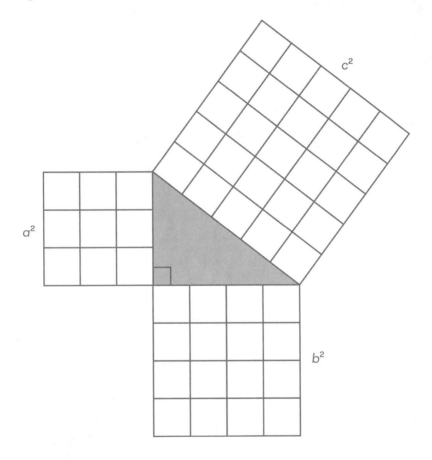

These are the side-length values turned into squares. *What happens if you add up all these units?*

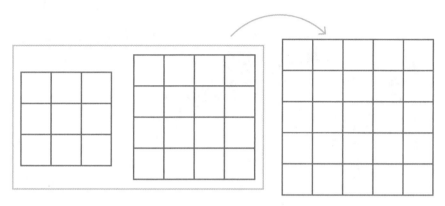

9 squares + 16 squares = 25 squares

Interesting. . . very interesting. When the side-lengths of the right triangle are put into square form, you see the Pythagorean Theorem is true.

That said, the Pythagorean Theorem has its limits. So, keep in mind:

- The Pythagorean Theorem works for ALL right triangles.

- If the squares of the side-lengths of a triangle don't add up to the square of the hypotenuse, it's not a right triangle.

Let's try it out! Use the Pythagorean Theorem to determine if the triangles on the next page are right triangles.

EXAMPLE A	EXAMPLE B	PROCEDURE
		Start by labeling each side of the triangle. Hint: Identify the longest side first.
		Enter these values into the Pythagorean Theorem equation: $a^2 + b^2 = c^2$
$(6)^2 + (3)^2 = (8)^2$	$(5)^2 + (12)^2 = (13)^2$	Evaluate the left and right side of each equation.
$36 + 9 = 64$	$25 + 144 = 169$	Determine if the left and right side of each equation make a true statement.
$45 \neq 64$	$169 = 169$	
Not true! This is not a right triangle.	True! This is a right triangle.	

As it turns out, the triangle in Example A isn't a right triangle. However, the side-lengths in Example B's triangle satisfy the Pythagorean Theorem, so it *is* a right triangle. Pretty cool, huh?

YOUR TURN!

Use the Pythagorean Theorem to determine if the three triangles below are right triangles.

1.

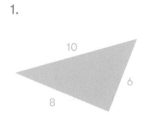

2.

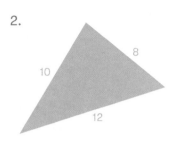

3. A triangle with side lengths 9, 40, and 41.

FINDING UNKNOWN SIDE-LENGTHS IN RIGHT TRIANGLES

Having a dependable formula for the side-lengths of a right triangle is super helpful. As we covered in the previous section, the Pythagorean Theorem can determine if a triangle is a right triangle. Next, you can explore using this formula to find the length of an unknown side when the other two sides are given.

TAKE A CLOSER LOOK

Study the triangle below. It's a model of a skateboard ramp that's going to be built in a new park in town. How could you use the Pythagorean Theorem to find its missing length?

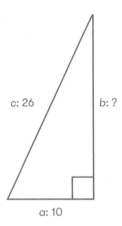

c: 26

b: ?

a: 10

First, it's important to make sure you can identify which are the legs and which is the hypotenuse in the triangle. Once you've done that, enter the values of a, b, and c into the Pythagorean Theorem equation:

$$a^2 + b^2 = c^2$$

$$(10)^2 + (b)^2 = (26)^2$$

PRIOR KNOWLEDGE

Finally, it's time to show off your skills with order of operations and inverse operations.

$$(10)^2 + (b)^2 = (26)^2$$ *Evaluate exponents first.*

$$\cancel{100} + b^2 = 676$$ *Combine terms.*

$$-\ 100 \qquad -\ 100$$ *Subtract 100 from both sides of the equation.*

$$b^2 = 576$$

$$\sqrt{b^2} = \sqrt{576}$$ *The inverse of "squaring" is a square root.*

$$b = 24$$

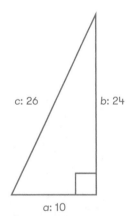

c: 26

b: 24

a: 10

Awesome! You've found the missing side of the ramp.

YOUR TURN!

Use your knowledge of the Pythagorean Theorem to solve for the following situations. Note: you can use a calculator for these!

1. The people who run the skate park are going to install a ramp at its entrance to make it wheelchair-accessible. The ramp needs to reach 3.5 feet in height and must start from 16 feet away. What is the length of the ramp? Round your answer to the nearest tenth of a foot.

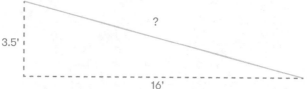

3.5'   ?

16'

2. You have a 15-foot ladder to reach a tree house you're building. The tree house is 11 feet off the ground. How far away from the base of the tree should you place the ladder? Round to the nearest foot.

15 FT

11 FT

?

THE DISTANCE BETWEEN TWO POINTS

The Pythagorean Theorem can also help you find the distance between two points on a coordinate plane. Although you've done this problem-solving before, you were limited to finding lengths between points that were perfectly horizontal or vertical to each other.

TAKE A CLOSER LOOK

Look at this simplified map of a nearby State Park. Each unit on the map equals one mile. The distance between the Lake (*Point A*) and the Campsite (*Point B*) is a diagonal line on the map, just like the hypotenuse of a triangle. Let's try using the Pythagorean Theorem to find the distance between Points *A* and *B*.

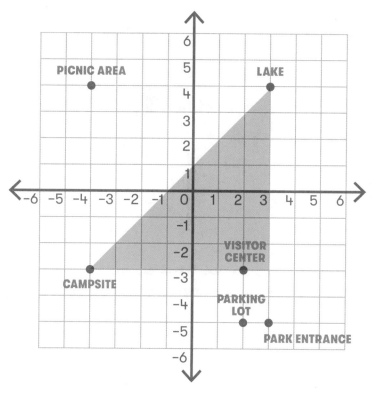

To start, you need to find the horizontal and vertical distances that separate Points A and B on the map.

- The vertical line down from Point A at the lake connects to the horizontal line from Point B at the campsite. It creates a right triangle between the lake, the campsite, and a point near the visitor center.

Next, measure the distance in miles of the horizontal and vertical lines. Label the sides of the right triangle, and get ready to use the Pythagorean Theorem.

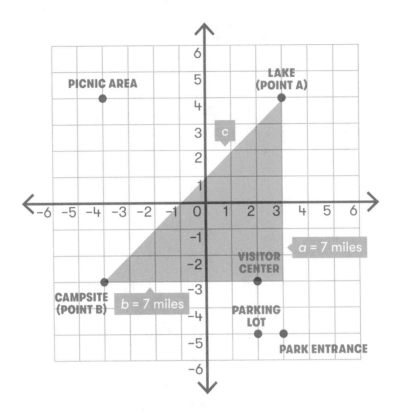

Great! Everything that needs a label has one, so you can enter the known side-lengths into the Pythagorean Theorem ($a^2 + b^2 = c^2$) and solve for the distance, c:

$$a^2 + b^2 = c^2$$

$(7)^2 + (7)^2 = (c)^2$ *Enter the known side-lengths and evaluate exponents first.*

$49 + 49 = c^2$ *Combine terms.*

$98 = c^2$

$\sqrt{98} = \sqrt{c^2}$ *The inverse of "squaring" is a square root.*

$c = \sqrt{98}$ or $c \approx 9.9$ *So, the distance from the lake to the campsite (triangle side c) is approximately 9.9 miles. Fantastic work!*

YOUR TURN!

Use the Pythagorean Theorem to find the distance between the coordinates given.

1. If C(-3,5) and D(3,0), what is the length of $\overline{CD}$? Round to the tenths place.

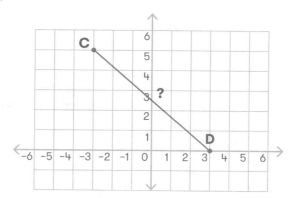

2. You decide to build a wooden box to store your comic book collection. All the corners of the box must have right angles. One side of your box is going to be 20 cm long and the other side will be 30 cm long. How long should the diagonal be so that the angle between the two sides measures 90 degrees? Round to the nearest whole number.

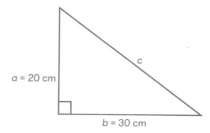

CHAPTER SUMMARY

CONGRUENCE

Figures are congruent if the angles and side-lengths are congruent.

Congruent figures are formed by the following transformations:

- Translations: slides (up, down, left, or right)
- Reflections: flip over a given reflection line
- Rotations: turn around a given point (*commonly the origin*)

SIMILARITY

Figures are similar when the objects are the same shape but different sizes. The corresponding side-lengths are proportional by a scale factor. The angles are congruent (equal) between the figures.

- **Dilations** create similar figures. Dilations create larger or smaller figures than the original figure by multiplying each side-length by the same scale factor, k.

- **Scale drawings** are often used to map areas that are much larger into smaller spaces, and if you want to magnify objects by a scale factor.

- **Scale factor** is a number that you use to multiply coordinates and/or side lengths to produce a similar figure.

ANGLE RELATIONSHIPS

- Corresponding angles: angles that are on the same side of the transversal but on each of the parallel lines.

  - Note: In the case of angle relationships, when we use the word "side," we mean position in relation to a line.

- Alternate interior angles: angles that are on opposite sides of the transversal line but are also on the inside of the parallel lines "sandwich." (Think of the parallel lines as the two pieces of bread.)

- Alternate exterior angles: angles that are on opposite sides of the transversal line that are also on the outside of the parallel lines "sandwich."

THE PYTHAGOREAN THEOREM

A formula that can only apply to right triangles. The formula is used to confirm a right triangle or to find a missing side-length.

$$a^2 + b^2 = c^2$$

$$\text{leg}^2 + \text{leg}^2 = \text{hypotenuse}^2$$

CHAPTER 11 VOCABULARY

alternate exterior angles: congruent angles that are on opposite sides of the transversal line, on the outside of two parallel lines

alternate interior angles: congruent angles that are on opposite sides of the transversal line, on the inside of the two parallel lines

congruence (symbol: ≅): equal in size and shape

corresponding angles: angles that are at the same location of each intersection

dilation: a transformation that creates similar figures by using the scale factor to increase the side-lengths or coordinates

hypotenuse: the longest side of a right triangle; this side is opposite the right angle

Pythagorean Theorem: states that the sum of the squares of the legs of a right triangle are equal in value to the square of the hypotenuse

reflection: a flip (or mirror) of an object/figure; the reflection occurs over a reflection line; it creates a congruent figure

right triangle: a triangle in which one of the angles forms a 90-degree (right) angle

rotation: a turn of an object/figure; there will be a degree and direction of turn around the origin or any coordinate in the plane; it creates a congruent figure

scale factor (k): a value used to create a dilation, this number is used to multiply all the vertices and sides to create a similar figure

similarity (symbol: ~): a figure/object that is the same shape but a different size than the original

transformation: a rigid motion that creates a similar or congruent figure

translation: a slide of an object/figure, a shift up, down, left, and right; it creates a congruent figure

transversal line: a line that cuts across other lines, usually parallel lines

CHAPTER 11 ANSWER KEY

SCALE DRAWINGS: SCALE FACTOR, SIDES, AND AREA (P. 358)

1. 72 inches × $\frac{1}{48}$ = 1.5 inches

2. 36 inches × $\frac{1}{48}$ = 0.75 inches

3.

DIMENSIONS	ACTUAL ROOM	2 BEDS	DRESSER	2 BEDS + DRESSER
Width	108	72	60	132

The limiting factor here is the width of the room. Since the widths of the two beds plus the dresser is greater than the total width of the room, you would NOT be able to fit two beds with the dresser in between them.

ROTATION, REFLECTION, AND TRANSLATION (P. 364)

1. a. ΔABC can be reflected over the y-axis.

   b. Trapezoid ABCD can be translated 6 units to the right and 3 units vertically.

SIMILARITY (P. 368)

1. Since both figures B and C are squares, with four 90° angles and equal sides, they are similar. We also know that the scale factor from B to C is $\frac{1}{4}$ since the side lengths are $\frac{1}{4}$ the size in figure C than in figure B.

2. Trapezoid ABCD and Trapezoid A'B'C'D' are similar because the side-lengths are proportional. The scale factor for all the side-lengths from Trapezoid ABCD to Trapezoid A'B'C'D' is $\frac{1}{2}$.

ANGLE RELATIONSHIPS (P. 375)

$\angle 1 = 135°$

$\angle 2 = 45°$

$\angle 3 = 45°$

$\angle 4 = 135°$

$\angle 5 = 135°$

$\angle 6 = 45°$

$\angle 7 = 45°$

$\angle 8 = 135°$

THE PYTHAGOREAN THEOREM (P. 381)

1. $(6)^2 + (8)^2 = (10)^2$

   $36 + 64 = 100$

   $100 = 100$

   This is a right triangle.

2. $(8)^2 + (10)^2 = (12)^2$

   $64 + 100 = 144$

   $164 \neq 144$

   This is not a right triangle.

3. $(9)^2 + (40)^2 = (41)^2$

   $81 + 1,600 = 1,681$

   $1,681 = 1,681$

   This is a right triangle.

FINDING UNKNOWN SIDE-LENGTHS IN RIGHT TRIANGLES (P. 383)

1.
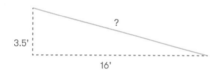

$a = 3.5 \quad b = 16 \quad c = ?$

$(3.5)^2 + (16)^2 = c^2$

$12.25 + 256 = c^2$

$268.25 = c^2$

$\sqrt{268.25} = \sqrt{c^2}$

$16.4 \approx c^2$

This ramp will be about 16.4 feet long.

2.
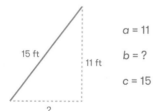

$a = 11$

$b = ?$

$c = 15$

$(11)^2 + (b)^2 = (15)^2$

$121 + b^2 = 225$

$b^2 = 225 - 121$

$\sqrt{b^2} = \sqrt{104}$

$b \approx 10.2$

You should place the ladder a little more than 10 feet from the base of the tree.

THE DISTANCE BETWEEN TWO POINTS (P. 387)

1.

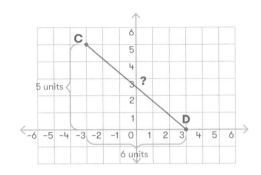

$(5)^2 + (6)^2 = (CD)^2$

$25 + 36 = CD^2$

$61 = CD^2$

$\sqrt{61} = \sqrt{CD^2}$

$7.8 \approx \overline{CD}$

2.

$(20 \text{ cm})^2 + (30 \text{ cm})^2 = c^2$

$400 \text{ cm}^2 + 900 \text{ cm}^2 = c^2$

$1300 \text{ cm}^2 = c^2$

$\sqrt{(1300 \text{ cm}^2)} = \sqrt{(c^2)}$

$36 \text{ cm} \approx c$

The diagonal should be about 36 cm.

NOTES

12 STATISTICS

In the sports world, statistical data helps answer questions and predictions about how players and teams might perform. If you wanted to know whether a left-handed basketball player has an advantage or disadvantage, you could go online and compare statistics between left-handed and right-handed players on the WNBA's database (or the NBA's). Statistics is a branch of math that studies, analyzes, and interprets data expressed in numbers in order to answer questions about them, like: *How many? How far? How long? How big?*

CHAPTER CONTENTS

STATISTICAL VARIABILITY

Sports are just one area where statistics are useful. In fact, statistics can help us understand and interpret nearly every aspect of life. The important thing is to ask the right questions.

Let's say you have a cousin who loves birding. One day, you meet up with her and her group of friends who are also birders. They want to know the number of eggs laid by American robins. After locating 8 nests, the group logs the number of eggs observed in each nest.

TAKE A CLOSER LOOK

In statistics, the questions you ask are just as important as the data you gather. **Non-statistical questions** result in only one possible answer. On the flip side, **statistical questions** result in—you guessed it—a variety of answers.

Looking at the two questions below, which of them is statistical?

1. How many robins' eggs were found in the third nest?

2. How many eggs does a robin lay?

data: a set of information *(usually numbers)* that represents a situation or parameters (e.g., number of birds watched)

non-statistical question: a question that only has one possible answer, collected from a single source of data

statistical question: a question with many possible answers, collected from a sample population

If you said question two, you're spot-on. The first question is non-statistical because it can only have one possible answer, as there would be a distinct, countable number of eggs. The second question is statistical because answers will be based on the collected data.

To answer the second question, you should consider data from all 8 nests. Since this is based on authentic information gathering, you can expect that not all the robins' nests show the same number of eggs.

Look at the chart on the next page.

NUMBER OF EGGS PER NEST

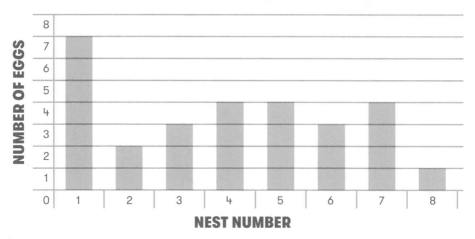

Here are some more examples of non-statistical and statistical questions:

NON-STATISTICAL QUESTION	STATISTICAL QUESTION
What's your name?	What's the most popular baby name?
Who's your math teacher?	Do more girls or more boys play soccer?
What's the temperature today?	What are the temperatures in January in Alaska?

TOOLS FOR SUCCESS

When determining if a question is statistical or non-statistical, it's important to remember:

1. Statistical questions should provide an adequate number of valid data—at least two or more results.

2. Non-statistical questions have no variability in their data and can only provide one valid result.

YOUR TURN!

Decide whether each question is a statistical question or a non-statistical question.

1. How many other people are in your math class?   ·st

2. What is the average height of your class?

3. About how many people are absent in your school each day?

4. How many people in your class have pets?

RANDOM SAMPLING

WHEN DO WE SAMPLE?

POPULATION

SAMPLE

Luckily for you, that afternoon spent birding will come in handy. For your school newspaper, you're writing an article about the best places nearby to go to watch birds. You feel stuck, though, because you're not sure how many people in town consider themselves birders, and with a looming deadline, there's no time to gather that information. It's nearly impossible for someone to gather all the data of an entire population to get an accurate sample. For your article, it's simply not realistic to find every birder in town. So, responses from a reliable sample (a portion of the population) are needed.

SAMPLE SPACE

To get valid data, you need to conduct a survey from a representative sample. A representative sample is the term used to describe the people you interview for a survey. Ideally, this smaller group of people should represent the whole population as best as possible, and reflect the larger group's diversity and range of varied qualities (for example, age, hair color, years of experience, specialties, and so on).

In this case, the whole population is everyone in town who knows the best locations for birding. You want the sample to give the same information you'd get if you were able to survey the whole population, and when it does, it's considered a representative sample.

How do you select an unbiased sample that represents the population accurately? Let's say you're given the following suggestions. *Which one is the best option for this specific birding survey?*

a. Asking people at your local grocery store

b. Asking students at your school

c. Asking students from the environmental club at your school

d. Asking senior citizens, since they like birds

The correct answer is C, because you're looking for people with a certain knowledge that this group is most likely to have. Options A, B, and D wouldn't lead to representative and reliable data.

representative sample: a smaller subset or group of a population that should represent the whole population as closely as possible

TAKE A CLOSER LOOK

Consider the following statistical situations. *Which of them could use population data? Which one would require sample data?*

1. You want to know the average height of giraffes in the Bronx Zoo.

2. You want to know the average height of an adult West African giraffe.

To answer the first question, you could measure the heights of the entire population of giraffes in the Bronx Zoo. It's safe to assume there's a fixed number of giraffes currently there, and that a zookeeper would have access to all of them.

*Giraffe Population
of the Bronx Zoo*

To answer the second question, though, you'd have to track down and measure the heights of *every* adult West African giraffe, but attempting to do that isn't realistic.

So, you'd need to collect a valid *sample* of adult West African giraffes.

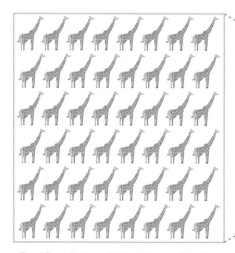

Total Population of West African Giraffes

*Sample Population of
West African Giraffes*

After measuring and averaging the sample heights, you'd have a reasonable estimate for the average height of West African giraffes.

YOUR TURN!

Would you be able to survey the entire population or would you do a sampling of the population based on the following situations? Explain your reasoning.

1. What was the average class score on Friday's math test?
2. How many sports drinks per week do students at your school consume?

VALID VS. NON-VALID SAMPLES

For a sample survey to be valid, it must be collected randomly. Random collection means each member of the sample is chosen by chance. Any part of that population being sampled has equal odds of being selected. If you're doing a survey about favorite school lunches, you need to sample the students who eat them—not shoppers at the grocery store. Just because the two groups have food in common doesn't mean data can be collected from the latter.

> random collection: a group of data that is collected without reason (i.e., blindly choosing)

TAKE A CLOSER LOOK

The question, then, is how can sample data be collected randomly? Consider the following example:

The owners of a local sporting goods store want to expand their kids' inventory. They decide to conduct a survey at the local middle school to find out what types of sporting activities local students are most interested in. The results of the survey will determine which items they'll stock in the store.

What would be the most reliable way to collect this information without surveying the entire school population?

a. Survey every fourth person that enters the post office.

b. Survey the student baseball and softball teams.

c. Survey every tenth student as they enter school.

- **Option A** isn't a valid sample because the sample members aren't all children.

- **Option B** also isn't a valid sample because the students weren't selected randomly, as the teams are sub-groups of the students at the school. This sample may also be too small to be reliable based on how many students attend the school. Because this sample isn't a true representation of the population, it would be considered a non-valid sample. It's also a biased sample since it's only the baseball and softball teams.

- **Option C** asks every tenth child at random as they enter school. This would give a better representation of the entire school and provide the most reliable data. So, this is a valid sample.

> **valid sample:** a subset of the entire population that accurately represents the entire population on a smaller scale
>
> **non-valid sample:** a subset of the entire population that does not give a true representation of the whole
>
> **biased sample:** a type of non-valid sample that occurs when individuals or groups of the entire population are not represented in the sample group

YOUR TURN!

A mobile pet groomer wants to expand his services to a new neighborhood. To collect reliable data:

1. Describe a valid method of collecting data without surveying the entire neighborhood.

2. Think about what statistical question could be asked and answered once the data is collected.

USING DATA TO MAKE INFERENCES AND GENERALIZATIONS ABOUT A POPULATION

Once data is collected, a number of inferences and generalizations can be made. Inference means drawing a conclusion or making a judgment. If you infer that something has happened, you don't experience the actual event. For example, when you analyze data from a survey about what pet types people have, you might infer that 30% of people have cats. When you make a statement about all (or most) of the people or objects together, you're making a generalization. For example, you could generalize from a survey that most students' favorite school lunch is pizza.

> **inference:** to draw a conclusion based on information/data that was not explicitly stated; making connections between background knowledge and evidence
>
> **generalization:** a statement or conclusion that is made for a situation or relationship based on data or repeated reasoning

TAKE A CLOSER LOOK

The bar graph below represents data that was collected at Yellowstone National Park. One hundred people who entered the park during August were asked: *"How many days did you go camping last year?"* Analyze the results of the "Days Spent Camping" data chart.

CAMPING DATA COLLECTED AT YELLOWSTONE NATIONAL PARK

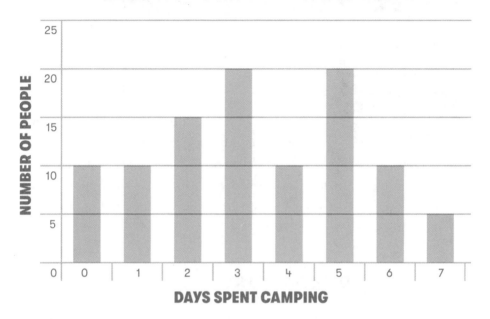

From the data you can infer:

- Twenty people spent 3 days camping, and another 20 people spent 5 days camping.

- Only 5 people spent 7 days camping, and 10 people didn't camp at all.

- You could also answer the question, "What's the average number of days this sample of people camped last year?" If the average is low, you could generalize that they don't go camping that often.

- The range of days spent camping by this sample is between 0 and 7 days. You could infer from the data that, in general, this group of people doesn't go camping more than 7 days per year.

Since this sample consists only of 100 people that were surveyed at Yellowstone National Park, you couldn't make inferences and generalizations to the population of the entire country about their days spent camping last year.

DISTRIBUTION OF DATA: MEAN, MEDIAN, MODE, AND RANGE

You're back visiting your bird-watching cousin again, and this time, you're helping to organize the data you and she have gathered.

There are countless types of charts and graphs to display and organize data: line graphs, scatter plots, pie charts, bar graphs, box and whisker plots, stem and leaf plots, and many more. Before determining which will best visualize the birding data you've collected, let's start by looking at a set of data for a group of birds.

PRIOR KNOWLEDGE

Data lists can be very long and sometimes difficult to read. A visual, like a **histogram**, can help you see and analyze data quickly. For this list of weights for 15 American robins, the numbers are very similar to each other, and not in order from least to greatest:

2.1 oz., 2.8 oz., 2.3 oz., 2.4 oz., 3.1 oz., 3.3 oz., 2.6 oz., 2.7 oz., 2.7 oz., 2.7 oz., 2.2 oz., 2.8 oz. 2.4 oz., 2.5 oz., 3.3 oz.

Presented as a list of numbers, it's a lot to process. But look what happens when you group the numbers by the frequency with which they occur—that is, in the form of a histogram.

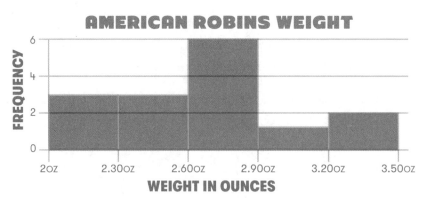

AMERICAN ROBINS WEIGHT

Suddenly, there's a shape to the data!

The bar of a histogram can have data points either inside the bar or on the edge of the bar. For this histogram, it's important to compare it to the list of data in order to be sure of the least and greatest values. Here's the data from least to greatest:

2.1, 2.2, 2.3, 2.4, 2.4, 2.5, 2.6, 2.7, 2.7, 2.7, 2.8, 2.8, 3.1, 3.3, 3.3

LEAST VALUE

GREATEST VALUE

Looking at the data in order helps you measure the variation of data using the range. Finding the difference between the least and greatest values gives you the data's range. When using range to measure data's variation, it's important to remember:

1. A smaller range means the data's distribution is less spread out.

2. A larger range shows that the data's distribution is more spread out.

For this data, the range of bird weights is from 2.1 to 3.3, a difference of 1.2 oz.

histogram: a visual display format in which particular quantities or ranges are grouped by frequency of occurrence, usually represented by bars of varying heights

distribution: the spread of the data points within the data set

range: the difference between the least and greatest value in the data set

FINDING THE MEAN (AVERAGE)

The center of the data helps us understand what the mean or average weight of the birds might be. Take another look at the histogram. *What is a good estimate for the average weight of American robins?* It looks like the center of the histogram is between 2.5 and 2.7 oz. Let's check to see if we're correct. The average (or mean) is the sum of all the weights divided by the number of birds:

Total of the Data Values ÷ Number of Data Values = Average of the Data Set

39.7 ÷ 15 = 2.66 ≈ 2.7 oz.

FINDING THE MEDIAN OF A DATA SET

- When you have an odd number of values, the median is the number in the middle of the data, which is also 2.7 oz.

2.1, 2.2, 2.3, 2.4, 2.4, 2.5, 2.6, 2.7, 2.7, 2.7, 2.8, 2.8, 3.1, 3.3, 3.3

least value   *greatest value*

This data set has an odd number of values, which is why the median has 7 values to the left and 7 values to the right.

- Let's look at another set of data for when there's an *even number of values.*

MEDIAN
↓

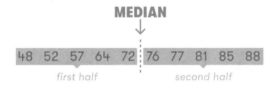

48 52 57 64 72 ⋮ 76 77 81 85 88

first half   *second half*

- Since we have an even number of data values, the median will be between the two middle numbers. To find it, calculate the average of the two middle numbers.

$$\frac{(72 + 76)}{2} = \frac{148}{2} = 74 = median$$

The median of the above data set is 74.

It may also be useful for you to know the **mode**—the number that occurs most often—of your data set. In the example with the odd number of values, the number 2.7 appears three times—at least once more than any other number. That is the mode.

Median, mean, and mode are the three measures of center. They are all ways of trying to understand and interpret data by defining the central position of the data set.

TOOLS FOR SUCCESS

You've already seen how histograms can effectively and simply display complex data in the example involving American robins on page 410. When considering whether a histogram is a useful way to display your data, it's important to remember:

1. It represents a frequency of distribution, similar to a dot plot, but in a bar chart form.

2. Each bar is grouped into ranges or intervals, not individual values.

3. Histograms can show data with larger ranges without being too wide.

mean: the average value for the entire data set (sum of value ÷ number of values in the data set)

median: the middle number of the data set once the list of values is in least to greatest order

mode: the number that occurs most often in your data set.

frequency: the number of times a particular quantity/data point is repeated in the data set (group)

measure of center/central tendency: measures the "center" or general behavior of the data set; includes mean, mode, and median

YOUR TURN!

Look at the data table below.

Find the mean (average), mode, range, and median for the following data for both male birds and female birds.

DATA TABLE	
WEIGHT OF MALE BIRDS (oz)	**WEIGHT OF FEMALE BIRDS (oz)**
35	19
36	19
27	20
35	20
32	21
26	22
28	22
31	22
30	23
35	23
33	24
27	26
28	27
36	27
32	28
36	29

MORE DATA DISPLAYS

DOT PLOTS, STEM AND LEAF PLOTS, BOX AND WHISKER PLOTS

Determining which type of data display to use often depends on the type of data you have. Let's begin with the simplest: the **dot plot**.

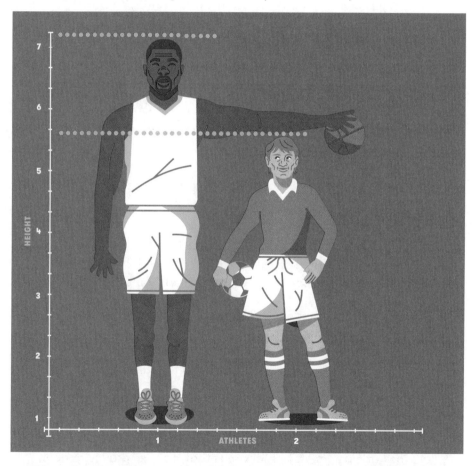

dot plot: a display format for representing repeated data points in a stacked format

If you wanted to compare the heights of a soccer team's players to those of a basketball team's players, you could create dot plots of their heights like these:

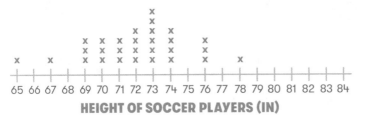

HEIGHT OF SOCCER PLAYERS (IN)

Key:

*Each dot (**x**) stands for a player, and the dot's location tells you that player's height in inches.*

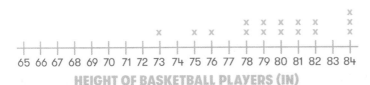

HEIGHT OF BASKETBALL PLAYERS (IN)

What do you notice about each of the two dot plots? What's the height of the shortest player on each team? The tallest ones? On average, how tall are the soccer players? The basketball players? Are there the same number of soccer players as basketball players?

These are just some of the questions you can answer by looking at the dot plots—and here are their answers.

- The dot plot for the soccer players not only has more dots, but most of the points are to the left of 77 inches. For the basketball players, most of the points are to the right of 77 inches.

- The shortest soccer player is 65 inches, and the shortest basketball player is 73 inches.

- The tallest soccer player is 78 inches, and the tallest basketball player is 84 inches.

- There are 29 soccer players and only 16 basketball players.

Now let's look at clusters of dots, or areas that look like groups of dots. *Where are most of the dots for the soccer players? For the basketball players? How does this help us compare information?*

There's a cluster of dots for soccer players between 72 and 74 inches with approximately the same number of dots on either side. This is where the mean height of the soccer players is located, about 72 inches. For the basketball players, this location is between 79 and 81 inches, or 80 inches if you were to calculate the mean. *How do these average heights compare?* By subtracting the means, you can see that the basketball players are on average 7.68 inches taller than the soccer players. That's more than half a foot!

The dot plots also tell you about the range of heights among the players: between 65 and 78 inches for soccer players, and between 73 and 84 for basketball players. Although there's a little bit of overlap with heights, it's clear that most of the basketball players are taller than the soccer players.

THE SHAPE OF DATA

The shape of the data refers to what the graph or dot plot looks like: *Are there more data points on the left, the right, or are they mostly in the middle with a few on each side?* Let's use dot plots to look at different clusters of points.

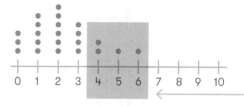

Here, the points are clustered to the left and get smaller in quantity as you move to the right.

*This dot plot has a **tail** on the right side.*

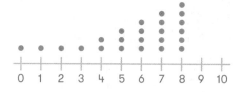

*This dot plot has points clustered to the right and a **tail** going to the left.*

This dot plot appears to be more even from the center, moving to the right and the left, away from the tallest set of points.

What about any gaps that might exist in a dot plot? What does this tell you about the data? The gaps in the points from left to right tells you that there are no data points that have those values. Sometimes gaps will be equally spaced, like the dot plots with tails above, meaning that only the whole numbers are used. But others, like the bottom dot plot, show you that there are decimal values for some of the data points.

YOUR TURN!

Describe some inferences, generalizations, and information that you can gather about the following dot plot about fuel economy.

FUEL ECONOMY FOR A RANDOM SAMPLE OF 2015 MODEL YEAR VEHICLES

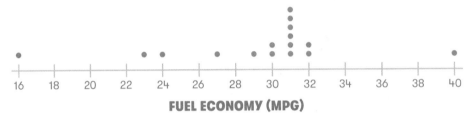

FUEL ECONOMY (MPG)

CHOOSING A DISPLAY

The environmental club at your school has some new data for you to look at. After measuring a field of mature trees, the club organized the data into an ordered list:

Measurement of Trees
(to the nearest foot)
11, 12, 13, 14, 17. 19, 20, 21, 22, 22, 23, 23, 24, 25, 26, 27, 27, 28, 28, 29, 30, 31, 31, 32, 33, 33, 34, 35, 42, 43, 43, 44, 45

It's important to consider the range of data when deciding which display to use.

Let's look at the range for this data.

$$\text{largest value} - \text{smallest value} = \text{range}$$

$$45 - 11 = 34$$

Since the range for this data is 34, if you were to use a dot plot, there would be a lot of values on the number line. Since the values don't repeat very often, there would be only a few places with stacked dots. A dot plot for this data set might not even fit on this page!

TAKE A CLOSER LOOK

You can group the tree heights into intervals of numbers, or numerical clusters, and then create a graph based on those groups. Typically, you want to create intervals that won't make too many groups. For example, let's say you use groups of 10: (10 to 19), (20 to 29), (30 to 39), and (40 to 49). This makes four intervals, which will create a good continuous display of the data without any gaps. Remember, all histograms are continuous!

A **stem and leaf display** also works really well for showing this organization of data:

> **stem and leaf display:** a display that is used for frequency of data values with a range over 10s, where the tens place and ones place are separated as "stem" and "leaf" respectively.

MEASUREMENT OF TREES (TO NEAREST FOOT)

1	1, 2, 3, 4, 7, 9
2	0, 1, 2, 2, 3, 3, 4, 5, 6, 7, 7, 8, 8, 9
3	0, 1, 1, 2, 3, 3, 4, 5
4	2, 3, 3, 4, 5

KEY: 4 (tens place) | 5 (ones place) = 45

Count the number of values in each group:

MEASUREMENT OF TREES (TO NEAREST FOOT)

1	1, 2, 3, 4, 7, 9	**6** (10–19)
2	0, 1, 2, 2, 3, 3, 4, 5, 6, 7, 7, 8, 8, 9	**14** (20–29)
3	0, 1, 1, 2, 3, 3, 4, 5	**8** (30–39)
4	2, 3, 3, 4, 5	**5** (40–49)

KEY: 4 | 5 = 45

Now that you have the number of data points for each interval, your intervals are equivalent in range and you have no gaps. Here's what the histogram and stem and leaf plot would look like.

HEIGHT OF MATURE TREES

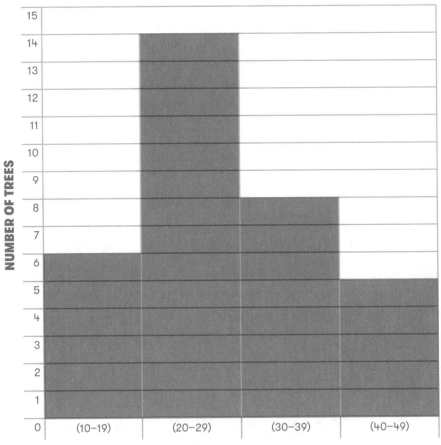

NUMBER OF TREES

HEIGHT OF TREES (TO NEAREST FOOT)

What can you say about the overall shape of this graph? What about the center?

The shape shows the largest cluster of points to be in the 20- to 29-foot interval, and that's also where the center of data is located. And, in creating the graph, you've already discovered the range (or spread of data). So, creating the histogram not only gives you a great visual, but it also helps you answer specific questions about the data!

🔍 TAKE A CLOSER LOOK

Let's take a closer look at stem and leaf plots. When you have a large group of data points, using a stem and leaf plot helps you show more by writing less!

Think about how a plant grows—not just the trees you've looked at so far, but all plants. For most of them, you can't have leaves without stems, since the stems grow first. Well, so does the stem and leaf plot. Each data point starts with the stem and finishes with the leaf, both representing place value (hundreds, tens, ones, etc.).

MEASUREMENT OF TREES (TO NEAREST FOOT)

STEM	LEAF
1	1, 2, 3, 4, 7, 9
2	0, 1, 2, 2, 3, 3, 4, 5, 6, 7, 7, 8, 8, 9
3	0, 1, 1, 2, 3, 3, 4, 5
4	2, 3, 3, 4, 5

Look at the example in the fourth stem. The first data point is 42 because the 4 in the stem represents the tens place and the 2 from the leaf is the ones place. If you write them next to each other, you'll get 42. The second data point in the fourth stem would be 43, then 43 again, and so on.

There are 14 numbers in the second stem. See if you can list all the numbers.

The numbers are: 20, 21, 22, 22, 23, 23, 24, 25, 26, 27, 27, 28, 28, 29.

How do you think the center, shape, and spread of this stem and leaf plot are similar to what we saw in the histogram? Let's take a look at the stem and leaf plot first.

STEM	LEAF
1	1, 2, 3, 4, 7, 9
2	0, 1, 2, 2, 3, 3, 4, 5, 6, 7, 7, 8, 8, 9
3	0, 1, 1, 2, 3, 3, 4, 5
4	2, 3, 3, 4, 5

Now let's compare it to a histogram:

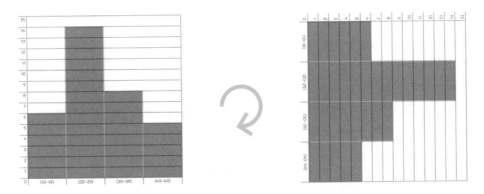

Can you see that if you were to rotate the histogram to the right that it looks just like the stem and leaf plot? Even though the stem and leaf plot represents the data in a kind of sideways fashion, you can still see the center, shape, and spread. You can almost immediately see that there are more numbers in the 20s than any other group of values. The fewest values occur in the 40s. No matter the type of display, the data will always have the same center, shape, and spread!

TOOLS FOR SUCCESS

When creating or reading a stem and leaf plot, it's important to remember:

1. The stems are going to be the greater place values for the data points, often the tens or hundreds place.

2. The leaves will be the next or last place value(s) to follow the stems.

3. If a stem is 0, it means that the data points are smaller than the place value of the other stems.

If a stem doesn't have any leaves, there's no data for that place value.

DOT PLOTS: A CLOSER LOOK

Just as we're ready to dig a little deeper into dot plots, your birdwatcher cousin calls, and she asks you to help with an important project: the Great Backyard Bird count. It's a nationwide bird census organized by the Audubon Society and Cornell University. Your job is to record the number of birds each person in your area has sighted. Your list:

3, 4, 4, 5, 5, 5, 6, 6, 7, 7, 7, 7, 7, 8, 8, 8, 10, 11, 11, 12

In the bird census, there are only 20 data points total, and the range is fairly small (12 – 3 = 9). It's this type of data set, small to medium, that works best for using dot plots. But, how do they work? We talked about some of the features when we compared heights of soccer and basketball players, but now we'll use just one dot plot to discuss specific features.

TAKE A CLOSER LOOK

Let's look at the range of data so we can create a good number line, similar to the way we created the histogram. Do you think we need decimals? Think about it this way: would you ever try to catch only parts of birds? No way! Decimals just don't work for this type of data because only whole birds count!

1. Start with a number line. The range was 3 to 12, so start the number line at 3 and end it at 12.

2. Add a dot for each data point above the corresponding number on the line. Each dot represents a person who saw that number of birds. You can stack the dots on top of each other if there's more than one data point for a particular number.

The stacking or vertical amounts above each number tell you the frequency of that value, and in this case the number of people that saw that many birds.

3. Look at the dots above the 4 in the number line below. This means that 2 people saw 4 birds. 3 people saw 5 birds, etc.

What do you notice? Why do you think a dot plot is a good display for this data? What does the gap mean?

Before talking about the center, shape, and spread for this data, let's look at how this can be displayed as a **box and whisker plot**.

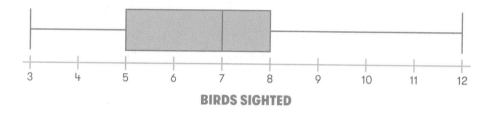

BIRDS SIGHTED

How does this box and whisker plot compare to the dot plot for the same data set? What is the same, and what is different?

> **box and whisker plot**: a display for organizing data sets in groups called quartiles. It is identifiable by the way it looks: a box with "whisker" lines extending from it

Let's first identify the pieces of the box and whisker plot:

1. The box represents half of the data points. Notice that the center, spread, and mean are inside the box. For this reason, a box and whisker plot is a good way to visualize data in terms of groups.

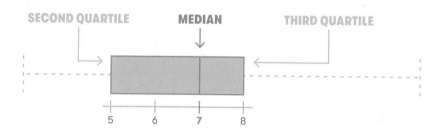

SECOND QUARTILE   MEDIAN   THIRD QUARTILE

2. The whiskers are attached to the box, one on either side, and they represent the other half of the data, split in two pieces. Notice the least and greatest values are in the whiskers.

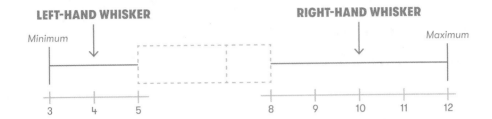

LEFT-HAND WHISKER   RIGHT-HAND WHISKER

Minimum   Maximum

3   4   5   8   9   10   11   12

If you look at either the dot plot or the box and whisker plot for this data set, you can see that the center is between 5 and 8, and the spread shows a range of 9 (difference from least to greatest).

What about the shape? Are any of the data points clustered to one side or another? Is one whisker significantly shorter/longer than the other? The center of the data is closer to the least value (3) than it is to the greatest value (12), so you can say that the shape of this data goes more to the left.

> **center of the data:** describes the "middle" of the data set, the general location where most of the data is located or clustered

YOUR TURN!

Below are examples involving dot plots, histograms, and stem and leaf plots.

1. The environmental club is measuring the circumference of saplings planted in a field last year. The results are displayed in the dot plot below.

FIRST YEAR SAPLIINGS

NUMBER OF SAPLINGS

2   3   4   5   6   7   8

TRUNK CIRCUMFERENCE (NEAREST INCH)

a. What circumference was found most frequently?

b. How many trees were measured to have a circumference of 5 inches or more?

c. What's the mean?

d. What's the median?

2. Organize the following tree heights in a stem and leaf plot. Then use the data to create a histogram.

20.3, 21.1, 22, 23, 24.2, 25, 26, 27.5, 27.8, 28, 28, 29, 29.9, 31, 33, 33, 34, 35.7, 35, 39.1, 39

HEIGHT OF TREES (TO NEAREST FOOT)

THE INTERQUARTILE RANGE

Let's look at the results of an archery tournament where 30 archers scored varying point totals based on their accuracy.

TOTAL ARCHERY POINTS

The average point total for an archer was 14.2 points.

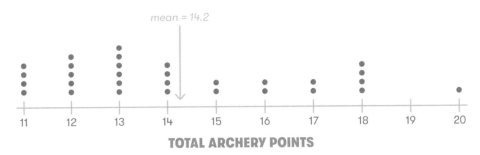

TOTAL ARCHERY POINTS

Both the median and the mean are in a cluster of points. Even though the median is less than the mean, they're close enough to each other that either can be used to talk about the center of the data set.

PRIOR KNOWLEDGE

As you saw earlier, range is a measure of variation. Unlike the center, measures of variation help you understand how the data is spread out.

In the archery data, the top score was 20 points and the lowest was 11.

$$20 - 11 = 9$$

$$range = 9$$

The range of points tells us that the difference between first value and last value was 9 points. To see if this spread is small or large in comparison to the data, we need to look a little more in depth at different clusters of data, this time using a box and whisker plot.

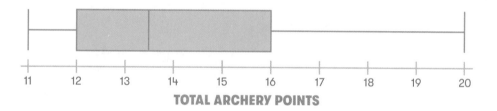

TOTAL ARCHERY POINTS

The minimum value and maximum value are easy to spot because they're at the end of the whiskers! But what does the box tell us?

$$median = 13.5$$

See how it can be labeled here:

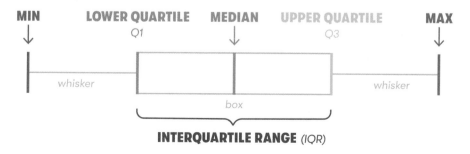

INTERQUARTILE RANGE *(IQR)*

You'll note that the median is right where we found it to be, at 13.5. Remember, box and whisker plots are a good way to show groups of data. Since the median is exactly half of the data set, we can split it again to get four groups; these clusters (groups) of information are called *quartiles*.

These quartiles can then be used to take a closer look at any given data set. You can use what's called the interquartile range (IQR) to get a more detailed measure of variability for the data. The IQR is most often used when a set of data contains extreme values called outliers.

> **interquartile range (IQR):** a more detailed measure of variability for the data set; it is the range within a quartile in a box and whisker plot
>
> **outlier:** a data point that does not behave the same as the majority of the data

TAKE A CLOSER LOOK

Let's use some data from the environmental club for a group of saplings to calculate the IQR.

FIRST YEAR SAPLINGS TRUNK DIAMETER (INCHES)

TOOLS FOR SUCCESS

Here's how you find the interquartile range:

1.2, 1.2, 1.2, 1.3, 1.3, 1.4, 1.4, 1.4, 1.8, 2.6, 2.6, 3.2, 3.2, 3.7, 4.1, 4.3, 4.3

Organize the data from least to greatest.

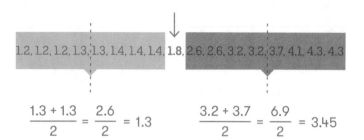

*Identify the **median**.*

$$\frac{1.3 + 1.3}{2} = \frac{2.6}{2} = 1.3 \qquad \frac{3.2 + 3.7}{2} = \frac{6.9}{2} = 3.45$$

Cut each half of the data in half, identifying those medians.

Now you have quartiles using these calculated values:

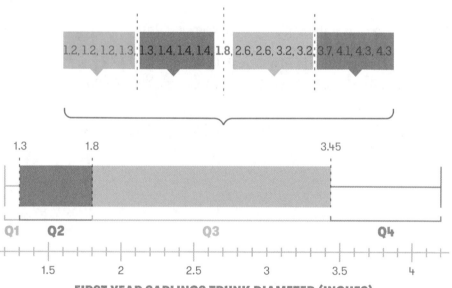

FIRST YEAR SAPLINGS TRUNK DIAMETER (INCHES)

To find the IQR, subtract Q_1 from Q_3.

$$Q_3 - Q_1 = IQR$$

$$3.45 - 1.3 = 2.15$$

$$IQR = 2.15$$

Nice work! This interquartile range of 2.15 focuses on the spread of data around the middle of the data.

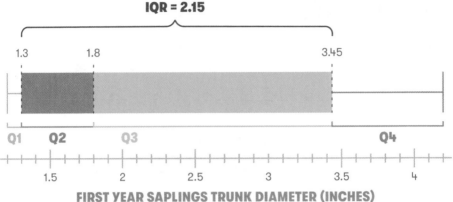

YOUR TURN!

Create a box and whisker plot for the following data:

Average Temperature in Pittsburgh in June:

79, 70, 73, 84, 83, 88, 75, 72, 76, 68, 68, 79, 84, 74, 75, 85, 67, 78, 69, 80

BOX AND WHISKER CHECKLIST

☐ First Whisker

☐ First Quartile: Median of First Half

☐ Median

☐ Third Quartile: Median of Second Half

☐ Last Whisker

FINDING MEASURES OF VARIATION

There's a lot of information surrounding the middle data of a set. The closer you look at the measure of variation, the easier it is to determine if your data is good. The best place to look is at the mean absolute deviation (MAD). When the MAD is close to zero, then the mean is said to be a good representation of the data as a whole. You're looking for the margin for error above or below the mean to be as small as possible, or the lowest gap.

> **mean absolute deviation (MAD):** value found from a dataset that is the average number between each data point and the mean

PRIOR KNOWLEDGE

The heights of first year saplings (young trees) were measured with the results listed in the chart below.

SAPLINGS	HEIGHTS (to the nearest half inch)
Tree A	22.5
Tree B	20
Tree C	21.5
Tree D	23
Tree E	24
Tree F	19.5
Tree G	20
Tree H	23.5

First let's start by finding the mean height of the saplings.

22.5 + 20 + 21.5 + 23 + 24 + 19.5 +
20 + 23.5 = 174

Find the sum of the data.

Mean = 174 ÷ 8 = 21.75" per tree

Divide by the number of data points.

Now for the satisfying part! It's time to calculate the mean absolute deviation. This will help you tell if 21.75 inches per tree is a good representation for this group of trees.

 TOOLS FOR SUCCESS

Find the difference between each data point and the mean.

SAPLINGS	HEIGHTS (to the nearest half inch)	DIFFERENCE OF HEIGHTS FROM THE MEAN (deviation)
Tree A	22.5	22.5 − 21.75 = 0.75
Tree B	20	20 − 21.75 = −1.75
Tree C	21.5	21.5 − 21.75 = −0.25
Tree D	23	23 − 21.75 = 1.25
Tree E	24	24 − 21.75 = 2.25
Tree F	19.5	19.5 − 21.75 = −2.25
Tree G	20	20 − 21.75 = −1.75
Tree H	23.5	23.5 − 21.75 = 1.75

0.75 + |−1.75| + |−0.25| + 1.25 +
2.25 + |−2.25| + |−1.75| + 1.75 = 12

List and add the absolute values for each of the differences.

12 ÷ 8 = 1.5

Divide the sum by the number of data points.

The *mean absolute deviation* is 1.5.

Here's how you interpret the MAD: you compare it to the overall range of data.

Since the MAD of 1.5 is a small number in relation to the range of the data set, the mean of 21.75 inches is a good representation for this set of data.

YOUR TURN!

1. The wingspans for some swallows, a protected bird species, were measured. The results are listed in the chart below.

SWALLOWS	WINGSPANS (to the nearest half inch)	DIFFERENCE OF WINGSPANS FROM THE MEAN (deviation)
Swallow A	11.5	
Swallow B	10	
Swallow C	11.5	
Swallow D	9.5	
Swallow E	12	

a. Find the range of this data.

b. Find the mean absolute deviation for the wingspans of this set of swallows.

c. Decide if the mean is a good representation for this data set.

2. Find the median, mean, and range of the data in the dot plot below.

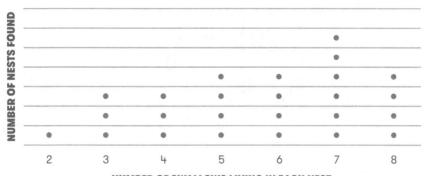

SWALLOWS LIVING IN EACH NEST

NUMBER OF NESTS FOUND

NUMBER OF SWALLOWS LIVING IN EACH NEST

COMPARING POPULATIONS

You've learned a great deal about statistics up to this point, and by far, the measures of center and variation have required the most calculations. Now, you'll take it one step further by comparing multiple populations.

TAKE A CLOSER LOOK

A man-made lake in a new community was stocked with equal populations of catfish and bass. After one year, data was collected to determine the status of the two populations. *Did the populations of catfish and bass remain fairly equal? Should the lake be restocked with one fish type more than the other?*

Random samples were collected by net in ten different areas of the lake. Each different type of fish was counted, with the results listed in the following table and dot plot.

FISH	NUMBER OF FISH NETTED									
CATFISH	60	43	58	69	50	37	68	46	55	65
BASS	51	46	48	60	45	46	58	46	34	33

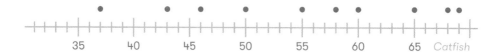

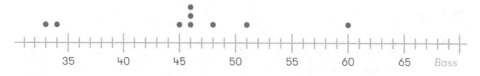

NUMBER OF FISH NETTED

Examine the distribution of both data sets on the dot plot. *How do they differ? How are they the same?* Calculating the ranges for both sets will help us talk about what we see in each dot plot and how they compare to each other.

Catfish Range: 69 – 37 = 32
Bass Range: 60 – 33 = 27

Although the ranges of the data for both fish are fairly close to one another, there's clearly a cluster of data for the bass just below 50, but the catfish seem to be more evenly spread across its range. The catfish have a greater maximum number of fish netted, while the bass have the lesser of the two minimums. Next, let's compare the average of the two sample data sets.

CATFISH MEAN	BASS MEAN
60 + 43 + 58 + 69 + 50 + 37 + 68 + 46 + 55 + 65 = 551	51 + 46 + 48 + 60 + 45 + 46 + 58 + 46 + 34 + 33= 467
551 ÷ 10 = 55.1	467 ÷ 10 = 46.7
mean = 55.1 catfish netted	mean = 46.7 bass netted

Mean Difference: 55.1 – 46.7 = 8.4

The mean difference between these sample means of 8.4 makes it appear that the total population of catfish is now more than the total population of bass. However, because of sampling variability, this may not be true, so we'd need to investigate more to say this for sure. Let's find the number of mean absolute deviations that separates the two samples to check how accurate our data is.

 TOOLS FOR SUCCESS

CATFISH	FISH	DIFFERENCE OF NUMBER FROM THE MEAN (deviation)
Net 1	60	60 − 55.1 = 4.9
Net 2	43	43 − 55.1 = −12.1
Net 3	58	58 − 55.1 = 2.9
Net 4	69	69 − 55.1 = 13.9
Net 5	50	50 − 55.1 = −5.1
Net 6	37	37 − 55.1 = −18.1
Net 7	68	68 − 55.1 = 12.9
Net 8	46	46 − 55.1 = −9.1
Net 9	55	55 − 55.1 = −0.1
Net 10	65	65 − 55.1 = 9.9

BASS	FISH	DIFFERENCE OF NUMBER FROM THE MEAN (deviation)
Net 1	51	51 − 46.7 = 4.3
Net 2	46	46 − 46.7 = −0.7
Net 3	48	48 − 46.7 = 1.3
Net 4	60	60 − 46.7 = 13.3
Net 5	45	45 − 46.7 = −1.7
Net 6	46	46 − 46.7 = −0.7
Net 7	58	58 − 46.7 = 11.3
Net 8	46	46 − 46.7 = −0.7
Net 9	34	34 − 46.7 = −12.7
Net 10	33	33 − 46.7 = −13.7

CATFISH	BASS
4.9 + |−12.1| + 2.9 + 13.9 + |−5.1| + |−18.1| + 12.9 + |−9.1| + |−0.1| + 9.9 = 89	4.3 + |−0.7| + 1.3 + 13.3 + |−1.7| + |−0.7| + 11.3 + |−0.7| + |−12.7| + |−13.7| = 60.4
89 ÷ 10 = 8.9 **MAD** = 8.9	60.4 ÷ 10 = 6.04 **MAD** = 6.04

Unsure where to start? Let's find the number of mean absolute deviations first.

55.1 − 46.7 = 8.4   *Find the difference of the two means.*

8.9 is the larger of the two MADs.

8.4 ÷ 8.9 = 0.943. . .   *Divide the difference of the two means by the larger of the two MADs.*

0.943. . . < 2   *Compare the number of means.*

Since the number of MADs is less than 2, there's not much difference between the population of catfish and bass in the entire lake. Looks like we don't need to add more of one type of fish to maintain an equivalent population of both fish.

Phew. You've learned a lot. Let's see how you tie it all together.

YOUR TURN!

A seventh-grade student was conducting a survey for his math project. He wanted to know if sixth and seventh graders spend the same amount of time playing video games. Ten sixth graders and ten seventh graders are randomly sampled to answer the question: How many hours do you spend playing video games each week? The results of the survey are listed below:

GRADE	NUMBER OF HOURS PLAYED WEEKLY									
6TH GRADE	10	15	11	12	18	20	10	15	13	16
7TH GRADE	21	13	15	25	16	17	25	10	28	10

Statistical question:

On average, is there a substantial difference in the amount of time that sixth graders and seventh graders spend playing video games?

1. Create a dot plot to represent the data set for both sample groups.

2. Calculate the mean, median, mode, and range for both populations.

CENTRAL TENDENCY	SIXTH	SEVENTH
RANGE		
MEAN		
MEDIAN		
MODE		

3. Find the difference in the mean time spent playing video games by grade.

4. Find the mean absolute deviation to verify your data.

5. Write a generalization about the two populations.

CHAPTER SUMMARY

STATISTICAL VARIABILITY

Statistical questions should provide an adequate number of valid data—at least two or more results. **Non-statistical questions** have no variability in their data and can only provide one valid result. Example: "Do you have brown eyes?" is non-statistical; "How many people in our town have brown eyes?" is statistical.

USING DATA TO MAKE INFERENCES AND GENERALIZATIONS ABOUT A POPULATION

- When you're collecting data to analyze a population, unless you can collect data from the entire population, you need to collect it from a **representative sample**. This a smaller group that should represent the whole population as closely as possible.

- A **random sample** is different than a representative sample in that it is chosen at "random" or by chance. For example, if you are choosing marbles from a bag of mixed colors and patterns, it's possible (though unlikely) that you'd choose all of the same variety if you are choosing *randomly*. If you were to choose a *representative* sample, you might choose one marble of each color and pattern

- Once data is collected, a number of **inferences** and **generalizations** can be made by looking at the "shape" of the data.

  - **Central Tendency:** This is the analysis of the way that data "behaves" in the center. We use these ideas to interpret data sets.

  - **Mean:** This is the average of the data set.

  - **Median:** This is the middle value of the data set.

  - **Mode:** The value that occurs most often in a data set.

- **Range:** This is the difference between the greatest and least (the technical terms for biggest and smallest) number in the data set. It also will tell you what number the data starts with and ends with.

DATA DISPLAYS

We discussed different representations that could be helpful based on the amount or type of data you're working with. It's important to choose your representation wisely. The representations are used to display frequency (how often something occurs).

- **Dot Plot:** This is mostly used when you have data that has a lot of repetition. This is based on repetition of single data points (i.e., numbers, colors).

- **Histogram:** We mostly use this connected bar graph model if we want to display data based on a continuous range.

- **Stem and Leaf Plot:** This format is mainly used to represent the number of times specific numbers or quantities arise in a data set. This plot will allow you to easily complete other representations. This is a great way to organize large sets of numerical data.

- **Box and Whisker Plot:** This plot does a great job of displaying the spread of the data. If there's clustering in the data, it shows up clearly in a box and whisker plot. The same is true for outliers in the data.

COMPARING POPULATIONS

You can analyze individual populations and compare two different populations by comparing the difference between their ranges, means, modes, and medians.

- Check the validity of your data by determining their mean absolute deviations (MADs): the average number between each data point and the mean.

CHAPTER 12 VOCABULARY

biased sample: a type of non-valid sample that occurs when individuals or groups of the entire population are not represented in the sample group

box and whisker plot: a display for organizing data sets in groups called quartiles. It is identifiable by the way it looks: a box with "whisker" lines extending from it.

center of the data: describes the "middle" of the data set, the general location where most of the data is located or clustered

data: a set of information (usually numbers) that represents a situation or parameters (e.g., number of birds watched)

distribution: the spread of the data points within the data set

dot plot: a display format for representing repeated data points in a stacked format

frequency: the number of times a particular quantity/data point is repeated in the data set (*group*)

generalization: a statement or conclusion that is made for a situation or relationship based on data or repeated reasoning

histogram: a visual display format in which particular quantities or ranges are grouped by frequency of occurrence, usually represented by bars of varying heights

inference: to draw a conclusion based on information/data that was not explicitly stated

interquartile range (IQR): a more detailed measure of variability for the data set; it is the range within a quartile in a box and whisker plot

mean absolute deviation (MAD): value found from a dataset that is the average number between each data point and the mean

measure of center/central tendency: measures the "center" or general behavior of the data set; includes mean, mode, and median

median: the middle number of the data set once the list of values is in least to greatest order

mean: the average value for the entire data set *(sum of value ÷ number of values in the data set)*

mode: the value that appears most frequently in a data set

non-statistical question: a question that only has one possible answer, collected from a single source of data

non-valid sample: a subset of the entire population that does not give a true representation of the whole.

outlier: a data point that does not behave the same as the majority of the data

random sample: a group of data that is collected without reason *(i.e., blindly choosing)*

range: the difference between the least and greatest value in the data set

representative sample: a small portion of a larger data set that should represent the larger data set's behavior

statistical question: a question with many possible answers that will be collected from a sample population

stem and leaf display: a display that is used for frequency of data values with a range over 10s, where the tens place and ones place are separated as "stem" and "leaf" respectively

valid sample: a subset of the entire population that accurately represents the entire population on a smaller scale

variability: the differences between the data points

CHAPTER 12 ANSWER KEY

STATISTICAL VARIABILITY (P. 401)

1. The question is *non-statistical* because there will be only one result in the data.

2. The question is *statistical* because you'll collect many results and then find the average.

3. The question is *statistical* because you'll collect many results and then find the average.

4. The question is *non-statistical* because there will be only one result in the data.

WHEN DO WE SAMPLE? (P. 405)

1. Since there's a limited number of students in the class, the entire population can be surveyed.

2. Each school has a lot of students, so it would be hard to survey the entire population about how many sports drinks they consume. This would be better if a sample of the population was surveyed.

VALID VS. NON-VALID SAMPLES (P. 407)

1. Survey two houses per street throughout the entire neighborhood.

2. You could ask something like *Do you have any animals that require grooming?* The answer to this question could tell you if there's enough of a pet population in the area to get enough business.

DISTRIBUTION OF DATA: MEAN, MODE, RANGE, AND MEDIAN (P. 414)

	WEIGHTS OF MALE BIRDS (OZ.)	WEIGHTS OF FEMALE BIRDS (OZ.)
MEAN	31.6875	23.25
MODE	35, 36 (both appear 3 times)	22
RANGE	10	10
MEDIAN	32	22.5

DOT PLOTS, HISTOGRAMS, STEM AND LEAF PLOTS, BOX AND WHISKER PLOTS (P. 418)

We can infer and generalize some information:

- MPG that is most often is 31 MPG. This is the mode.

- The two outliers are 16 and 40 MPG.

- The range is 24.

- We can generalize that most cars have similar MPG.

DOT PLOTS, HISTOGRAMS, STEM AND LEAF PLOTS, BOX AND WHISKER (PP. 426–427)

1. a. 7 inches
   c. 5.44 inches

   b. 18 trees
   d. 6 inches

2.

STEM	LEAF
20	3
21	1
22	0
23	0
24	2
25	0
26	0
27	5, 8
28	0, 0
29	0, 9
30	
31	0
32	
33	0, 0
34	0
35	0, 7
.	
39	0, 1

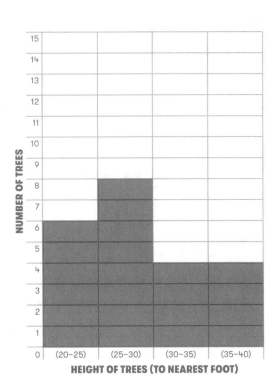

FINDING MEASURES OF CENTER (P. 432)

Average Temperature in Pittsburgh in June:

79, 70, 73, 84, 83, 88, 75, 72, 76, 68, 68, 79, 84, 74, 75, 85, 67, 78, 69, 80

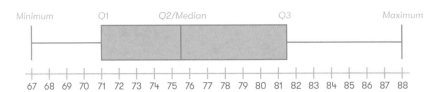

FINDING MEASURES OF VARIATION (P. 435)

1.

SWALLOWS	WINGSPANS (to the nearest half inch)	DIFFERENCE OF WINGSPANS FROM THE MEAN (deviation)
Swallow A	11.5	11.5 − 10.9 = 0.6
Swallow B	10	10 − 10.9 = −0.9
Swallow C	11.5	11.5 − 10.9 = 0.6
Swallow D	9.5	9.5 − 10.9 = −1.4
Swallow E	12	12 − 10.9 = 1.1

a. The range of wingspans is 2.5 (from 12 – 9.5).

b. To find the mean absolute deviation, you need the mean first:

$$11.5 + 10 + 11.5 + 9.5 + 12$$
$$= 54.5$$

$$\text{Mean} = \frac{54.5}{5} = 10.9 \text{ inches per swallow}$$

List and add the absolute values for each difference (from chart):

$$|0.6| + |-0.9| + |0.6| + |-1.4| + |1.1|$$
$$= 0.6 + 0.9 + 0.6 + 1.4 + 1.1$$
$$= 4.6$$

Divide by the number of data points:

$$\text{Mean Absolute Deviation} = \frac{4.6}{5} = 0.92$$

c. Since the mean absolute deviation is close to zero (0.92), the mean (10.9) is a good representation for this set of data.

2. First, use the dot plot to create a list of the data:

2, 3, 3, 3, 4, 4, 4, 5, 5, 5, 5, 6, 6, 6, 6, 7, 7, 7, 7, 7, 7, 8, 8, 8, 8

Median: 6 swallows per nest

$$\text{Average (mean)}: \frac{141}{25} = 5.64 \text{ swallows per nest}$$

Range: 6 (8 – 2)

COMPARING POPULATIONS (PP. 440–441)

Statistical question answer: answers will vary but should include statements that acknowledge some overlapping. The distribution of sixth graders' data is clustered toward the center, whereas the seventh graders' data is more distributed across the plot with time trending on the higher end.

1.

HOURS SIXTH GRADERS SPEND PLAYING VIDEO GAMES WEEKLY

HOURS SEVENTH GRADERS SPEND PLAYING VIDEO GAMES WEEKLY

2. Sample Central Tendencies

CENTRAL TENDENCY	SIXTH	SEVENTH
RANGE	10	18
MEAN	14 hours	18 hours
MEDIAN	14	16.5
MODE	10 & 15	10 & 25

3. It appears that seventh graders play video games on average 4 more hours than sixth graders.

4. To find mean absolute deviation:

SIXTH GRADERS	#	DIFFERENCE OF NUMBER FROM THE MEAN (deviation)
1	10	10 – 14 = –4
2	15	15 – 14 = 1
3	11	11 – 14 = –3
4	12	12 – 14 = –2
5	18	18 – 14 = 4
6	20	20 – 14 = 6

SEVENTH GRADERS	#	DIFFERENCE OF NUMBER FROM THE MEAN (deviation)
1	18	21 – 18 = 3
2	18	13 – 18 = –5
3	18	15 – 18 = –3
4	18	25 – 18 = 7
5	18	16 – 18 = –2
6	18	17 – 18 = –1

7	10	$10 - 14 = -4$	7	18	$25 - 18 = 7$
8	15	$15 - 14 = 1$	8	18	$10 - 18 = -8$
9	13	$13 - 14 = -1$	9	18	$28 - 18 = 10$
10	16	$16 - 14 = 2$	10	18	$10 - 18 = -8$

SIXTH GRADERS	SEVENTH GRADERS
$\lvert-4\rvert + 1 + \lvert-3\rvert + \lvert-2\rvert + 4 + 6 + \lvert-4\rvert + 1 + \lvert-1\rvert + 2 = 28$	$3 + \lvert-5\rvert + \lvert-3\rvert + 7 + \lvert-2\rvert + \lvert-1\rvert + 7 + \lvert-8\rvert + 10 + \lvert-8\rvert = 54$
$28 \div 10 = 2.8$ **MAD = 2.8**	$54 \div 10 = 5.4$ **MAD = 5.4**

It appears that the seventh grader's sample data has much more variability (5.4) than the sixth grader's sample data (2.8). For better results, another survey could be done with a larger sample (greater than 30) for each grade.

5. The difference between the two means: $18 - 14 = 4$

The larger of the two MADs: 5.4

$$\frac{4}{5.4} \approx .74$$

For the sample mean to represent the total population of sixth and seventh graders at this school, the mean absolute deviations should be greater than 2.

The MADs separating the sample mean of time spent between sixth and seventh graders is less than 2. So, there's not much difference in the variability. It can't be assumed that, on average, all seventh graders spend more time playing video games than all sixth graders in this school.

PROBABILITY

Here's some good news for almost everyone! If you've ever played a board game in your life, it's very likely that you've already gained some understanding of probability. The likelihood of an event occurring can be introduced through rolling dice or flicking a spinner. When outcomes (results) have an equal chance of happening, each player has the same likelihood of winning or getting the desired outcome.

PROBABILITY

Let's say that one rainy day at home, you and a friend invent a game called "The Great Pet Competition." The rules are:

THE GREAT PET COMPETITION

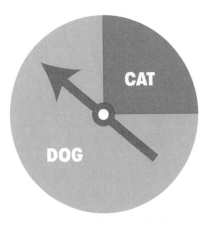

1. Each person chooses either "Dog" or "Cat," both of which are represented on a spinner.

2. The players take turns spinning the spinner. If it lands on their chosen animal, they get 1 point. If it lands on the other animal, they get 0 points.

3. The first player to earn 10 points is the winner!

outcome: a target event

🔍 TAKE A CLOSER LOOK

Now, study the spinner's design. What do you think the likelihood is of it landing on "Dog" versus "Cat"?

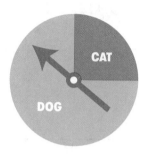

Visually, you can see that "Dog" takes up much more space on the spinner than "Cat." So, it's safe to say that the likelihood of landing on "Dog" is greater than the chance of landing on "Cat."

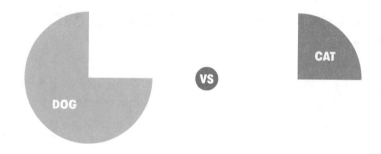

🥾 PRIOR KNOWLEDGE

Probability describes the chance, or likelihood, of an event occurring. As a number, probability is expressed as a fraction or decimal from 0 to 1, or as a percentage from 0% to 100%. The likelihood of an event occurring can be visualized on a probability scale.

IMPOSSIBLE	LESS LIKELY	EQUALLY LIKELY	MORE LIKELY	CERTAIN
0	$\frac{1}{4}$	$\frac{1}{2}$	$\frac{3}{4}$	1
0%	25%	50%	75%	100%

Look back at the spinner from "The Great Pet Competition." Where would the likelihoods of spinning "Dog" and "Cat" fall on this probability line?

Use the number line below to predict the likelihood of spinning a "Dog" or a "Cat":

How did you choose your predictions? How do the percentages help you understand which is more likely?

THE RANGE OF PROBABILITY: FROM IMPOSSIBLE TO CERTAIN

The "Dog" piece of the spinner represents three-fourths ($\frac{3}{4}$) of the circle, which is more than 50%. The "Cat" piece represents one-fourth ($\frac{1}{4}$) of the circle, which is less than 50%.

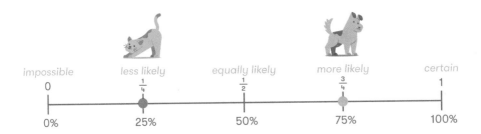

Since the area of the spinner for the "Dog" is about $\frac{3}{4}$ (or 75%) of the spinner, for any single spin, it's *more likely* you would land on "Dog." The area of the spinner for the "Cat" is about $\frac{1}{4}$ (or 25%) of the spinner. For any single spin, it's *less likely* you would land on "Cat."

Take a few minutes to practice these ideas of probability. Use the terms *impossible, less likely, equally likely, more likely,* and *certain* to describe the likelihood of the following events. Then assign a value from 0 to 1 according to the likelihood of the event happening.

a. _____ Your friends will use at least one social media app today.

b. _____ The month after February will be March.

c. _____ The Sun will rise in the west.

d. _____ You'll star in a TV series someday.

e. _____ The coin being flipped will land on heads or tails.

Let's see how these events look on a probability graph.

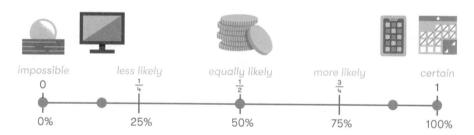

Now, let's break down how we got here for two of the trickier ones:

a. It's *almost certain* that your friends will use a social media app today, but can you be 100% certain? Internet connections can fail, batteries die, and devices can be misplaced. These small possibilities affect the likelihood of this event to be *almost* certain.

d. It's *very unlikely* that you'll get to star in a TV series someday, for a wide range of reasons. Although this event is *nearly* impossible, there's still a chance you'll become an actor.

TOOLS FOR SUCCESS

When determining the likelihood of an event occurring, it's important to remember:

- The chance or likelihood of an event occurring is a number on a scale from 0 to 1.
- It can be written as a fraction, a decimal, or a percentage.
- Impossible events have a probability of 0 (or 0%).
- Certain events have a probability of 1 (or 100%).
- Equally likely events have a probability of 0.5 ($\frac{1}{2}$ or 50%).

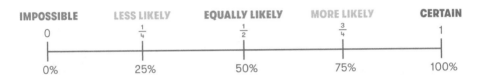

YOUR TURN!

Place the letters representing the events below on the probability scale according to their likelihood of occurring. Then assign a value from 0 to 1 according to the likelihood of the event happening.

a. _____ You'll win the lottery.

b. _____ The Sun will rise in the east.

c. _____ A football team will win the coin toss at the beginning of the game.

d. _____ A coin tossed will land on its side.

e. _____ It will rain gold.

THEORETICAL VS. EXPERIMENTAL PROBABILITY

BASICS AND THEORY

There are no age restrictions when it comes to Halloween, so you and some friends decide to go trick-or-treating. The night has been full of treats, until you arrive at your math teacher's house and she has a trick for you! She holds up a bag of candy and recites the following:

Three colors of candy,
In my bag so dandy.
Name a color and draw the same,
And all three colors you may claim.
Name a color and draw it not,
And leave here with an empty pot!

You have to guess which color you're going to pull from the bag before you can even look at it! Your math teacher isn't the only one with a trick up her sleeve. You ask for a practice round first, and your teacher allows it. You and your group of friends pull the following results:

RESULTS		TOTALS	
PICK	**COLOR**	**COLOR**	**TOTAL**
1	Red	Red	3
2	Blue	Blue	5
3	Yellow	Yellow	2
4	Blue		
5	Red		
6	Blue		
7	Red		
8	Blue		
9	Blue		
10	Yellow		

TAKE A CLOSER LOOK

You asked for a practice round to find out the likelihood of picking each color. With the 10 results from your experiment, you can use some rules and math symbols to show the likelihood, or the probability, that you will get the color you want.

PROBABILITY OF AN EVENT $\longrightarrow$ $P\ (Target\ Event) = \dfrac{Target\ Event}{Total\ Possible\ Events}$

For example, a lot of blue candies were picked. What was the probability of picking blue in your experiment?

$$P\ (Blue) = \underset{\underset{\text{Total picked}}{\uparrow}}{\overset{\overset{\text{Blues picked}}{\downarrow}}{\dfrac{Blue\ Candies}{Total\ Candies}}} = \dfrac{5}{10}\ or\ \dfrac{1}{2}$$

$$P\ (Blue) = \dfrac{5}{10}\ or\ 0.5\ or\ 50\%$$

How can you describe the likelihood of choosing blue? At 50%, you're equally likely to get blue as you are another color.

Using the tables from your experiment, try to find *P (Red)*. Set up the probability:

$$P\ (Red) = \frac{Red\ Candies}{Total\ Candies} = \frac{3}{10}$$

$$P\ (Red) = \frac{3}{10}\ \text{or } 0.3\ \text{or } 30\%$$

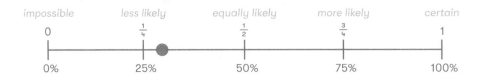

As you can see, the likelihood of getting an orange candy is slightly more than *less likely* and less than *equally likely*. So, this would be considered *unlikely*.

What about *P (Yellow)*? Set up the probability:

$$P\ (Yellow) = \frac{Yellow\ Candies}{Total\ Candies} = \frac{2}{10}\ \text{or } \frac{1}{5}$$

$$P\ (Yellow) = \frac{2}{10}\ \text{or } 0.2\ \text{or } 20\%$$

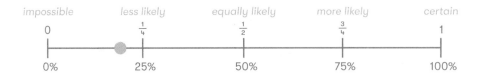

The likelihood of getting a yellow candy is slightly less than *less likely* and more than *impossible*. This would be considered *very unlikely*.

You've now figured out all three probabilities separately. When combined, they add up to 1 (or 100%).

$$P\ (Blue) + P\ (Red) + P\ (Yellow)$$

$$50\% + 30\% + 20\%$$

$$100\%$$

Here's another question: *What's the probability of not picking yellow?*

Obviously, you know that if you didn't pick yellow, you ended up with blue or orange. Check it out in visual terms:

So, by combining P (Blue) and P (Red), you'll have P (not Yellow).

$$P\ (not\ Yellow) = P\ (Blue) + P\ (Red)$$

$$P\ (not\ Yellow) = 50\% + 30\%$$

$$P\ (not\ Yellow) = 80\%$$

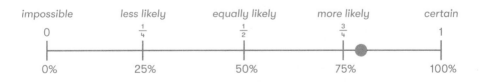

As you can see, the likelihood of not getting a yellow candy is slightly more than *more likely* and less than *certain*. It's close enough, though, that this would be considered *more than likely*.

ANOTHER PATH

P (not Yellow) could also be found by subtracting *P (Yellow)* from the whole 100%. Here's a visual again:

100%

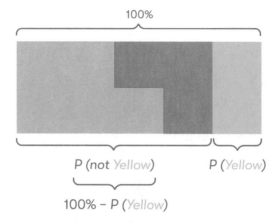

P (not Yellow)

P (Yellow)

100% – *P (Yellow)*

As you saw earlier, *P (not Yellow)* is the result of all the other outcomes besides *P (Yellow)*.

$$P\text{ (not Yellow)} = 100\% - P\text{ (Yellow)}$$

$$P\text{ (not Yellow)} = 100\% - 20\%$$

$$P\text{ (not Yellow)} = 80\%$$

So, each of your friends says they'll pick a blue piece of candy because it had the highest likelihood in your experiment.

It's almost time to make your final pick, but before you do, you ask your math teacher to see all of the bag's contents. She allows it, and you're able to see the color totals, including the ones you chose earlier that were put back into the bag:

COLOR	FREQUENCY	FRACTION	DECIMAL	PERCENT
Blue	30	$\frac{30}{60} = \frac{1}{2}$	0.5	50%
Red	18	$\frac{18}{60} = \frac{3}{10}$	0.3	30%
Yellow	12	$\frac{12}{60} = \frac{1}{5}$	0.2	20%

PREDICTING WHAT'S GOING TO HAPPEN VS. ANALYZING WHAT HAPPENED

These values are very similar to the likelihoods found in the experiment you did with just 10 picks. The table on the previous page shows the theoretical probability, the probability that an event *should* happen, while the experimental probability from before was what *actually* happened. When you need to know what to expect, you use theoretical probability. When you *analyze* what happened, you use experimental probability.

> **theoretical probability**: the likelihood of an event based on what could happen based on the parameters (*i.e., sides of a coin or faces of a die*)
>
> **experimental probability**: the likelihood of an event based on actual events

TAKE A CLOSER LOOK

Let's go one step further. *How many times should a blue candy be picked if there were 16 picks done at random?* Assume that after each pick you'd put the candy back in the bag and start over. You can think of it as, since one pick is $P(Blue) = \frac{1}{2}$, how would 16 times that amount be calculated?

$$P(Blue) = \frac{1}{2} \times 16$$

$$= \frac{16}{2} \text{ Blue Candies}$$

$$= 8 \text{ Blue Candies}$$

This means, in theory, there should be 8 blue candies selected out of 16 picks. It all comes back around to that 50%! Nice work!

You made the statistically sound choice, guessed you would pick a blue candy, and got one! For all your hard work, your math teacher brings out a giant plate of chocolate chip cookies for you and your friends to enjoy!

YOUR TURN!

Rolling a single, 6-sided die can result in a side showing 1, 2, 3, 4, 5, or 6.

1. What's the probability of rolling each value?

NUMBER	FRACTION	DECIMAL	PERCENT
1			
2			
3			
4			
5			
6			

2. Are each of the outcomes fair or unfair? Explain.

3. If you randomly roll the die 60 times, how many times should the die land on 4?

PROBABILITY OF COMPOUND EVENTS

LIST FORM

One day at camp, your counselors are arranging trips for campers. Each camper will be randomly selected for the type of trip they'll take and the length (number of days) of the trip. There are four kinds of trips, and each will last 1, 2, or 3 days.

Since the selections are random, how can you figure out the probability of each outcome?

SIMPLE EVENT 1 Activity (4 Choices)	SIMPLE EVENT 2 Number of Days (3 Choices)
Trail Hiking	1
Horseback Riding	2
Rock Climbing	3
Whitewater Rafting	

TAKE A CLOSER LOOK

The more choices there are, the more the probability of combining the options can be affected. When two or more simple events, each with two or more choices, are combined in order to create one event, that's known as a compound event. So, how do you find the probability of compound events?

> simple event: a single outcome or event (e.g., flipping a coin)
>
> compound probability: the likelihood of a combination of two simple events occurring

First, create a table and organize all the possible combinations of outcomes.

For example, "Trail Hiking for 1 day" is one outcome (T1). "Whitewater Rafting for 3 days" is another outcome (W3).

SIMPLE EVENT 1 Activity	SIMPLE EVENT 2 Number of Days	OUTCOME	PROBABILITY
Trail Hiking	1	T1	
Trail Hiking	2	T2	
Trail Hiking	3	T3	
Horseback Riding	1	H1	
Horseback Riding	2	H2	
Horseback Riding	3	H3	
Rock Climbing	1	R1	
Rock Climbing	2	R2	
Rock Climbing	3	R3	
Whitewater Rafting	1	W1	
Whitewater Rafting	2	W2	
Whitewater Rafting	3	W3	

ANALYZE THE RESULTS

Now that all the combinations are in list form, you can analyze the results:

a. Consider all the possible combinations—this is called the sample space. *How many possible outcomes are there (how big is the sample space)?*

b. You really want to go on the trail hike for 3 days, so that's your first choice. *What's the probability of that happening?*

c. Your second choice would be to go whitewater rafting for 2 or 3 days. *What's the probability of that combination?*

For specific probabilities, find the number of combinations that fit your choice, then divide by the total possibilities.

Since there are 12 trips possible, there are 12 compound events. Simple Event 1—the type of trip—has 4 options. Simple Event 2—the length of the trip—has 3 options. Notice how these are related to 12? 4 × 3 = 12.

Trail Hiking: 1, 2, or 3 days	T1, T2, T3	
Horseback Riding: 1, 2, or 3 days	H1, H2, H3	4 sets of 3
Rock Climbing: 1, 2, or 3 days	R1, R2, R3	4 × 3 = **12**
Whitewater Rafting: 1, 2, or 3 days	W1, W2, W3	

12 combinations

$$P\ (T \text{ and } 3) = \frac{\textit{Number of Times "Trail Hiking" and "3 days"}}{\textit{Number of Total Combinations}}$$

There's only 1 outcome out of 12 where you could pick "Hiking" and "3 days."

SIMPLE EVENT 1 Activity	SIMPLE EVENT 2 Number of Days	OUTCOME	PROBABILITY
Trail Hiking	1	T1	$\frac{1}{12}$
Trail Hiking	2	T2	$\frac{1}{12}$
Trail Hiking	3	T3	$\frac{1}{12}$
Horseback Riding	1	H1	$\frac{1}{12}$
Horseback Riding	2	H2	$\frac{1}{12}$
Horseback Riding	3	H3	$\frac{1}{12}$
Rock Climbing	1	R1	$\frac{1}{12}$
Rock Climbing	2	R2	$\frac{1}{12}$
Rock Climbing	3	R3	$\frac{1}{12}$
Whitewater Rafting	1	W1	$\frac{1}{12}$
Whitewater Rafting	2	W2	$\frac{1}{12}$
Whitewater Rafting	3	W3	$\frac{1}{12}$

P (Hiking and 3 Days) $= \frac{1}{12}$

You may notice that each of the events (Simple Event 1 and Simple Event 2) are equally likely.

ANOTHER PATH

When you want to figure out the probability of compound events, you can multiply the probability of each individual event. So, to find the probability of "Trail Hiking" and "3 days," you'd set up the equation like this:

$$P(H3) = P(H) \times P(3)$$

The probability of randomly choosing "Trail Hiking" is 1 out of 4:

Trail Hiking

Horseback Riding

Rock Climbing

Whitewater Rafting

$$P(H) = \frac{1}{4}$$

The probability of randomly choosing "3" is 1 out of 3:

1 day

2 days

3 days

$$P(3) = \frac{1}{3}$$

So, to find the probability of hiking for 3 days,

$$P(H3) = P(H) \times P(3)$$

$$P(H3) = \frac{1}{4} \times \frac{1}{3}$$

$$P(H3) = \frac{1}{12}$$

Your second choice is whitewater rafting for 2 or 3 days—the word "or" is used when you accept more than one outcome. This means you include W2 as well as W3. As you know, there's only 1 outcome out of 12 for whitewater rafting for 2 days and 1 outcome out of 12 for whitewater rafting for 3 days.

$$P (W2) = \frac{1}{12}$$

or

$$P (W3) = \frac{1}{12}$$

Whitewater rafting for 2 or 3 days

This means there are a total of 2 combinations out of 12 for your second choice.

$$P (W2 \text{ or } W3) = \frac{2}{12} \text{ or } \frac{1}{6}$$

YOUR TURN!

One of your friends at camp really doesn't want to go rock climbing. Using the list above, find the probability that:

1. They're assigned rock climbing for 1, 2, or 3 days.

2. They're *not* assigned rock climbing for 1, 2, or 3 days.

TREE DIAGRAMS

After 3 days on white water, the hungry campers who went rafting all meet up at a pizza place. The pizza makers can create any combinations they want with the following ingredients:

Dough: white (W) or wheat (T)

Cheese: mozzarella (M) or cheddar (C)

Toppings: pepperoni (P), sausage (S), onions (O), or mushrooms (U)

TAKE A CLOSER LOOK

What's the probability that the chefs will make your favorite pizza with *white* dough (W), *mozzarella* cheese (M), and *pepperoni* (P)? Before we can figure that out, let's first create a tree diagram to represent all the possible combinations.

1ST OPTION *Dough*	2ND OPTION *Cheese*	3RD OPTION *Toppings*	COMBINATIONS
		P	WMP
	M	S	WMS
		O	WMO
		U	WMU
W		P	WCP
	C	S	WCS
		O	WCO
		U	WCU
		P	TMP
	M	S	TMS
		O	TMO
		U	TMU
T		P	TCP
	C	S	TCS
		O	TCO
		U	TCU

In total, there are 16 different pizza combinations that can be made. Each branch of the tree leads to a unique combination of dough, cheese, and toppings. You can even spot the combination you're craving (*white* dough, *mozzarella* cheese, and *pepperoni*).

tree diagram: a type of probability diagram that is primarily used when there are multiple options or attributes that converge (or combine)

1ST OPTION *Dough*	2ND OPTION *Cheese*	3RD OPTION *Toppings*	COMBINATIONS
		P	(WMP)
	M	S	WMS
		O	WMO
W		U	WMU

Explore the full tree diagram to see some of the other possible combinations. *Where do the following combinations appear?*

- *Wheat* dough with *cheddar* cheese and *onions*
- *White* dough with *cheddar* cheese and *mushrooms*

Now you can figure out the probability that one of the pizzas tonight is your favorite! Let's start off with an easy question: *What's the probability that your pizza will have white dough?*

- Since there are only 2 dough choices—and half the tree is white dough—it's 50%.

1ST OPTION *Dough*	2ND OPTION *Cheese*	3RD OPTION *Toppings*	COMBINATIONS
		P	WMP
	M	S	WMS
		O	WMO
		U	WMU
W		P	WCP
	C	S	WCS
		O	WCO
		U	WCU

What about a pizza with white dough and mozzarella cheese?

- You've already got the 50% from the white dough, so follow along that branch to the mozzarella cheese. What do you see? Since there are only 2 choices for cheese as well, there's a 50% probability it's one or the other. The intersection of type of dough

(0.5) and cheese probabilities (0.5) can be multiplied to get 25%.

$$P(W) \times P(M) = 0.5 \times 0.5 = 0.25 = 25\%$$

1ST OPTION Dough	2ND OPTION Cheese	3RD OPTION Toppings	COMBINATIONS
		P	WMP
		S	WMS
	M	O	WMO
		U	WMU
W		P	WCP
		S	WCS
	C	O	WCO
		U	WCU

Any pizza pie with wheat dough and mozzarella cheese represents 4 out of the 16 total options, which is $\frac{1}{4}$ or 25% of the total number of pizza possibilities.

Almost there! Finally, let's add in your topping choice of pepperoni.

Keep following your branch and note each event's probability:

1ST OPTION Dough	2ND OPTION Cheese	3RD OPTION Toppings	COMBINATIONS
		P	WMP
		S	WMS
	M	O	WMO
		U	WMU
W		P	WCP
		S	WCS
	C	O	WCO
		U	WCU

Now, of the 25% ($\frac{1}{4}$) of the pizza with white dough and mozzarella cheese, only one option has pepperoni, which is 25% ($\frac{1}{4}$) of the given options. This is 1 out of 16 possibilities or 6.25%.

ANOTHER PATH

Here it's broken down, step by step.

The probability of getting *white* dough: $P(W) = \frac{1}{2}$

The probability of getting *mozzarella* cheese: $P(M) = \frac{1}{2}$

The probability of getting *pepperoni*: $P(P) = \frac{1}{4}$

Look for "WMP" in the Combinations column; it's *one* of *sixteen* combinations. Like you did before, you'll need to multiply to find the probability of this compound event:

$$P(WMP) = P(W) \times P(M) \times P(P)$$

$$= \frac{1}{2} \times \frac{1}{2} \times \frac{1}{4}$$

$$= \frac{1}{16} = 0.0625 \text{ or } 6.25\%$$

Perfect! The likelihood that you'll get your favorite pizza with white dough, mozzarella cheese, and pepperoni is about 6%.

All this pizza math helps you realize there's another combination you'd be just as happy with: white dough, mozzarella, and sausage. *What's the probability of P (WMS)?*

$$P(W) = \frac{1}{2}$$ *Find the individual probabilities first.*

$$P(M) = \frac{1}{2}$$

$$P(S) = \frac{1}{4}$$

$$P(WMS) = P(W) \times P(M) \times P(S)$$

$$P(WMS) = \frac{1}{2} \times \frac{1}{2} \times \frac{1}{4}$$ *Then multiply.*

$$P(WMS) = \frac{1}{16} = 0.0625 \text{ or } 6.25\%$$

Great! Look familiar?

So, what's the probability that they'll serve at least one of your favorite combinations?

$$P \text{ (WMS } \textbf{or } WMS) = ?$$

It's not as boggling as it looks! Remember, if you'll accept one outcome or another, you can add the two probabilities together.

$P \text{ (WMS } \textbf{or } WMS) = P \text{ (WMS)} + P \text{ (WMS)}$

$$= \frac{1}{16} + \frac{1}{16}$$

$$= \frac{2}{16}$$

$$= \frac{1}{8}$$

Note: Make a common denominator, if necessary.

Excellent! Now you know there's a $\frac{1}{8}$ or 12.5% chance you'll get to enjoy one of your favorite pizza types!

YOUR TURN!

Find the probabilities of the two combinations you located on the diagram earlier:

1. $P \text{ (TCO)} = ?$

2. $P \text{ (not WCM)} = ?$

3. What's the probability of getting either one of these combinations?

$$P \text{ (TCO } \textbf{or } WCP) = ?$$

DATA TABLES

A data table is another method of organizing and interpreting the probability of compound events. Look back at your camp's system for camper's trip types and length. In order to create a data table from this information, the possible outcomes were put into list form:

CHOICE 1 Activity	CHOICE 2 Number of Days	OUTCOME
Trail Hiking	1	T1
Trail Hiking	2	T2
Trail Hiking	3	T3
Horseback Riding	1	H1
Horseback Riding	2	H2
Horseback Riding	3	H3
Rock Climbing	1	R1
Rock Climbing	2	R2
Rock Climbing	3	R3
Whitewater Rafting	1	W1
Whitewater Rafting	2	W2
Whitewater Rafting	3	W3

data table: a type of organizational diagram of information

TAKE A CLOSER LOOK

Now, look at the possible combinations in the data table below:

Outcomes of 1ˢᵗ Event

	WHITEWATER RAFTING	ROCK CLIMBING	TRAIL HIKING	HORSEBACK RIDING
DAY 1	W1	R1	T1	H1
DAY 2	W2	R2	T2	H2
DAY 3	W3	R3	T3	H3

Outcomes of 2ⁿᵈ Event (vertical label on left)

The outcomes of the first event are listed horizontally at the top of the table. The outcomes of the second event are listed vertically, along the left side of the table. All the possible combinations are then coordinated in the cells below.

For example, "Rock Climbing" and "3 days" is located where these two choices intersect.

Outcomes of 1ˢᵗ Event

	WHITEWATER RAFTING	ROCK CLIMBING	TRAIL HIKING	HORSEBACK RIDING
DAY 1	W1	R1	T1	H1
DAY 2	W2	R2	T2	H2
DAY 3	W3	→ R3	T3	H3

Outcomes of 2ⁿᵈ Event (vertical label on left)

You can also use a data table to find the probability of multiple outcomes. What's the probability that a camper will pick a one-day or two-day horseback riding expedition? Shade the cells that apply.

		WHITEWATER RAFTING	ROCK CLIMBING	TRAIL HIKING	HORSEBACK RIDING
Outcomes of 2nd Event	DAY 1	W1	R1	T1	H1
	DAY 2	W2	R2	T2	H2
	DAY 3	W3	R3	T3	H3

Count the cells and write the number over the total possible outcomes:

$$P\,(H1 \text{ or } H2) = \frac{2}{12} = \frac{1}{6} \approx 0.1\overline{6} \approx 1.7\%$$

The reason tables can be so useful is because they provide a quick visualization of the information. The more you work with probability and data, the more you'll get to know if you prefer tree or table diagrams.

YOUR TURN!

You're planning to visit some national parks with your friends during summer vacation. Each person wants to go to a different national park, and no one can agree about the length of the vacation. To look at all the possible options, you get together and put the possible trip combinations into a frequency table:

	YELLOWSTONE	GRAND CANYON	ACADIA	EVERGLADES
4 DAYS				
5 DAYS				
6 DAYS				
7 DAYS				

1. Complete the data table to help visualize your sample space.

2. What's the probability that you'll visit Everglades National Park for four days?

3. What's the probability that you'll visit Yellowstone Park?

4. What's the probability that your vacation will last one week?

CHAPTER SUMMARY

PROBABILITY

Probability is the likelihood of a particular event taking place. Probability is measured in whole numbers, fractions, decimals, and percentages. Use this double number line to help you with the likelihood of events.

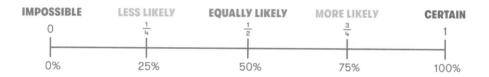

THEORETICAL VS. EXPERIMENTAL PROBABILITY

There are two different types of probabilities that help us analyze situations.

- **Theoretical Probability:** This is based on all the possible events. For example, there's a 50/50 chance of getting heads or tails when you flip a coin.

- **Experimental Probability:** This is the actual probability based on the events that occurred.

PROBABILITY OF COMPOUND EVENTS

Sometimes you'll need to measure probabilities of multiple or simultaneous events. For this, organizing the possible outcomes is very important. Here are some options for organization:

- **List Form:** This format is great if you prefer making continuous lists and then combining them into one list. This works really well when you only have two simple events to compare.

CHOICE 1 Activity	CHOICE 2 Number of Days	OUTCOME
Trail Hiking	1	T1
Trail Hiking	2	T2
Trail Hiking	3	T3
Horseback Riding	1	H1
Horseback Riding	2	H2
Horseback Riding	3	H3
Rock Climbing	1	R1
Rock Climbing	2	R2
Rock Climbing	3	R3
Whitewater Rafting	1	W1
Whitewater Rafting	2	W2
Whitewater Rafting	3	W3

- **Data Table:** This format is great if you like to work horizontally and vertically and you have multiple options.

Outcomes of 1ˢᵗ Event

	WHITEWATER RAFTING	ROCK CLIMBING	TRAIL HIKING	HORSEBACK RIDING
DAY 1	W1	R1	T1	H1
DAY 2	W2	R2	T2	H2
DAY 3	W3	R3	T3	H3

Outcomes of 2ⁿᵈ Event

- **Tree Diagram:** This format works great when you have more than 2 choices, like we did for the pizza problem. But you can use it for simpler problems too.

1ST OPTION Dough	2ND OPTION Cheese	3RD OPTION Toppings	COMBINATIONS
		P	WMP
	M	S	WMS
		O	WMO
		U	WMU
W		P	WCP
	C	S	WCS
		O	WCO
		U	WCU
		P	TMP
	M	S	TMS
		O	TMO
		U	TMU
T		P	TCP
	C	S	TCS
		O	TCO
		U	TCU

CHAPTER 13 VOCABULARY

compound probability: the likelihood of a combination of two simple events occurring

data table: a type of organizational diagram of information

experimental probability: the likelihood of an event based on actual events

outcome: a target event

probability: the likelihood of an event or outcome

random event: an event or occurrence whose outcome cannot be predicted, for example, rolling a die

simple event: a single outcome or event (i.e., flipping a tails)

theoretical probability: the likelihood of an event based on what could happen based on the parameters (i.e., sides of a coin or faces of a die)

tree diagram: a type of probability diagram that is primarily used when there are multiple options or attributes that converge (or combine)

CHAPTER 13 ANSWER KEY

PROBABILITY (P. 458)

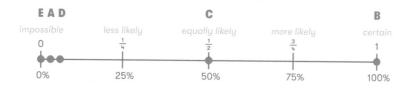

PREDICTING WHAT'S GOING TO HAPPEN VS. ANALYZING WHAT HAPPENED (P. 466)

1. The probability of rolling each value will be the same.

$$P\ (Rolling\ 1) = \frac{1}{6} = 0.16 = 16.6\%$$

$$P\ (Rolling\ 2) = \frac{1}{6} = 0.16 = 16.6\%$$

$$P\ (Rolling\ 3) = \frac{1}{6} = 0.16 = 16.6\%$$

$$P\ (Rolling\ 4) = \frac{1}{6} = 0.16 = 16.6\%$$

$$P\ (Rolling\ 5) = \frac{1}{6} = 0.16 = 16.6\%$$

$$P\ (Rolling\ 6) = \frac{1}{6} = 0.16 = 16.6\%$$

2. Theoretically the outcomes are fair. Each value has an equal chance of being the result of a random roll.

3. Theoretically, 4 should come up one in six times, or 10 times out of 60.

PROBABILITY OF COMPOUND EVENTS
LIST FORM (P. 472)

1. There are 3 "Rock Climbing" outcomes out of 12, or

$$P(M\ 1, 2, 3) = \frac{3}{12} = 0.25 = 25\%$$

You could also find it as $P(M1\ or\ M2\ or\ M3) = \frac{1}{12} + \frac{1}{12} + \frac{1}{12} = \frac{3}{12}$

2. The probability of any outcome besides "Rock Climbing" leaves the remaining 9 out of 12 possibilities, or $\frac{9}{12} = 0.75 = 75\%$.

You could also find any outcome besides "Rock Climbing" by subtracting the "Rock Climbing" probability away from 1 (or 100%). In mathematics, this is called finding the *complement* of an event.

$$1 - \frac{3}{12}$$

$$= \frac{12}{12} - \frac{3}{12}$$

$$= \frac{9}{12} \text{ or } 0.75 \text{ or } 75\%$$

TREE DIAGRAMS (P. 478)

1. $P(TCO) = \frac{1}{2} \times \frac{1}{2} \times \frac{1}{4} = \frac{1}{16}$

2. $P(not\ WCM) = \frac{1}{2} \times \frac{1}{2} \times \frac{3}{4} = \frac{3}{16}$

3. $P(TCO\ \textbf{or}\ WCM) = \frac{1}{16} + \frac{1}{16} = \frac{2}{16} = \frac{1}{8}$

DATA TABLES (P. 481–482)

1.

	YELLOWSTONE	GRAND CANYON	ACADIA	EVERGLADES
4 DAYS	Y4	G4	A4	E4
5 DAYS	Y5	G5	A5	E5
6 DAYS	Y6	G6	A6	E6
7 DAYS	Y7	G7	A7	E7

2. $P\,(E4) = \dfrac{1}{16} \approx 6\%$

3. $P\,(Y4 \text{ or } Y5 \text{ or } Y6 \text{ or } Y7) = \dfrac{1}{16} + \dfrac{1}{16} + \dfrac{1}{16} + \dfrac{1}{16} = \dfrac{4}{16} = 25\%$

4. $P\,(Y7 \text{ or } G7 \text{ or } A7 \text{ or } E7)$

$= \dfrac{1}{16} + \dfrac{1}{16} + \dfrac{1}{16} + \dfrac{1}{16} = \dfrac{4}{16} = \dfrac{4}{16} = 25\%$

14 BIVARIATE DATA

Let's say you need to convince your parents that playing video games isn't affecting your grades, and that eating ice cream before dinner doesn't affect your appetite. How can you do this? By gathering data that allows for two variables—called bivariate data—you can make claims about relationships to support your ideas. But keep in mind that you may not always get the results you're looking for!

CONSTRUCTING, EXAMINING, AND INTERPRETING SCATTERPLOTS

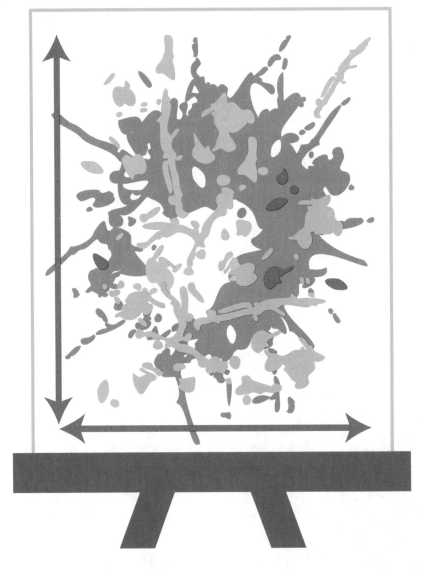

In this chapter, we'll look at comparing data to see if there's a relationship. We'll compare two sets of data called bivariate data. One way to examine data is through using scatterplots.

A scatterplot is a way to display and study values of bivariate data. First, you plot each pair of values on a coordinate plane. Then, you examine the scatter or the behavior of the points—all while looking for patterns associated with the two quantities.

> **bivariate data:** a data set that includes two variables (Note: *bi-* means "two")
>
> **scatterplot:** a coordinate plane with bivariate data displayed

PRIOR KNOWLEDGE

Before you go on and scatter some plots, take a minute to think about the variables you're comparing. Scatterplots may or may not show a cause-and-effect relationship between the variables.

- Cause-and-Effect Relationship: The amount of time driving in a car and the distance traveled.
- Non-Cause-and-Effect Relationship: The number of days in a month and the amount of rainfall.

TAKE A CLOSER LOOK

This past summer, you spent a lot of time outside—and each day, the ice cream truck was there too—rain or shine. Because you're becoming quite the data-collector, each day you tracked the outside temperature highs *and* the number of ice-pops sold. Visually, you show the data you collected as such:

OUTSIDE TEMPERATURE (°F)	NUMBER OF ICE POPS SOLD
77°	89
94°	156
97°	152
87°	131
79°	97
76°	46
86°	128
89°	124
73°	70
92°	141
90°	136
83°	106

- How do you know which variable should be on the x-axis (input) and which variable should be on the y-axis (output)?

After looking over the data, it would seem like the output, the "Number of Ice-Pops Sold," might be the result of the input: the "Outside Temperature." So, you could easily claim that the hotter the day, the more ice-pops that'll be sold. Seems like a good bet!

- For graphing purposes, we can include the Outside Temperature (input) along the x-axis and the Number of Ice-Pops Sold (output) on the y-axis.

Quick Tip: The best way to decide which is the input (x-axis) is by asking yourself, which one is out of my control (i.e., time, temperature, etc.)?

SUMMER HEAT AND ICE-POP COMPARISON

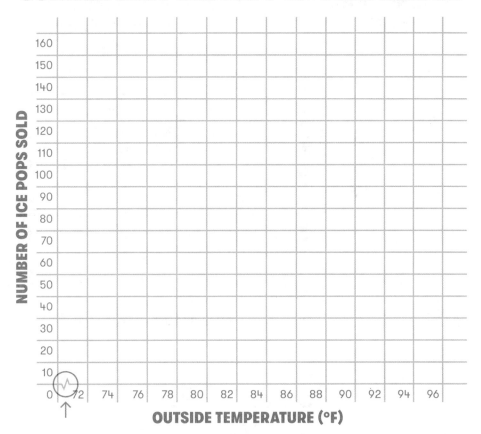

Note: The zigzag symbol on the x-axis is called an **axis break**. It allows you to skip smaller values you don't need and start closer to the lowest actual input value.

Now that you have the graph set up, you can go ahead and plot the pairs of data as you would coordinates, (x, y).

OUTSIDE TEMPERATURE (°F)	NUMBER OF ICE-POPS SOLD
77°	89
94°	156
97°	152
87°	131
79°	97
76°	46
86°	128
89°	124
73°	70
92°	141
90°	136
83°	106

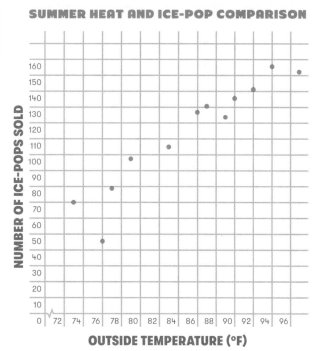

SUMMER HEAT AND ICE-POP COMPARISON

NUMBER OF ICE-POPS SOLD

OUTSIDE TEMPERATURE (°F)

ANALYZING SCATTERPLOTS

When analyzing scatterplots, look for direction, clusters of data points, and any patterns. This will allow you to make and support a claim about the relationship between the two variables.

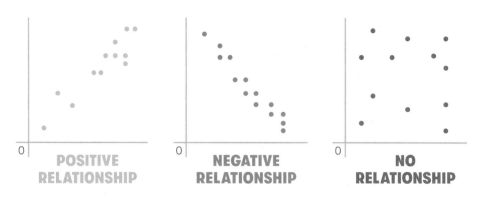

POSITIVE RELATIONSHIP

NEGATIVE RELATIONSHIP

NO RELATIONSHIP

cluster: a group of data points that are close together

With this new information in hand, let's return to the Summer Days and Ice-Pops Sold story.

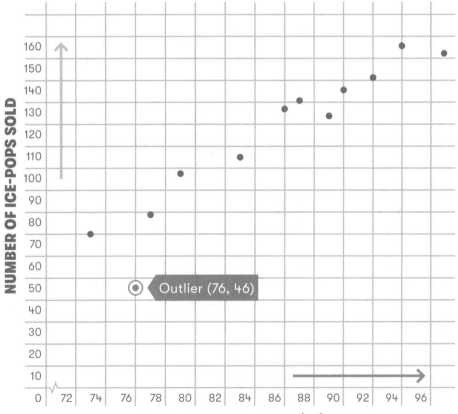

Do you notice a pattern or any exceptions to that pattern in the data?

- There seems to be a grouping of data in a pattern going up and to the right. This means it is a positive relationship.

- The one point, (76°, 46), seems to be all by itself and is considered an outlier. (Reminder: an outlier is any data point that doesn't fit or behave like the rest of the data.)

Finally, think about how the pattern and outlier might be interpreted. Here are some key questions to consider:

- *Does the pattern suggest any relationship between these two variables?*

The pattern of data seems to show that as the inputs ("Outside Temperature") are increasing, the outputs ("Number of Ice-Pops Sold") are also increasing. So, you can make the claim that there's a positive relationship between the temperature outside and the number of ice-pops sold. More people are buying ice-pops on warmer days.

OUTSIDE TEMPERATURE ↑
NUMBER OF ICE-POPS SOLD ↑

- *Can you think of a reason for the outlier? Why would a temperature of 76° result in only 46 ice-pops sold when similar temperatures sold many more?*

It seems like there are other factors that would affect the number of ice-pops sold on the 76° day. Maybe it was raining, or maybe the seller ran out of ice-pops. These and other variables might be causing effects on the number of ice-pops sold.

So, what does this mean? It shows that temperature alone can't always determine the exact cause of ice-pops sold—although it's definitely an important factor.

APPLY WHAT YOU'VE LEARNED

Let's apply what we have learned so far and look at this new graph. Try to:

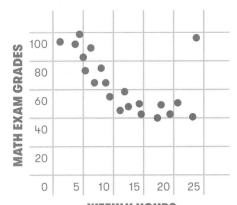

1. Identify the variables.

2. Examine the scatter for patterns and outliers.

3. Consider if a relationship might exist between the two variables.

Your answers should look something like this:

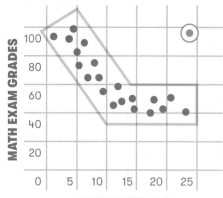

WEEKLY HOURS
PLAYING VIDEO GAMES

1. The input variable is "Weekly Hours Playing Video Games" and the output variable is "Math Exam Grades."

2. There seems to be a pattern trending down and to the right. There appears to be an outlier at approximately (25, 97).

3. There might be a relationship between the two variables where more time spent playing video games corresponds with lower grades on a math exam. The outlier is a student who played a large amount of video games but still scored high on the exam.

TOOLS FOR SUCCESS

When interpreting scatterplots, it's important to remember:

1. Inspect the scatterplot for patterns and/or outliers.

2. Consider if the data suggests a relationship between the two variables.
   a. Does the data have any clusters?
   b. Can the relationship be described as positive or negative?

**POSITIVE
RELATIONSHIP**

**NEGATIVE
RELATIONSHIP**

YOUR TURN!

Each morning, you go walking for one hour and record the time you start as well as the number of dogs you pass on your walk. Using the data below, complete the following:

1. Construct a scatterplot.

2. Identify any clusters, patterns, and/or outliers.

3. Determine if a relationship exists between the two variables.

STARTING TIME	NUMBER OF DOGS SEEN
7:30 A.M.	8
8:15 A.M.	5
9:30 A.M.	4
9:45 A.M.	3
10:00 A.M.	2
8:00 A.M.	7
7:15 A.M.	8
7:00 A.M.	9
10:30 A.M.	1
8:45 A.M.	4

NUMBER OF DOGS SEEN @ TIMES PER DAY

NUMBER OF DOGS SEEN

STARTING TIME

(x-axis: 7 A.M., 8 A.M., 9 A.M., 10 A.M., 11 A.M.; y-axis: 0–10)

LINEAR AND NONLINEAR RELATIONSHIPS

PRIOR KNOWLEDGE

In a scatterplot, the main behaviors to consider are linear and nonlinear.

- In a **nonlinear relationship**, the output doesn't change in direct proportion to a change in any of the inputs. A nonlinear relationship doesn't create a straight line but instead creates a curve.

- In a **linear relationship**, the output increase is in direct proportion to a change in any of the inputs. It creates a straight line when plotted on a graph.

> **nonlinear relationship:** the rate of change (ratio between the change in the dependent and independent variables) is not constant, and the relationship creates a curve
>
> **linear relationship:** the rate of change (ratio between the change in the dependent and independent variables) is constant, and the relationship creates a line

On a scatterplot, the data might not form a straight line (linear relationship), but you may see a general linear pattern. Here are examples of scatterplots with linear relationships:

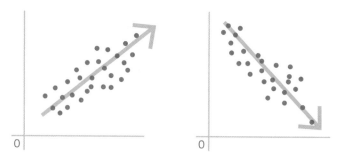

Combining this with the idea of direction, you can label each:

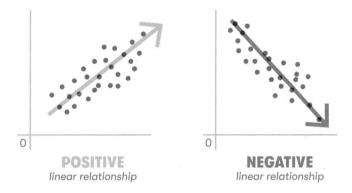

POSITIVE
linear relationship

NEGATIVE
linear relationship

Not all relationships in scatterplots are linear. It's still possible for data to form a pattern that represents a different type of relationship. For example,

NONLINEAR RELATIONSHIPS

Since the scatterplots don't form a straight line, their data is said to have a *nonlinear* relationship.

 TOOLS FOR SUCCESS

When examining scatterplots, it's important to remember:

1. The direction of the data will be a:

   • **Positive relationship** if an increase in inputs makes an increase in outputs.

   • **Negative relationship** if an increase in inputs makes a decrease in outputs.

2. The shape of the data will be:

- **Linear** if the data's change appears to be in a constant pattern.

- **Nonlinear** if the data's change doesn't appear to be in a constant pattern.

YOUR TURN!

Look at the scatterplots below and determine:

1. Is there a relationship between the two variables?

2. If so, does it appear to be positive, negative, linear, or nonlinear?

a.

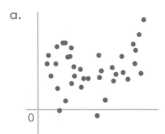

b.

c.

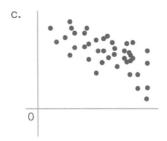

LINE OF BEST FIT

A line of best fit for a data set is one line that best fits, or passes through, most of the data. The line of best fit allows us to construct a linear equation to best represent the data and its direction, which you can use to make predictions about future outcomes.

TAKE A CLOSER LOOK

A line of best fit is drawn through the majority of the data points. The line should go in the direction of the data points to the best of your ability. This is an approximate and reasonable middle of the data.

Tip: Try to balance the number of data points above and below the line of best fit that you're drawing.

> **line of best fit:** a line that most closely models, or passes through, the data for a linear relationship

YOUR TURN!

For the following data set, which option do you think is the line of best fit? Why?

a.
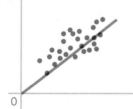

b.

c.
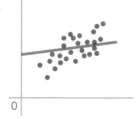

d.
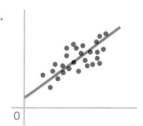

EQUATION OF THE LINE OF BEST FIT

For our purposes, we'll focus on scatterplots that are linear, so the line of best fit's equation will be linear. For linear equations, you'll need to know the slope and y-intercept of the relationship.

Let's return to the original example where we looked at Summer Heat and Ice-Pops Sold. We found a relationship between the number of ice-pops sold and the outside temperature. Let's examine some data on the number of hot chocolates sold each day as it relates to the outside temperature.

OUTSIDE TEMPERATURE	NUMBER OF HOT CHOCOLATES SOLD
77°	50
94°	2
40°	75
87°	9
79°	30
76°	46
86°	10
89°	12
73°	50
55°	70
90°	3
83°	20

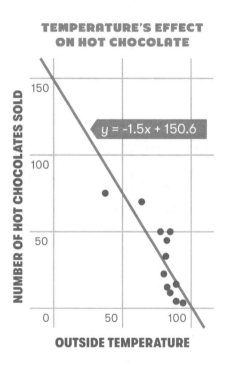

TEMPERATURE'S EFFECT ON HOT CHOCOLATE

$y = -1.5x + 150.6$

NUMBER OF HOT CHOCOLATES SOLD

OUTSIDE TEMPERATURE

Remember, you're able to find the line of best fit using slope-intercept form ($y = mx + b$):

$$y = -1.5x + 150.6$$

This equation is the rule that creates the line of best fit. The equation is an **estimate** based on the general behavior (direction and shape) of the line. The equation offers a way to predict other values that are not part of your data.

estimate: an educated guess based on context

PRIOR KNOWLEDGE

The slope (*m*) represents the constant change of the output for each increase in input. So, with your hot chocolate data, what does the slope of −1.5 represent?

This means a slope of −1.5 predicts a decrease of 1.5 in the number of hot chocolates sold for every increase in temperature. You could also say this is the rate of change.

Slope or Rate of Change: −1.5 hot chocolates per day

The *y*-intercept (*b*) represents the output when the input is 0. You could say it's the starting amount (initial value). So, in this context, what does the *y*-intercept of +150.6 represent?

If the *y*-intercept is +150.6, it means that at 0 degrees a store will sell 150.6 (about 151) hot chocolates.

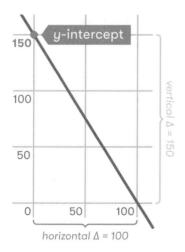

y-intercept: 150.6 hot chocolates

Next, how can you check the accuracy of the line of best fit?

Slope or Rate of Change:

$$\frac{-150}{100} = -1.5$$

−1.5 hot chocolates per day

TAKE A CLOSER LOOK

As you did earlier, you can check the line's fit by visually verifying it on the scatterplot. Now that you have an equation, though, you can use input values to create and check outputs. Using the integers 40, 55, 73, 86, and 94, you find:

OUTSIDE TEMPERATURE x	NUMBER OF HOT CHOCOLATES SOLD $y = -1.5x + 150.6$ Line of Best Fit (Predicted Model)	NUMBER OF HOT CHOCOLATES SOLD (Actual Data Points)
40	90.6	75
55	68.1	70
73	40.5	50
86	21.6	10
94	9.6	2

The line of best fit predicts inputting 55° will get you 68.1 hot chocolates. *Does this seem reasonable?*

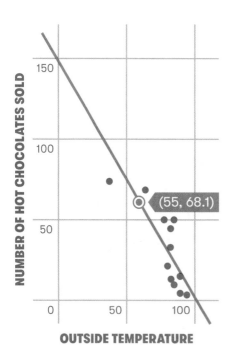

OUTSIDE TEMPERATURE

As you can see, the predicted point (55, 68.1) falls "in line" with the actual data in that area. So, it does appear to be a good predictor!

A line of best fit is also useful in predicting results for input value outside of the ones you have.

For example, how many hot chocolates do you think the store would sell if it were 30°? Checking the data, you see that there's no data point with an input of 30°. So, you turn to your trusty equation:

$$y = -1.5x + 150.6$$

You input the value of 30° for x and evaluate:

$$y = -1.5(30) + 150.6$$

$$y = 105.6$$

So, according to the equation, if the temperature is 30° outside, then the store should sell about 106 hot chocolates.

TOOLS FOR SUCCESS

When finding and interpreting a line of best fit for a scatterplot with a linear relationship, it's important to remember:

1. The line is drawn as close as possible to all the data.

2. The linear equation (slope-intercept form) will provide a way to predict output values.

3. The slope of the line approximates the change in each output for each change in the input.

YOUR TURN!

Each week you and your friend hike the nearby trails. You record your time and distance for each trip and display them in the scatterplot below.

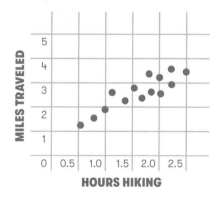

HOURS HIKING

1. Draw a line of best fit for the data in the scatterplot.

2. Interpret the slope and y-intercept of the line of best fit's equation.

$$y = 1.2x + 0.5$$

3. Use the line of best fit's equation to predict the number of miles you and your friend would hike in 3 hours.

TWO-WAY
FREQUENCY TABLES

Campers will have two sets of options for their activities on an upcoming trip. They get to vote for one activity from each option:

- **Mountain options:** hiking or zip-lining
- **River options:** kayaking or whitewater rafting

Example: Your vote is to go zip-lining on the mountain and whitewater rafting in the river.

TAKE A CLOSER LOOK

After 120 campers vote for their preferences, you get involved to help organize the results. One good way to arrange this data is in a **two-way frequency table**.

A two-way frequency table organizes and counts the frequency of data for two categories. It will allow you spaces for all the possible combinations.

> **two-way frequency table:** a display for frequencies of two categorical variables; they are connected to a whole amount and the relative percentages

To organize the results from the vote, you set up a blank two-way table with sample titles.

	Mountain Option 1	Mountain Option 2	TOTALS
River Option 1			
River Option 2			
TOTALS			**TOTAL VOTES**

Next, the key thing is to label the rows and columns with the correct activities and totals.

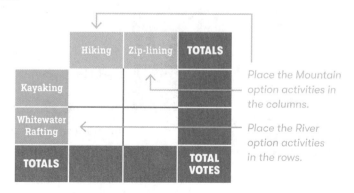

	Hiking	Zip-lining	TOTALS
Kayaking			
Whitewater Rafting			
TOTALS			**TOTAL VOTES**

Place the Mountain option activities in the columns.

Place the River option activities in the rows.

Now you can use the numbers for each result to fill in the two-way table. Using the results on the right, you can fill in the table.

	Hiking	Zip-lining	TOTALS
Kayaking	24	36	
Whitewater Rafting	28	32	
TOTALS			TOTAL VOTES

Results from your camp's votes:

Hiking and Kayaking: 24

Zip-lining and Kayaking: 36

Hiking and Whitewater Rafting: 28

Zip-lining and Whitewater Rafting: 32

Next, the totals for each row and each column can be calculated. Simply add across for the rows and add down for the columns.

	Hiking	Zip-lining	TOTALS
Kayaking	24	36	60
Whitewater Rafting	28	32	60
TOTALS	52	68	TOTAL VOTES

We'll add vertically and horizontally to gather our totals.

Vertical example: 24 + 28 = 52, so there are 52 votes for hiking.

Horizontal example: 24 + 36 = 60, so there are 60 votes for kayaking.

Finally, total votes can be calculated and placed in the bottom right cell (red cell below). To get the total votes, add the bottom row across or add the last column down. Given how many campers voted, *what number do you think these will total to?*

	Hiking	Zip-lining	TOTALS
Kayaking	24	36	60
Whitewater Rafting	28	32	60
TOTALS	52	68	120

TOTAL VOTES ⟶

Yes! There were 120 campers that voted, so it makes sense that 120 is the total for both the last column and last row.

Now that the data is neatly organized, you can determine your camp's interest level in the different activities.

Consider:

    a. What combination of activities is preferable by most?

    b. What combination of activities is least preferable?

    c. Which location had an equal number of votes for its activity?

    d. If you had to pick one combination of mountain and river activities for the camp, what would it be and why?

After studying the two-way frequency table, you figure out:

    a. The combination of activities with the highest number of votes was *zip-lining* and *kayaking* with 36.

    b. The combination of activities with the lowest number of votes was *hiking* and *kayaking* with 24.

    c. The *river* location has equal votes for each activity.

    d. Since the combination of mountain and river activities with the highest number of votes was *zip-lining* and *kayaking*, that would be the most popular choice.

YOUR TURN!

The administrators of a new school are deciding on two choices for school colors. To get opinions from the students, they surveyed all seventh and eighth graders. The color options are: *royal blue, gold, red,* and *silver*.

The results of the survey are listed below:

Seventh graders for royal blue: 78   **Seventh graders** for gold: 56

Eighth graders for royal blue: 62   **Eighth graders** for gold: 75

Seventh graders for red: 85   **Seventh graders** for silver: 67

Eighth graders for red: 44   **Eighth graders** for silver: 33

1. Using the survey results, complete a two-way frequency table below. How will you label the rows and columns?

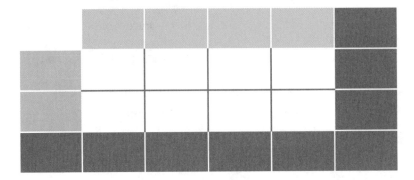

2. Which two colors were favored by the most seventh graders?

3. Which two colors were favored by the most eighth graders?

4. Which two colors were favored the most in total (by both seventh and eighth graders)?

5. Which two colors do you think the school should pick? Why?

RELATIVE FREQUENCY

As you just saw, creating two-way tables with the counted totals in each cell is helpful. When you're comparing numbers, though, it can be even more helpful to turn the counts into percentages.

Two-way frequency tables in percent form are called two-way relative frequency tables. Percentages are a useful way to relate, or compare, data.

two-way relative frequency table: a two-way frequency table that uses percentages as a means of comparison

🔍 TAKE A CLOSER LOOK

Looking at your camping data, were there any choices that had the majority (more than half) of camper votes? Let's look at how you would convert these amounts into percentages.

YOUR CAMP	Hiking	Zip-lining	**TOTALS**
Kayaking	24	36	60
Whitewater Rafting	28	32	60
TOTALS	52	68	120

Since there are a total of 120 campers, each of these amounts should be divided by 120.

YOUR CAMP	Hiking	Zip-lining	**TOTALS**
Kayaking	$\frac{24}{120} \approx 20\%$	$\frac{36}{120} \approx 30\%$	$\frac{60}{120} \approx 50\%$
Whitewater Rafting	$\frac{28}{120} \approx 24\%$	$\frac{32}{120} \approx 27\%$	$\frac{60}{120} \approx 50\%$
TOTALS	$\frac{52}{120} \approx 43\%$	$\frac{68}{120} \approx 57\%$	$\frac{120}{120} \approx 100\%$

Looking at the data, now you see a majority of the campers want to go zip-lining.

YOUR FRIEND'S CAMP:

You meet a friend from another camp who also took part in a vote for their activity. Here are his results:

FRIEND'S CAMP	Hiking	Zip-lining	TOTALS
Kayaking	22	28	50
Whitewater Rafting	13	31	44
TOTALS	35	59	94

Looking at your friend's camp's data, how does his data compare to yours?

You may notice the amounts are lower, but that may be because they have fewer campers. This is where turning the data into percentages would help since you would be comparing percentages to percentages.

FRIEND'S CAMP	Hiking	Zip-lining	TOTALS
Kayaking	$\frac{22}{94} \approx 23\%$	$\frac{28}{94} \approx 30\%$	$\frac{50}{94} \approx 53\%$
Whitewater Rafting	$\frac{13}{94} \approx 14\%$	$\frac{31}{94} \approx 33\%$	$\frac{44}{94} \approx 47\%$
TOTALS	$\frac{35}{94} \approx 37\%$	$\frac{59}{94} \approx 63\%$	$\frac{94}{94} \approx 100\%$

What number would you need to divide each of these amounts to get a percentage?

Your friend's camp has 94 campers in total, so that's what you should divide by.

Good work! You can now see these data in a more familiar form. Compare your camp's data to your friend's.

YOUR CAMP	Hiking	Zip-lining	TOTALS
Kayaking	$\frac{24}{120} \approx 20\%$	$\frac{36}{120} \approx 30\%$	$\frac{60}{120} \approx 50\%$
Whitewater Rafting	$\frac{28}{120} \approx 24\%$	$\frac{32}{120} \approx 27\%$	$\frac{60}{120} \approx 50\%$
TOTALS	$\frac{52}{120} \approx 43\%$	$\frac{68}{120} \approx 57\%$	$\frac{120}{120} \approx 100\%$

FRIEND'S CAMP	Hiking	Zip-lining	TOTALS
Kayaking	$\frac{22}{94} \approx 23\%$	$\frac{28}{94} \approx 30\%$	$\frac{50}{94} \approx 53\%$
Whitewater Rafting	$\frac{13}{94} \approx 14\%$	$\frac{31}{94} \approx 33\%$	$\frac{44}{94} \approx 47\%$
TOTALS	$\frac{35}{94} \approx 37\%$	$\frac{59}{94} \approx 63\%$	$\frac{94}{94} \approx 100\%$

a. Which camp has a greater percentage of campers that want to go kayaking?

Your friend's camp does, at 53%, compared to your camp at 50%.

b. Which camp has a greater percentage of campers that want to go hiking?

Your camp does, 43% to 37%.

c. Which camp has more campers?

Again, your camp does, 120 campers to 94 at your friend's camp.

How did seeing the data as percentages affect your ability to compare?

YOUR TURN!

Convert the table for the new school's color choice into a two-way relative frequency table. Then answer the questions below using the completed table.

	Royal Blue	Gold	Red	Silver	TOTALS
Seventh Graders	78	56	85	67	286
Eighth Graders	62	75	44	33	214
TOTALS	140	131	129	100	500

	Royal Blue	Gold	Red	Silver	TOTALS
Seventh Graders					
Eighth Graders					
TOTALS					

1. What percentage of the total were seventh graders who chose red? Royal blue?

2. What percentage of the total were eighth graders who chose royal blue? Gold?

3. What percentage of the total vote was represented by seventh graders?

4. What percentage of the total vote was represented by eighth graders?

5. Which two colors do you think the school should pick? Why?

CHAPTER SUMMARY

CONSTRUCTING, EXAMINING, AND INTERPRETING SCATTERPLOTS

This is a form of graphs based on actual experiments or events. When you graph the coordinates from the data set, they will look scattered.

- You can have different types of relationship trends: positive, negative, and no relation; this is based on the direction that the majority of the coordinates are going on the graph.

- You can also decide how strong the relationship is based on how close the points are to one another.

LINE OF BEST FIT

The line of best fit refers to the equation and a sketch for a line that best represents the data set from the scatterplot. Lines of best fit can be used for linear and nonlinear relationships, but in this chapter, we only covered linear relationships.

TWO-WAY FREQUENCY TABLES

Use a two-way frequency table to organize information, usually something having to do with surveying people for their likes and dislikes for two different areas of interests or for groups. (i.e., sports or arts, eighth graders or seventh graders). You can also use these tables for percentages.

KEEP PRACTICING

Throughout this book, you explored the big ideas of middle school math. With all this information, begin to think about how useful these ideas can be in the real world—and in your everyday life. Ratios and relationships: that is the main event here.

- What happens when you have to share with your friends and/or siblings?
- What happens when you have to make a prediction about how something will likely turn out?
- How do you plan to organize your room?
- What about that upcoming birthday party you are having? How many supplies should you buy?

This is just a sampling of questions that you can answer with all the mathematical knowledge you've learned and reviewed in this book. Happy problem solving!

CHAPTER 14 VOCABULARY

bivariate data: a data set that includes two variables

cluster: a group of data points that are close together

estimate: an educated guess based on context

line of best fit: a line that most closely models, or passes through, the data for a linear relationship

linear relationship: the rate of change (ratio between the change in the dependent and independent variables) is constant, and the relationship creates a line

positive linear relationship: occurs when both variables in a data set trend in the same direction. The data points spread upward to the right.

negative linear relationship: occurs when one variable in a data set increases and the other decreases. The data points spread downward on the right side.

no relationship: there is no correlation between the two variables in a data set. The plots are "all over the place."

nonlinear relationship: the rate of change (ratio between the change in the dependent and independent variables) is not constant, and the relationship creates a curve

scatterplot: a coordinate plane with bivariate data displayed

two-way frequency table: a display for frequencies of two categorical variables; they are connected to a whole amount and the relative percentages

two-way relative frequency table: a two-way frequency table that uses percentages as a means of comparison

CHAPTER 14 ANSWER KEY

CONSTRUCTING, EXAMINING, AND INTERPRETING SCATTERPLOTS

ANALYZING SCATTERPLOTS (P. 501)

1.

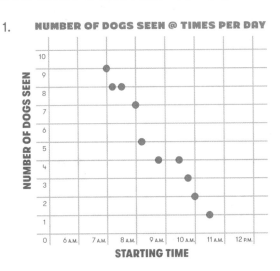

NUMBER OF DOGS SEEN @ TIMES PER DAY

2. The data has a downward trending pattern with no outliers.

3. There appears to be a relationship between the two variables showing fewer dogs seen as morning time increases.

LINEAR AND NONLINEAR RELATIONSHIPS (P. 504)

a.   1. Yes, there appears to be a relationship between the two variables in the data.

2. The relationship isn't positive or negative and is nonlinear.

b.   1. Yes, there appears to be relationship between the two variables in the data.

2. The relationship is positive and linear.

1. Yes, there appears to be relationship between the two variables in the data.

2. The relationship is negative and linear.

LINE OF BEST FIT (P. 505)

a. Option A isn't the line of best fit. It's **too low**; many more data points are above the line than below it.

b. Option B isn't the line of best fit. It's **too high**; many more data points are below the line than above it.

c. Option C isn't the line of best fit, but its direction does seem to represent the direction of the data.

d. Option D is the line of best fit. It seems to be going through the middle of the data and follows the increasing trend.

LINE OF BEST FIT (P. 509)

1.

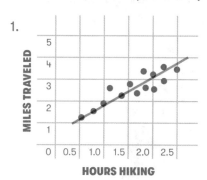

2. The slope of 1.2 represents an additional 1.2 miles traveled for each additional hour of hiking. The y-intercept says at 0 hours you've hiked 0.5 miles. Although this isn't possible, the y-intercept makes the rest of the equation more accurate for the data.

3. In 3 hours, the line of best fit's equation says you would hike 4.1 miles.

$$y = 1.2(3) + 0.5$$

$$= 3.6 + 0.5$$

$$= 4.1$$

TWO-WAY FREQUENCY TABLES (PP. 513–514)

1.

	Royal Blue	Gold	Red	Silver	TOTALS
Seventh Graders	78	56	85	67	286
Eighth Graders	62	75	44	33	214
TOTALS	140	131	129	100	500

2. Red and royal blue

3. Gold and royal blue

4. Royal blue and gold

5. The eighth graders favored *royal blue* and *gold*; it also got the highest number of votes in the overall total for both seventh and eighth graders. But—there are more seventh graders than eighth graders (286 vs. 214). They favored *red* and *royal blue*. So: no clear answer.

RELATIVE FREQUENCY (P. 518)

	Royal Blue	Gold	Red	Silver	TOTALS
Seventh Graders	$\frac{78}{500} \approx 16\%$	$\frac{56}{500} \approx 11\%$	$\frac{78}{500} \approx 17\%$	$\frac{67}{500} \approx 13\%$	$\frac{286}{500} \approx 57\%$
Eighth Graders	$\frac{62}{500} \approx 12\%$	$\frac{75}{500} \approx 15\%$	$\frac{44}{500} \approx 9\%$	$\frac{33}{500} \approx 7\%$	$\frac{214}{500} \approx 43\%$
TOTALS	$\frac{140}{500} \approx 28\%$	$\frac{131}{500} \approx 26\%$	$\frac{129}{500} \approx 26\%$	$\frac{100}{500} \approx 20\%$	$\frac{500}{500} \approx 100\%$

1. 17% of the total were seventh graders who chose red, and 16% of the total were seventh graders who chose royal blue.

2. 12% of the total were eighth graders who chose royal blue, and 15% of the total were eighth graders who chose gold.

3. 57% of the total vote was represented by seventh graders.

4. 43% of the total vote was represented by eighth graders.

5. It really is a toss-up between red with royal blue and royal blue with gold because gold and red basically tied.

ABOUT THE CREATORS

Concetta Ortiz is a high school Math Instructional Lead at the New York City Department of Education in Brooklyn, New York. She has been working in public education for a decade, spending eight of those years as a middle school math teacher. She has a passion for connecting math content to context and continues that work through her leadership role.

Matthew Fazio is a mathematics teacher and tutor who integrates his real-world experience into curriculum design and delivery. Matt earned a Bachelor of Science in Finance from the University of Florida, a Master of Arts in Adolescent Education from the City University of New York's Hunter College, and an Early Career Fellowship from Math for America.

Sideshow Media is a print and digital book developer specializing in illustrated publications with compelling content and visual flair. Since 2000, Sideshow has collaborated with trade publishers, institutions, magazines, and private clients to deliver well-crafted books on a wide variety of subjects, in virtually every format. Sideshow excels at making complicated subjects accessible and interesting to young readers and adults alike. Sideshow is led by its founding partner, Dan Tucker. Visit www.sideshowbooks.com.

Carpenter Collective is a graphic design and branding studio led by partners Jessica and Tad Carpenter. They focus on bringing powerful messages to life through branding, packaging, illustration, and design. They have worked with clients ranging from Target, Coca-Cola, and Macy's, to Warby Parker, Adobe, and MTV, among many others. They've earned a national reputation for creating powerful brand experiences and unique visual storytelling with a whimsical wink. See more of their work at carpentercollective.com.

NOTES